City Contented City Discontented

A HISTORY OF MODERN HARRISBURG

Harrisburg History and Culture

Eric Papenfuse and Catherine Lawrence, Series Editors

With a commitment to preserving the diverse history of Pennsylvania's capital region, the Midtown Scholar Press proudly inaugurates this series, dedicated to exploring the people, places, ideas, and experiences that have shaped Harrisburg and its environs over time. By recovering the contested stories of the past, the publications will help create a shared heritage that illuminates today's social relations and political culture. The series seeks to educate and inspire readers, to elucidate and inform contemporary public discourse, and to transform the possibilities of civic life in the future by strengthening bonds of community.

City Contented City Discontented

A HISTORY OF MODERN HARRISBURG

by Paul Beers

Originally published as 120 columns in the Harrisburg Patriot and the Harrisburg Evening News from February 1983 to March 1984

Edited by Michael Barton
with American Studies Graduate Students at Penn State Harrisburg

Midtown Scholar Press

Front Cover Illustration *(from a stereoview in a private collection)***:** *This rare stereopticon view of an active crowd at Harrisburg's shoreline is titled "River Carnival, September 7, 1908." Mayor Vance McCormick was the first to imagine such a seasonal event, and boat parades began in 1907. Then, in 1916, Telegraph publisher E.J. Stackpole, Sr., organized the first Kipona festival. Politician Harve Taylor was its planner and banker George Reily its admiral. This scene of women in white dresses, men in straw boaters, and babies in wicker carriages evokes E.L. Doctorow's description, in his novel* Ragtime, *of turn-of-the-century America:*

The population customarily gathered in great numbers either out of doors for parades, public concerts, fish fries, political picnics, social outings, or indoors in meeting halls, vaudeville theatres, operas, ballrooms. There seemed to be no entertainment that did not involve great swarms of people. Trains and steamers and trolleys moved them from one place to another. That was the style, that was the way people lived.

Published by Midtown Scholar Press, Harrisburg, Pennsylvania

Design by Fathom Studio, Mechanicsburg, Pennsylvania

Typeset in Goudy Old Style by Boggs & Company, Harrisburg, Pennsylvania

Printed in the United States of America on acid-free paper by
Advanced Color Graphics, State College, Pennsylvania

10 9 8 7 6 5 4 3 2 1

A catalogue record for this book is available from the Library of Congress.

ISBN: 978-0-9839571-0-2

CONTENTS

Paul Beers, HISTORIAN AT LARGE

A Foreword by Michael Barton

I first ran into Paul B. Beers—or I should say his newspaper columns—when I moved from Philadelphia to Harrisburg in 1980 and subscribed to The Patriot. I quickly discovered that this crafty journalist was the proverbial Indian guide who could lead me through the dense forest of the city's past and present life. Not only was he invaluable to the newcomer, but I found that the old-timers in town swore by him too, or occasionally at him.

Paul began writing his "Reporter at Large" columns on June 9, 1961. They appeared at first in the Evening News and were added to the Patriot some years later. His assignment continued Harrisburg journalism's tradition of giving space to a local history columnist, which started in the early 20th century. Those early essayists, usually lacking a byline, wrote under such inviting headings as "Short Walks in and about Harrisburg," "Streets and Corners," "Evening Chat," "Short Stories of Our Harrisburg," "Looking the Town Over," "Historic Harrisburg," "Glimpses of Old Harrisburg," "Mirrors of Harrisburg," "Then and Now," and "Harrisburg of Yesterday." These columnists were among the leading practitioners of local history in their time. But Paul was popular in his time because he also spoke to, and about, the city's contemporary residents. If you were mentioned in his column, that made you somebody, even if you were just one among the thousands of locals he cited. When he announced his retirement from

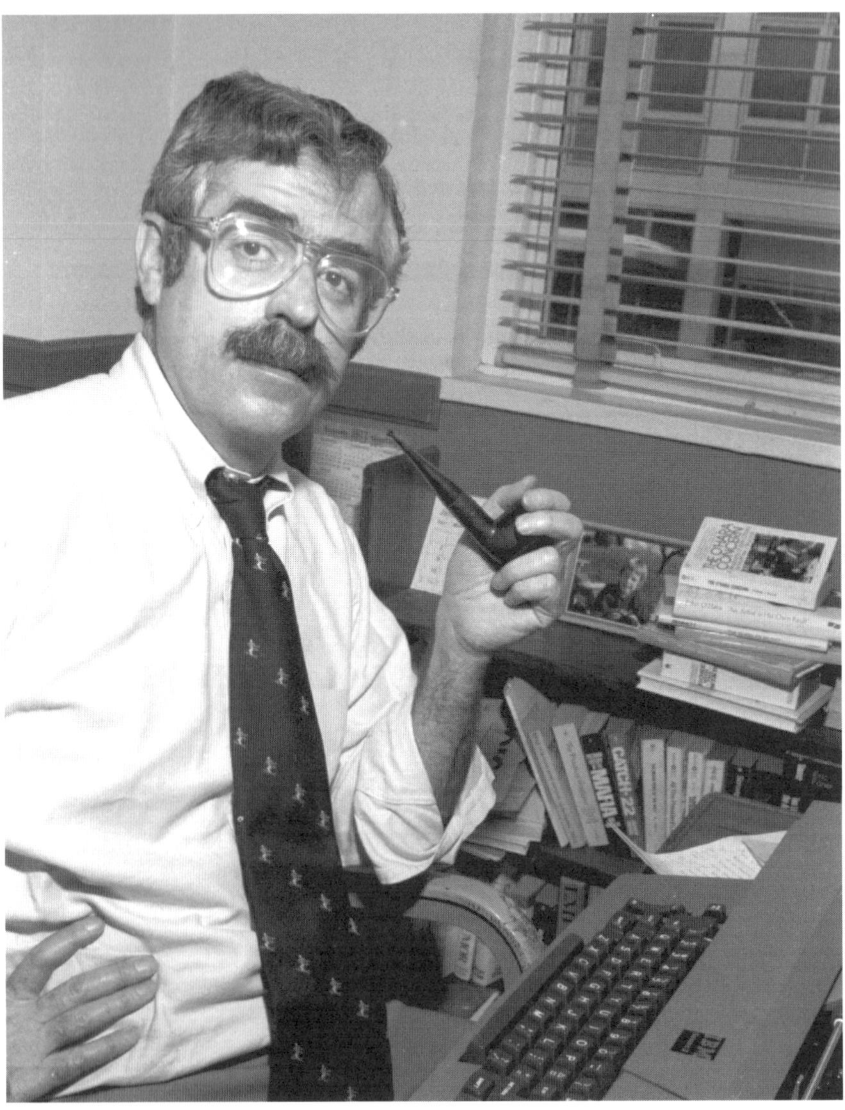

Paul B. Beers non-chalantly at work in 1977. We know the approximate date of the photo because we have identified the artifact in front of him—an "IBM Selectric typewriter," once standard equipment for journalists. Also, there is a calendar behind him.

"Reporter at Large" on December 30, 1985, he said he had written 3,599 columns, or over 3,000,000 words, in 25 years. Paul had many rules for his columns, but he said he followed only two consistently: he never used the first person singular, and he never wrote about his dog. "This columnist fortunately never owned a dog nor had a dog own him," he declared in his farewell pronouncement.

From February 1983 to March 1984, Paul devoted a string of 120 columns to interpreting Harrisburg's modern history. For over a year, on Mondays, Wednesdays, and Fridays, he lectured and entertained us about our past. As he saw it, Harrisburg greatly needed to be modernized in the early 1900s, and by World War I its leaders had famously improved the city. Then Harrisburg was greatly troubled again in the late 1960s, but it was making another notable comeback by the 1980s. Paul called those two recoveries Renaissance I and II, organizing his series into two sections of 60 columns each. He believed the two periods were not identical or equally laudable, however, so he titled the first section "City Contented" and the second "City Discontented." Paul has given us, in other words, a general theory of 20th-century Harrisburg.

Because these columns were previously available only on microfilm or found in incomplete collections of clippings, I thought it essential that they be brought back into print as a book, especially at this moment in the city's history when "challenges," as they say, loom large and historical perspective should be instructive. In addition, readers should consider this publication our personal tribute to Paul.

Certain characteristics of these columns are worth highlighting. First, as often as Paul was a methodical historian, readers will see that he was an opinionated observer. To be specific, *City Contented, City Discontented* takes an unapologetically "progressive" approach to its subject. Paul had pronounced sympathy for minorities, workers, and the little guy. He could be hard on majorities, managers, and big guys, particularly if they lived in the suburbs. But if he was sometimes class-conscious in his analysis, he was no class warrior. After all, he lived in Bellevue Park, Harrisburg's most comfortable neighborhood, so he knew professionals and power brokers well enough to call them friends and allies. Of Harrisburg's movers and shakers in the past, he could be considerate, too. He wrote, for instance, that "Front Streeters lacked the luxury to disassociate themselves from the real world. It was, after all, only a block away, and the slums just a few blocks farther. Many were Victorian enough to be eager humanitarians, satisfying their self-esteem and upholding their family's reputation by performing social service." While his instincts were populist, Paul could still admire wealthy men—if they fulfilled their patrician duties to the people. Cagey politicians and sharp businessmen are other figures who sometimes got the best lines in his columns—if they did their job for the common good.

As for his opinions about particular social groups, he took undisguised swipes at "Dutchmen"—central Pennsylvania men of German descent. His references to them were often close to caricature. Dutchmen, he wrote, are "dour," "tight-lipped," and "docile," and he scolded "Dutch culture's notorious reputation for stand-fastness." Paul found support for his feelings about Dutchmen in the stories of John O'Hara, one of his favorite authors. Near the end of the "City Contented" section, Paul wrote:

Harrisburg obliviously rode the wave of its prosperity and advantages, and it did so, as the characters in O'Hara's...novels, by basking on incessant busyness, exaggerated family and neighborhood togetherness, mindless familiarities, and daily portions of easy contentment. Its biases weren't seriously challenged.

But Paul also appreciated the stability and moderation Dutchmen could bring to the community, so they were not the actual villains in his history. The real villainy, he opined, was "negativism," no matter who showed it.

A second distinctive quality of these columns is that they take ideas and the historian's mission seriously. Paul quotes academics and brings up their theories, which is unusual for a columnist. He possessed scholarly credentials, in that he had published political history with Penn State Press a few years earlier. At the same time, his commitment to readability and sheer facticity is marvelous, and there is hardly a sentence without a concrete datum or two, or more. Professsors would have to point out, however, that he does not usually give the sources for his facts. We have to wonder, where did he get all those details, such as "When the 1890 Fleming Mansion became the Civic Club in 1916, at least 62 of its ladies lived on Front Street." Okay, he probably pried the number out of the membership directory, but where is that document now? And how did he compile the facts quickly enough to produce three columns a week? The answer must be that Paul was a seasoned reporter, accustomed to getting the story, writing it quickly, and meeting a deadline. He had to have ransacked old newspapers for details. His reporter's notebooks must have been the source for much of his best writing, by virtue of his 25 years of interviewing, listening, and looking around. One of his associates told me that, like any good reporter, Paul cultivated sources in the city and in state government whom he did not name. Whatever our questioning, Paul would be entitled to reply that his journalism should be treated as the first draft of history, not as the definitive version. Inevitably, his results will stand on their merits.

Third, one cannot miss Paul's poetic sensibility. Appreciate this imagery as he seems to be riding along in an engineer's cab:

Running like great black cats, the locomotives went off into the night. Tight-lipped Dutchmen at the throttle would ease them across the Rockville Bridge, puffing their grayish clouds into a cinder-color sky in a sight of almost unimaginable beauty.

And then at the Cove, just north of Summerdale, the engineers would floor the old girls and they'd purr in rapid rhythms up to 100 mph—anticipating the thrill of their grandsons, the hot-rodders.

Then comes his Olympian observation:

In a panoramic view from above, glistening steel rail radiated from Harrisburg in all directions like a galaxy. Main lines, sidings, and classification yards were designed into an orderly pattern, not the pandemonium of the modern highway sprawl. The railroads were Euclidean geometry combined with the might of Vulcan. Sensible, conservative people understood the railroads.

He writes so well, so lively, that you forget you're just reading a newspaper. When he's not pleasing you with poetry, he's laying out just the right quotation, or jolting you with his own zingers. The supreme compliment to popular historians applies here: while he informs you, he keeps you turning pages.

Another defining trait of the columns is the presence of Paul's skepticism, his profession's inoculation against catching the conventional wisdom. That attitude is demonstrated in the following passage:

The cherished myth is that conservative Harrisburgers dislike government. It is a comforting ideology, espoused at today's Tuesday Club as it was at such old watering holes as the Jones House, Lochiel Hotel, Harrisburg Club, Esquire Bar and country club grills. But it is premeditated hokum.

He realized that mankind is fallen, glory is fleeting, and the newspaper goes on the floor of the bird cage at the end of the day. But, ultimately, Paul was willing to be un-skeptical and non-judgmental about anyone in town. In his last column, he wrote,

Way back the collective voice of Harrisburg whispered: "This is a crazy place. We're stubborn, standoffish, often narrow minded, silly and, boy are we self-righteous. But we're also lively, tolerant, have a damn great sense of humor, and when the chips are down and people are forthright we'll stick together. You try to understand us, and you'll get to love us. Is it a deal?

Over the years countless readers made a deal with him, and the entire community was the beneficiary.

Finally, something else to remember is that his commentaries are current for his times and therefore they are yesterday's news for us. When he says "now," he is referring to the late 1970s or the early 1980s, a generation ago. The economic statistics he uses have not been adjusted for today's inflation. However, seeing Harrisburg's once current events as if they were in a rear view mirror is not necessarily a disadvantage for us. Now as we read we can better judge if Paul's hopes and anxieties were on target, and we can reflect on his theory of Renaissance II. In short, we need yesterday's news in order to understand today's headlines. But I greatly wish that Paul could be writing this introduction instead of me, so that he could update or even revise his findings. Oh, for his dissection of our current mayoral politics! And his "Crime Scene Investigation" of the incinerator!

Paul started his career in journalism as a stringer for the Philadelphia Inquirer and the Bulletin, although at that time he was mainly occupied as a student at Girard College High School. He graduated from Girard in 1949 and from Wilkes College in 1953, in Wilkes-Barre, his home town. He served as a Journalist Third Class in the U.S. Navy until 1955, then earned a master's degree in 1956 from the Columbia University Graduate School of Journalism. He joined the Patriot-News staff in 1957 and was named Associate Editor of both newspapers in 1981. He retired from the Patriot-News company in 1985 and the next year was appointed Historian of the Pennsylvania State Legislature, a fitting last act for his professional life.

He won awards from the Pennsylvania Newspaper Publishers Association and the American Political Science Association. He was a Pulitzer Prize nominee and a Professional Journalism Fellow at Stanford. He once mentioned to me that he was a finalist for a Nieman Fellowship at Harvard, which is a wonderful plum for a serious journalist. Besides those achievements, Paul was the author of five books published by local and university presses. They are, *The Pennsylvania Sampler: A Biography of the Keystone State and its People* (Stackpole, 1970); *The Republican Years* (Patriot-News Co., 1971); *Profiles from the Susquehanna Valley: Past and Present Vignettes of its People, Times and Towns* (Stackpole, 1973); *Profiles in Pennsylvania Sports: Athletic Heroes and Exploits from Past and Present in the Commonwealth Where Sports Are Almost Everyone's Passion* (Stackpole, 1975); and *Pennsylvania Politics Today and Yesterday: The Tolerable Accommodation* (Pennsylvania State University Press, 1980). Those works continue to be highly valued and frequently cited. Toward the end he was working on a sixth book, his assessment of five recent governors. The chapters on Dick Thornburgh and Bob Casey are said to be complete.

Paul Benjamin Beers passed away on January 24, 2011, at age 79. He had been a resident for a number of years at Homeland Center in Harrisburg, diagnosed with Alzheimer's disease. I was doing the final editing on the manuscript at the time he died. He did not know the book was in development, and we had planned to present it to him in the spring. Now, regretfully, it must serve as a memorial rather than a gift. But his influence survives, and it should grow. To use a reviewer's trope, future historians will have to confront his work, and my prediction is they will embrace it. For our time, these columns should be considered the standard history of Harrisburg from the turn of the century to the 1980s.

Preparing Paul's writings was a school project. Four graduate students at Penn State Harrisburg—Nancy Jones, Megan McGee, Danielle Pfeiffer, and Sarah Hopkins—helped me transcribe and edit a portion of the columns during the spring and summer of 2009. In the fall of 2009, six students in my American Studies graduate seminar in local history helped edit and transcribe the remaining columns; they were Cecelia McNaughton, Rachael Zuch, Billy Jackson, Lyndsay Morrison, Sheila Rohrer, and Linda

Alonzo. As I intended, the editorial tasks helped them learn while they worked. I take the responsibility for the final editing and this introduction. I have read the columns very carefully and proofread the transcriptions, but I cannot guarantee the accuracy of all the names and numbers. Indeed, for the sake of the record, I invite readers to correct it.

At the Historical Society of Dauphin County, Steve Bachman, Ken Frew, Barbara Tiesch, and some anonymous helpers were indispensable in making sure we possessed all the columns. This project would still be waiting in a file cabinet if not for the assistance of those researchers. Cate Barron, Executive Editor at the Patriot-News Co., was a key facilitator, arranging permission for us to republish the Beers columns. Paul's friends, his son Philip, and representatives of the estate also provided their permission and vital assistance. Eric Papenfuse was eager for the Midtown Scholar Press to publish the manuscript, and for that we are most grateful. All profits from the sale of this book will go to Harrisburg Area Community College and the Historical Society of Dauphin County, two of Paul's designated charities.

Our editing of the columns was light-handed. We corrected the obvious typographical errors in the text, fixed misspellings, and added missing words. On occasion we have provided clarifications inside brackets [ ]. Paul's rhetorical style was his own, and he discovered or invented words such as eruditic, epigenisis, seclusive, struthious, lambented, and perditious. We left those alone. Economical journalism is inclined to avoid commas and abbreviate whatever it can, and we tolerate those practices here. One hyphen in particular was an editorial vexation. Paul's columns usually did not hyphenate the "Penn Harris" hotel, which I had seen other places written as "Penn-Harris." I checked the Reminiscences of the hotel's developer, E.Z. Wallower, and found that he always hyphenated his establishment's name. Moreover, memorabilia from the hotel's early years—specifically, a room key and a salad dish, both found on eBay's website—also show the hyphen. But, judging from the signage, the management did not hyphenate the name after the Penn Harris was relocated from Harrisburg to Camp Hill in 1964, when it was re-branded as a motor inn. One could justify either treatment, but again, respecting his judgment, I have decided to stay with Paul's deletion of the hyphen.

The columns were not titled in their original version; they were simply numbered from 1 to 120. To provide a useful table of contents, however, I have created a title for each of them, using pertinent wording from Paul's text. All the original columns featured small photographs to illustrate them, but finding all of those again was virtually impossible, so I have chosen a number of similar or suitable images and captioned them. In sum, one would have to say that Paul's writing doesn't really need an editor. What it does deserve is a throng of readers again, and we sincerely hope this book will attract them.

City CONTENTED

1.

OLD HOME WEEK

AND

RENAISSANCE I

IT WAS HARRISBURG HYPERBOLE, but when Mayor Edward Z. Gross proclaimed Harrisburg for Old Home Week as "the most prosperous and hustling city of its size in the country," his constituents agreed. Those were bully times.

Since frontier days, Harrisburgers had been a moderate, temperate folk, usually more apathetic and unappreciative of their community than boastful. Texans they're not. But this was 1905, and their city was in flower.

Genuine progress had been achieved, with rash expectations generated for the future.

A medium-sized American city with Harrisburg's capabilities, it was believed, could become the exciting hub of a thriving metropolis, not just another stop on the railroad. A new urban concept of regional municipal cores was evolving for prosperous towns a half-day's journey from the big cities and a half-hour from their own rural components. These regional centers would have orchestras, hotels, newspapers and sports teams like the big cities, but also farmers markets, fairs, specialized industries and neighborhoods like the old inland, upstate settlements they once had been. Such revitalized cities would be manageable, stable, affluent and contented.

The "City Beautiful Movement" was sweeping America, prodded by reformers committed to Katharine Lee Kates' popular lyrics of the day about "alabaster cities gleam, undimmed by human tears."

New Haven was doing municipal planning, as was Harrisburg. Toledo went so far as to throw out the old politicians and put its police on Civil Service. Harrisburg's politics were far better in the 1900-1920 era than they would be for decades afterward, but the town wasn't about to junk its hallowed principles of patronage for "Snivel Service," as some called it.

Not a backwater nor one-horse burg any longer, Harrisburg at the turn of the 20th Century would think of itself as the gem of the Susquehanna—urbane, cultured and attractive for that new breed of American go-getters. And Harrisburgers felt rich, and quickly getting richer. From 1900-1905 more than $5 million was invested in putting up 2,500 new structures in town, while from 1903-1910 seven new banks opened to share in the stepped-up business.

Old Home Week of Oct. 1-7 of 1905 would celebrate a hustling town that during the Gaslight Nineties had shot up by 10,000 so its population at the dawn of 1900 was just over 50,000—what the freemen of Periclean Athens numbered, or what Harrisburg would be in 1980 when the unexpected counter-cycle accelerated. The city would add 14,000 more persons between 1900 and 1910, and then 11,800 more the following decade.

A year before the 1920 census was available, the Harrisburg Chamber of Commerce surmised that the population figure would be 125,000—or 35,000 more than Harrisburg ever reached. Herman P. Miller, a developer of Bellevue Park, foresaw Harrisburg hitting 150,000. During the first 10

Old Home Week attracted an estimated 350,000 visitors in 1905 and let the city cheer itself.

years of the century, Bell Telephone increased phone service from 1,247 to 6,034 and predicted the city's population by 1930 might be 200,000.

Old Home Week was the town's cheering itself. Never before—nor never again—would it be so ecstatic. The Board of Trade, which in a decade became the Chamber of Commerce, invested $15,000 in Old Home Week, and an estimated 350,000 visitors and former residents were attracted. This was, after all, "a wide-awake, up-to-date modern city with more than 20 miles of excellently paved streets," announced The Patriot.

Citizens decorated their homes and shops with patriotic bunting. A "Triumphal Arch" was erected at the entrance of the new Market Street Bridge. The arch was only plaster, but it was bedecked with 15,000 lights.

Almost 100,000 persons, or nearly two-thirds of the metropolitan area, crowded center city to see a 5,000 person parade that was five miles long. The Grand Opera House staged "Uncle Tom's Cabin." There was a masquerade ball and a carnival. And then 6,500 gathered at City Island to watch the famed Carlisle Indians, quarterbacked by a swift, 140-pound Tuscarora named Frank Mt. Pleasant, shut out the unscored-upon Penn State Nittany Lions, 11-0.

The celebration's guest of honor, Gen. Horace Porter, spoke at Reservoir Park. He had grown up on Front Street as the son of Gov. David Rittenhouse Porter, became the chief aide in the Civil War to U. S. Grant, and won the Congressional Medal of Honor. Now he was ambassador to France.

To conclude the proud week, the Pennsylvania National Guard fired a 17-gun salute from the State Arsenal. Delighted Harrisburgers had a granite monument for Old Home Week erected in River Front Park. It is the last symbol of the occasion, but not the last reminder of the exuberance, the palpable optimism that was Harrisburg's Renaissance I.

2.

CITY BEAUTIFUL

Harrisburg: The City Beautiful, Romantic and Historic, as George P. Donehoo entitled his book, lasted from 1900 to 1930, or when the first clues emerged, though not recognized at the time, that the city was losing its pre-eminence.

This was the epoch of sunny horizons in which, as Dr. Donehoo stated: "The striving for better things in material surrounding is...an evidence and a token of what man is in his soul and of what he is seeking to attain. Someday he will be what he seeks to be."

Such purity, or naiveté, was heard from the highest places, such as the White House and the Governor's Mansion. Woodrow Wilson and Martin G. Brumbaugh, both pious sons of ministers, were the only Ph.D.s to hold their respective offices, and they believed sincerely in humankind's progress, almost perfectibility. To them, as to many, World War I was more opportunity than it was carnage.

Donehoo, himself an esteemed clergyman from Second Street, was married to a physician, Dr. Virginia B. Donehoo, one of the first woman doctors in town. He wrote his book in 1926 for The Telegraph Press of Edward J. Stackpole Sr., the newspaper publisher who was a stalwart backer of Harrisburg improvement, what was called "The Harrisburg Idea" or Renaissance I.

Buoyant and a bit smug, Donehoo saw the rebuilding and getting ahead as the attributes of secular salvation, and he helped proselytize this gospel of civic enterprise preached by his fellow community leaders.

"Harrisburg had existed from the days of John Harris and had been content with the 'things that are,'" wrote Donehoo. "Then suddenly it awoke to a blessed discontent with the 'things that are' and went after the 'things that ought to be.' The old town commenced to sink into the memories of the past and the new city of Harrisburg began to materialize."

It was the era of George F. Babbitt and his proud towers of Zenith aspiring above the morning mist. Teddy Roosevelt shouted "Bully," and Americans cheered. Sure, Philadelphia was "corrupt and contented," as Lincoln Steffens wrote in 1904, and in greedy, industrial Pittsburgh 40 of the 88 councilmen were under indictment for fraud. But Donehoo and thousands of others believed that humankind could achieve what it desired in its soul—though some of these values were no loftier than that of robbing the public treasury, such as the Capitol Draft Scandal right in Harrisburg.

Harrisburg was John O'Hara's Fort Penn, owned by "the best blood... families who by custom get things without even asking for them, because the people of Fort Penn acknowledged some kind of superiority."

Writing in 1949, O'Hara could sneer at such "superiority," but the Harrisburgers of 1900-1920 respected it, because in many cases it was an earned superiority. Much of the gentry did invest in and work for "the civic progress" that in their conviction was part of the logical, irreversible social evolution creating a Zion on the banks of the Susquehanna.

Commerce, as espoused by those like Donehoo, would replace meekness as the divine means to inherit the earth. Given its acquisitive German, Scotch-Irish and even Irish capitalists, the first third of the 20th century in Harrisburg was indeed one of exuberant civic self-assurance.

Harrisburg entered the new century sprinting. It had enjoyed the most prosperous year in its history in 1899. Blough Manufacturing, off Reily Street, in eight years went from one to almost 400 sewing machines, had a 150 percent increase in the sale of sunbonnets and was pioneering ready-to-wear garments. The buggy whip business in town was good, too.

In the next 20 years, Harrisburg's prosperity, buttressed by railroading, steel and growth in government, would improve even more.

The combined population of Dauphin and Cumberland counties passed the 200,000 mark in 1900, and the City of Harrisburg had 30 percent of that population. By 1920, with a growth of more than 25,000 persons, Harrisburg was up to 75,917—truly a metropolitan hub with a record 36 percent of the residents of the region.

Harrisburg leaped during the two decades to being the sixth largest Pennsylvania city, ahead of Wilkes-Barre which began to see its fortune in coal decline. Harrisburg was not only the state capital and the magnet for the affluent, the middle and the working classes, but it was Pennsylvania's growth city. And it was conveniently located on the keystone corridor between Philadelphia and Pittsburgh.

Better things were happening, and it was natural that George Donehoo and his brethren would think the Harrisburg soul as well would be improved.

3.

THE HANDSOMEST BUILDING HE EVER SAW

THE FIRST CHALLENGE for Harrisburg at the dawn of the 20th century was to save the capitol. Since 1812 Harrisburg had been the seat of state government, and now Philadelphia wanted that honor back.

Whither the Capitol, whither Harrisburg? With only 300 state employees in those days, the distinction of being the capital city was far greater than the economic advantages. But as sailors were to Norfolk, so bureaucrats had become to Harrisburg.

For the first 10 years after state government moved from Lancaster, the legislators held their four-month annual session in Dauphin County Courthouse, while three successive governors worked out of their rented houses.

It was a banner day in 1822 when the red-brick Capitol on the acropolis opened with its handsome portico topped by a clock. A low iron fence surrounded the grounds, which sloped upward to the two-story Capitol with its dome. The Capitol was of Harrisburg and yet apart from it, as the Vatican is to Rome, and Harrisburgers thought it would be just as eternal.

Then at high noon on Feb. 2, 1897, the 75-year-old Capitol burned down, a loss to taxpayers of $1.5 million. The blaze supposedly started in the faulty fireplace of the lieutenant governor who was out to lunch. An inferno erupted, routing legislators in session. An estimated 500 tons of paper and documents went up in flames, yet no one was severely injured.

Within eight days, the solons gathered at nearby Grace Methodist Church, and immediately the Philadelphia delegation submitted bills to relocate the capital to their city, where it had been until 1799.

So threatened, Harrisburgers united. Top leadership politicked as it has never done since for the good of the town, led by Congressman Marlin Olmsted and Senate President Samuel J. M. McCarrell, later judge. A House vote of 103-75 on May 8, 1901, saved Harrisburg—and coming five months after the famous "civic awakening" speech by Mira Lloyd Dock before the Harrisburg Board of trade, the vote also saved the crusade for city improvement.

Insiders knew, of course, that the legislators were against Philadelphia, and not for Harrisburg. Upstaters and Pittsburghers had little appreciation for Harrisburg's tepid hospitality. What they shared was a cordial dislike of Philadelphia as a den of Boies Penrose's iniquitous politics.

The new Capitol as "the handsomest building I ever saw" was dedicated by President Theodore Roosevelt on Oct. 4, 1906, in what was Harrisburg's proudest day.

It was one of the grandest projects of its time in the nation. For $13 million—half the assessed valuation of Harrisburg—the Capitol was solidly constructed and extravagantly furnished. Added to the Capitol lore was that it also became the nation's No. 1 public graft scandal—$4 million unrecovered and siphoned off by Eastern Pennsylvania politicians, not a Harrisburger in the bunch.

The brazen defrauding of taxpayer money didn't overly bother Harrisburgers. The shame of the grafters was quickly dispelled, their names

The censored Capitol statues. George Grey Barnard said, "I would put pajamas on Venus if it would save the cause of art."

and reputations blotted out. But the marmoreally monumental Capitol endured, soon achieving a transcending ageless splendor, like a bejeweled dowager queen.

What really propelled Harrisburg into the disturbing 20th century was the unveiling of the Capitol nudes on Oct. 4, 1911. These 27 life figures—representing "Law Unbroken" and "broken Laws"—were sculpted by George Grey Barnard and placed at the Capitol entrance. "Pagan art," some Harrisburgers wrote indignantly to The Patriot. It was, after all, two years before Marcel Duchamp's "Nude Descending a Staircase" made headlines at the controversial New York Armory Show.

The nudes frolicked merrily before State Street's church row, and as late as 1963 there was a legislative attempt to replace them with dutiful historic figures of Abraham Lincoln and Thomas Jefferson. A Pittsburgh senator bewailed that the innocence of visiting schoolchildren must not be besmirched.

Barnard (1863-1938) was from Bellefonte, studied under Auguste Rodin in Paris and became a teacher of Jacob Epstein. He was in the 1913 Armory Show and the year his Harrisburg nudes were unveiled he started a museum in New York which he sold to the Rockefellers for the Cloisters.

Barnard did the models of his Harrisburg statuary in Paris. Anticipating a negative reaction in his native state, he added fig leaves to the gentlemen in the final soft Italian marble. "I would put pajamas on Venus if it would save the cause of art," he said.

He expected to receive $700,000, or the largest sculpture commission ever paid in the United States, but the adamant Legislature gave him only $180,000 and would have thrown the sculpture out if experts from Columbia University and the Metropolitan Museum of Art hadn't certified its worthiness. Not embittered, Barnard later had himself buried in Harrisburg Cemetery to be near his masterpieces.

4.

AN EDIFICE OF SOVEREIGNTY

THE MASSIVENESS OF THE NEW CAPITOL—a secular cathedral, really—fostered a spirit of thinking big into admiring Harrisburgers.

A feeling of bully brawniness took hold in a town that previously had modest mansions and humble shops. St. Patrick Cathedral down State Street was under construction while the capitol was being built. It, too, is huge, with that ineffable space that gives worshippers a sense both of spiritual expansion and community bonds.

American architecture at the turn of the century sought to reflect the nation's assertiveness and also its inner need for social order in a confusing era of rapid industrialization, urban dislocations and massive immigration. Europeans with their named printed on signs around their necks got off the train at Steelton to work at the mill, and in the distance they could see the majestic dome of the Capitol of their new homeland. For older Americans, the Pennsylvania Capitol was a patriotic partner of the U.S. Capitol, completed in 1867.

The new Harrisburg Capitol originally had 633 rooms and was 23 times larger than the old red-brick Capitol. It sat upon a two-acre expanse of Vermont granite—hauled into Harrisburg in 1,100 carloads. The building's half-mile circumference made it larger than St. Paul's Cathedral of London or Westminster Abbey.

To many provincial Harrisburgers at the turn of the century, the Capitol olive-colored dome was awesome, certainly the most impressive work of architecture they had ever seen.

The dome was modeled after St. Peter's of Rome. It is supported by seven million bricks, or almost a year's production from the Bigler Brickyard off Cameron Street.

The lighted dome soars 272 feet, topped by the 14-foot-5-inch female figure symbolic of the Commonwealth, but always called "Miss Penn." It wasn't until the 291-foot City Towers opened in 1975 that Harrisburg had a taller structure, but the Capitol on its 34-foot elevation still overshadows City Towers. The 334-foot Harristown building for the Department of Education at 333 Market Street in 1980 became the tallest building in Pennsylvania between Philadelphia and Pittsburgh, but in optical perspective it does not appear to out-sky the more gigantic Capitol two blocks away.

There are 335 steps to the top of the Capitol, and for the building's 75th anniversary in 1981, Rep. Kenneth E. Brandt of Falmouth led a climb up them to Miss Penn's golden toe, Harrisburg's first Himalaya expedition.

Among its many splendors, the new Capitol had the world's finest lighting system, and in 1906 likely the world's most expensive one—$2 million's worth that cost $4 million, because its overly elaborate chandeliers and other fixtures were illegally weighted to fetch a higher price for the favored contractors.

Gov. Samuel W. Pennypacker was so thrilled with the Rotunda, its grand staircase modeled after the 1875 Paris Opera House, that he had all the lights turned on the night before the dedication. To this day on rare occasions when the opulent Rotunda is fully illuminated, the glittering effect from the chandeliers and the interior of the radiant dome is like the sparkling brightness of a thousand diamonds.

Oddly, the building had its critics at its birth, not at its maturity. "A monstrous botch of bad arrangement...and most bloated bad taste," wrote Owen Wister, the Philadelphia novelist and muckraker, who disliked the Capitol's "great aimless bulk, its bilious, overeaten decoration, its swollen bronzes, its varicose chandeliers." Violet Oakley did her most famous murals for the Capitol, especially for the Supreme Court chamber, but by 1950 even she conceded, "Distance undoubtedly lends enchantment to the Capitol."

Yet there remains distinct grandeur to the building, that proper sort of grandiosity that hasn't succumbed to modern functionalism and pretentious commercial design. This Capitol is not the work of cost accountants who lease by the square foot, calculate planned obsolescence, and compute depreciation. This is an edifice of sovereignty that heralds the spirit of a past generation imbued with such secure optimism in its nation-building intentions that nothing less than manifest destiny was its creed.

5.

THE BIGGEST CENTRALIZED STATE GOVERNMENT IN AMERICA

THE SPLENDID NEW CAPITOL wasn't 20 years old before state government, to the joy of Harrisburgers, outgrew it and needed expansion.

Pennsylvania fashioned the biggest centralized state government in America, more concentrated than New York's, California's or anybody else's. The lure of patronage and the strategy to isolate the distrusted big city machines encouraged upstaters to make the Capitol their political bastion.

Ten successive Republican administrations, from 1895 through 1934, increased state government. Patronage masters like Harrisburg's Simon Cameron, Ed Beidleman and M. Harvey Taylor could always find a berth for a worthy supporter's sure vote.

The cherished myth is that conservative Harrisburgers dislike government. It is a comforting ideology, espoused at today's Tuesday Club as it was at such old watering holes as the Jones House, Lochiel Hotel, Harrisburg Club, Esquire Bar and country club grills. But it is premeditated hokum.

John Harris himself was the first to appreciate government and its blessings, by setting aside "four acres and 13 perches" for the Capitol in 1791.

U.S. Sen. William Maclay, Harris' son-in-law, was the mastermind behind the family's machinations for immortality. When he laid out the city, he reserved "The Hill" for the eventual Capitol, and later sold to the commonwealth from his own holdings an additional 12 acres for $36,430 to make the scheme a reality.

As caustic as he was brilliant, Maclay was the first of the city's numerous shrewd legal entrepreneurs, and it is fitting that his Front Street home today is the headquarters of the Pennsylvania Bar Association as it furthers its constituents' privileges via government.

It was Maclay who devised Harrisburg's surefire plot for defeating the envious ambitions of rival sister cities by keeping the capital domain provided with land and buildings as quickly as the state government's

Views of the splendiferous Capitol were the most popular Harrisburg postcards.

insatiable appetite demanded. Harrisburg could be a good neighbor and an avaricious one, Maclay would have said if he had put such pragmatic thoughts in writing.

That lesson had to be relearned after the 1897 Capitol fire. Before the Civil War, the Capitol sought to expand toward the river, between North and South Streets, but local property holders wanted $24,400 and the state wouldn't pay. As the new Capitol was being dedicated in 1906, Harrisburg Sen. John E. Fox had the Legislature authorize $1.6 million for more land and construction at its backdoor.

At the turn of the century, the Capitol had about 300 employees working under a governor paid $10,000. There were 11 departments and 14 boards and commissions. The attorney general was paid $3,500; clerks, $1,400 and night watchmen, $900. The annual budget was $17 million, and its $8 million balance was more than enough to pay off the state debt of $6.8 million.

In two decades, to Harrisburg's delight, that state budget grew to $46 million, the state debt to $50 million, and the payroll to about 1,400. There were 20 departments, 24 commissions, 15 boards and 24 different tax funds. The governor was paid $16,500; top stenographers, $4,000, and custodians, $1,800.

This spending and hiring was genuine Republicanism. The depressed Democrats never had more than 15 senators or 55 House members at any one time to make a difference.

Between 1912 and 1919, under the guidance of Capitol architect Arnold W. Brunner and landscape architect Warren H. Manning, the commonwealth spent $2.3 million for almost 30 acres of the old Eighth Ward, from Walnut to North Streets. Some 598 buildings on 331 properties, including five churches, two synagogues, Hickok Manufacturing, the

Paxtang Flour and Feed and a cigar factory, were cleaned out for what became the South Office, North Office, Forum and Treasury buildings.

Harrisburg's original black neighborhood was razed. Wesley Union AME Zion Church had been founded in 1829 and from 1862 to 1917 was where The Forum is today. Immigrant German and Irish laborers had moved into the ward as early as 1826 to build the Pennsylvania Canal, near today's Main Line tracks. That canal closed in the winter of 1901. An early Jewish community also lived in the ward.

The one immovable object in the complex was the Brelsford meat processing plant, opened in 1883, that became Swift and Company. As many as 500 hogs daily were slaughtered there. On butchering days, the abattoir odors wafted over the Capitol, and at least once during the 1950s swine escaped across Seventh Street to mingle with the public servants. Eventually, in April of 1970, the slaughterhouse was razed and a central air-conditioning unit and parking lot were put in its place.

For a busier, more prosperous Harrisburg, man and beast gave way.

6.

ITINERANT GOVERNORS

SINGLE-MINDED AS HARRISBURG POLITICIANS always were about bigger state government and patronage, they often were inconsiderate of the well-being of the governor.

Lieutenant governors for years took hotel rooms. It wasn't until 1971, when Milton Shapp sent Lt. Gov. Ernest P. Kline to the Indiantown Gap Mansion, that these public servants didn't pay rent. Many Harrisburg politicians thought of the governor as an itinerant, and were heedless of his domestic desires.

The attitude might trace back to the fact that no Harrisburger ever became governor. The bosses, like Simon Cameron, Ed Beidleman and M. Harvey Taylor, never wanted to be upstaged by promoting anyone of their own, though Beidleman was counted out in Pittsburgh in the 1926 primary for the big job. Not to be discriminating, these bosses also ignored the U.S. Senate seat for Harrisburg colleagues, though Simon and son Don Cameron held it themselves for 40 years.

Not providing a first-rate Governor's Mansion was a serious oversight for Harrisburg politicians. Gov. David L. Lawrence about 1960 expressed what many previous governors might have felt. He said he didn't enjoy living in the old Governor's Mansion, he thought Harrisburgers' disrespect of state government insulting, and he wouldn't mind moving some

Keystone Hall, the governor's residence downtown, was a grand brownstone, but, considered inadequate to its task, it met the wrecker in 1960.

state offices and employees to other, more appreciative towns. Lawrence didn't threaten, but his words were scary.

The first three governors in Harrisburg, 1812-1822, didn't even have an office. That wasn't too critical for Gov. Simon Snyder, because he could carry most of his files in his pocket. The state budget was only $336,189.15, there were fewer than 50 employees, and taxes during the War of 1812 were so lucrative that the balance at the end of the year was an incredible $10,531 higher than the original total budget.

There wasn't even an official mansion for the first 11 governors. State Rep. John Kunkel in 1851 did seek an appropriation for one, but it wasn't until 1858 that an $11,000 house was purchased where Executive House is today.

At last in 1864 the Old Governor's Mansion at 313 N. Front St. was bought for $30,000, and Andrew G. Curtin moved in. Sensing that if a permanent mansion weren't acquired a governor someday might want to move the capital, the City of Harrisburg provided $20,000 in cash to pay the widow for her home. The city exacted the promise from the commonwealth that if the capital ever were moved from Harrisburg, it would be repaid its $20,000.

The brownstone front to the old mansion was added in the 1880s, the same time two successive governors, Robert E. Pattison and James A. Beaver, saw their young sons, both juniors, die at the mansion. A pallor descended, and the mansion never gained liveliness until fun-loving George H. Earle had a pinball machine installed during the Great Depression.

Harrisburgers, if not governors, thought the mansion a classy place. Kids lined up on the steps Christmas morning to receive traditional "belsnickels" candy gifts from governors. Councilman DeWitt Fry had the same 313 address on S. Front Street, so he put a brownstone stoop on his house to resemble the Governor's Mansion.

Rep. John A.F. Hall, later Harrisburg's mayor, in 1927 vainly sought $500,000 for a new mansion. By then the state was in the midst of spending $200,000 to refurbish the old place with its 23 rooms, 11 bathrooms, 196 chairs, 19 fireplaces and nine clocks, all in four floors covering two rowhouse properties.

As Gov. Edward Martin was spending $36,658 for a summer mansion at Indiantown Gap during World War II, Sen. Harvey Taylor just weeks before Pearl Harbor had the commonwealth buy two properties at Front and Maclay streets for $185,000. Gov. Dick Thornburgh at the 1979 Gridiron Dinner quipped that the state got "a public housing project on the flood plain of the Susquehanna." Taylor didn't care where a new governor's mansion should go, even Reservoir Park. City hall, however, reminded the state that if it went up on Front Street, it was taking $100,000 out of municipal tax revenues.

Lawrence in 1960 sold the old mansion for $85,000 and moved to Indiantown Gap. His successor, William W. Scranton, complained that the 54-mile roundtrip to the Capitol made the Gap "a little more convenient for the governor of New Jersey" than for himself.

At last for Christmas of 1968, Gov. Raymond P. Shafer moved into the new $2.4 million mansion at 2035 Front St., designed by a 78-year-old architect from Swarthmore. The monthly mortgage payments for 30 years are $12,133, so it will cost a final $4.37 million—or a few dollars more than the combined pay of all 38 governors in Harrisburg.

It took 22 years to get the Taj Mahal. The new Governor's Mansion required five more years than that.

7.

MIRA LLOYD DOCK AND THE "HARRISBURG IDEA"

FIVE DAYS BEFORE CHRISTMAS of 1900, the "Harrisburg Idea," or Renaissance I, was born. The unlikely Joan of Arc for Harrisburg was Mira Lloyd Dock.

It was Miss Dock's illustrated lecture that evening before the Harrisburg Board of Trade that constituted, in the words of her friend, J. Horace McFarland, "the last blow...toward breaking the stone of Harrisburg's indifference."

The gallant lady told the respected burghers that their city was anything but beautiful and romantic, and was, in fact, unhealthy. Conservationist McFarland noted that Mira took to the ramparts for a "crusade against ugliness."

Miss Dock was a stocky Front Street spinster in her mid-40s. Her family, for whom Dock Street was named, was not wealthy but was applauded for achievements in medicine.

An uncle, Dr. George Dock, as far back as the 1860s and 1870s, fought futilely for pure drinking water in Harrisburg.

The Docks were another in that peculiar Harrisburg tradition of large families who ceased marrying and reproducing. Their neighbors, the banking McCormicks, had five bachelor sons. Mira was one of six Docks who remained single.

She became a European traveler, an accomplished photographer, an arts lover, an amateur forester and botanist, and a friend of noted contemporaries such as Gifford Pinchot and literature's William Dean Howells. Mira also was a superb clubwoman in an age when towns like Harrisburg had serious women's organizations with assertive grand dames to lead them. Mira, as much as anyone, founded the Wednesday Club, for it was at her home at 1427 N. Front Street that its first meeting was held on May 17, 1882. She also was a founder of the Civic Club.

Yet she would be just another name in the annals of Harrisburg if she hadn't been an activist in the City Beautiful Movement.

Urban enhancement was something new. Educated civic leaders, joining with progressive planners, architects, physicians and a few politicians, recognized a public calling that had a priority over their professional self-interest. The ravages of the Industrial Revolution—an accumulation of a half-century's worth of blight, dirt and indigence—needed to be redressed.

Chicago's world fair of 1893, the Columbian Exposition, launched the City Beautiful Movement with its glorious slogan, "Make Culture Hum." The National Municipal League was founded in 1894, and the Conference for Good Government started the following year. Daniel H. Burnham's Chicago Plan of 1896 and then Burnham's inspired redesign of the Washington Mall showed what could be done. Soon cities like Philadelphia, Seattle and Cleveland were modernizing their streets, transportation, waterfronts, parks, railroad stations, health facilities like water filtration and hospitals, and the necessities and amenities that contribute to the aesthetics of urban living.

Mira Lloyd Dock was a uniquely noticeable and influential leader of Harrisburg's City Beautiful movement.

Do-goodism was part of the movement, but it also had a hardcore capitalistic investment base and a preference for the pragmatic in its proposals and designs. "The cash value of cleanliness and beauty" was just as important as aesthetics, Miss Dock proclaimed.

Germanic Harrisburg, with its certainty that cleanliness is next to godliness and almost as important as material comfort, was especially susceptible to the arguments of Miss Dock, McFarland and others that the community was not only dirty but unhygienic. It was. Moonshine from Perry County was safer to drink than the piped-in Susquehanna.

Miss Dock's speech goaded the Board of Trade, founded in 1886, into action -quite unusual, because it is the first known incident of a woman in male-dominated Harrisburg influencing public policy. The lady had made a "graphic contrast of our filthy and unattractive civic conditions compared with our opportunities for natural beauty," McFarland said.

The Board of Trade told Mira that if her "Harrisburg Idea" were to work, $5,000 was necessary in seed money. John V.W. Reynders, the superintendent of the bridge department at the Steelton mill, was the first to respond, writing to the Harrisburg Telegraph and pledging $100. Within 10 days the $5,000 was subscribed, and a week later a committee of seven, chaired by Vance McCormick, was formed. Four days later -or just 18 days after the Reynders letter of May 3, 1901—the Harrisburg League for Municipal Improvements was organized.

Ironically, Mira Lloyd Dock, the catalyst of the project, inexplicably left town in 1903 to live her last 42 years with relatives in Graeffenburg and then Fayetteville, towns that had many of its young people moving to exciting cities like Harrisburg.

8.

VANCE MCCORMICK AND THE MUNICIPAL LEAGUE

IN THE SPRING OF 1901, City Councilman Vance McCormick was only 29, but he was chairman of the Municipal League, a year away from becoming mayor and proprietor of The Patriot, and his mind and level of intensity were on a par with his family and banking connections.

Though privately close-fisted, McCormick as a young man was publicly generous. His Municipal League's $5,000, even in 1901, could do little. What the city should do is borrow $525,000.

"It must be confessed that Harrisburg has not pushed herself to the front with the energy that she should," he said. "There has been too much indifference to the public welfare in a selfish desire to benefit the individual."

He pointed out that Harrisburg could well afford such civic investment spending, as there were only five cities in the nation with lower municipal taxes.

The Municipal League functioned until McCormick's death in June 1946, when he was its last president. J. Horace McFarland was its secretary all 45 years. E.Z. Wallower, the spirited capitalist who would build the Penn Harris Hotel, was its early chairman of the executive committee. Architect William Lynch Murray and Dr. Roy Stetler were its last vice presidents. Murray, appropriately, would launch the Greater Harrisburg Movement in the 1960s and lead the way to Renaissance II.

For its "Awakening of Harrisburg," McCormick's Municipal League wasted no time in going after its slumbering city.

Within a month of its own formation, the league hired two of the nation's most respected consultants—landscape architect Warren H. Manning of Boston and sanitary engineer James H. Fuertes. Manning, a protégé of Frederick Law Olmsted of Central Park fame, was a friend of McFarland's in the national conservation movement. He took one look at Harrisburg and said, "There is not a finer natural site for a city anywhere on the continent." Fuertes, having just completed the textbook on water filtration, planned Harrisburg's and Steelton's new water system.

Local expertise rallied to the cause. Dr. George Reily Moffitt Sr., the bacteriologist at Harrisburg Hospital, reviewed as many as 1,000 local typhoid cases a year. While health statistical reporting was new and inexact at the time, Harrisburg one year had a known 27 deaths from typhoid fever and 13 from diphtheria. There were probably more of these childhood afflictions than there were adult Harrisburgers writhing with syphilis and gonorrhea. A more frightening comparison is Harrisburg's typhoid caseload with the polio epidemic of a generation later, when the entire commonwealth in its peak year of 1952 had 1,965 new polio victims.

It didn't surprise Harrisburgers that its epidemics seemed to be a constant, not just periodic, occurrence. A half-million people upstream dumped their untreated waste into the Susquehanna, and Harrisburgers drank the unfiltered water. Of Harrisburg's own sewage, what garbage wasn't discarded along the river bank, 60 percent went into the Susquehanna and 40 per-

Vance C. McCormick ran for governor in 1914, after his successful stint as mayor. He lost, but then managed Woodrow Wilson's winning re-election campaign in 1916.

cent into Paxton Creek. During summer droughts, the foul-smelling river produced an odoriferous "Susquehanna Punch" that rivaled the "Schuylkill Punch" which gave Philadelphians diarrhea and worse.

With these facts at hand and Harrisburg's dependable battalion of "no-sayers" contained, McCormick had the audacity to up his recommended bond issue from $525,000 to $1.1 million. That huge sum was more than the city in its history had spent on public facilities. It probably was half what the entire West Shore was worth at the time.

McCormick, with the arrogance of an aristocrat, got the bond issue on the ballot for Feb. 18, 1902—the same day he was running for mayor. It would be nine months, less three days, since the Municipal League was formed. Harrisburg never before—nor ever again—did anything worthwhile with such urgency.

With braintrusters like McFarland, Wallower, Edward Bailey, William Jennings, W.K. Alricks and smart lawyers like Robert Snodgrass, Ehrman B. Mitchell Sr. and Spencer C. Gilbert, young McCormick was as cunning as when he had quarterbacked Yale's undefeated team or coached the Carlisle Indians. He called the bond issue and his mayoralty candidacy the "Anti-Typhoid Ticket."

A 25-year-old ward healer from Shipoke named Harve Taylor must have shaken his head at the way such a Democrat was outdistancing his Republicans. Teetotaler McCormick once gave Taylor a bottle of ginger ale to pitch illegally for the Harrisburg Academy. Now the man was talking real money, like $1.1 million. Harve always respected Vance McCormick after that.

9.

THE MOST SPIRITED ELECTION IN HARRISBURG HISTORY

THE "ANTI-TYPHOID TICKET" OF 1902—a record $1.1 million bond issue and Vance McCormick for mayor—spawned the most spirited election in Harrisburg history.

Both newspapers, the Telegraph of Edward J. Stackpole Sr. and the Patriot, which McCormick would purchase in six months, tried to outdo the other in enthusiasm for municipal improvement. This was Stackpole's first local election as a new publisher, and he sought to establish himself as a civic spokesperson. McCormick as chairman of the Municipal League could advocate a tie-in package—the bond issue and himself.

Republican Stackpole—he and his sons would never support a Democrat in their lives—avoided the embarrassment of backing the cocky Democrat McCormick by endorsing his opponent, Dr. Samuel F. Hassler, an excellent physician who specialized in contagious diseases and later for 16 years would be the city's director of public safety.

"Mr. McCormick is a rich man only in the sense that he has money," editorialized The Patriot, still owned by the Orr family but ready to be bought by that McCormick money. "He works more hours every day than most men of less estate." It intimated that "Handsome Sam" Hassler, only 34, was less of a Harrisburger than McCormick, because he lived a few blocks away at Second and State Streets from the 29-year-old Front Streeter.

The Municipal League raised $10,221.55 to fight for the bond issue. It distributed more than 200,000 circulars and other campaign advertisements, yet finished with a $331.91 balance.

One of the leaflets contained a Patriot editorial entitled, "The Crisis—Prosperity a Brilliant Future, Or a Public Failure a Doomed City." The editorial warned that if the river, creek and sewers weren't modernized, "The people will continue to drink polluted water and the death rate from the dread typhoid will continue to increase, until each summer will come an epidemic that will carry off hundreds."

The Telegraph got Gov. William A. Stone to speak out: "Let your bathtub run full of city water any morning without filtering it and then look at it. You might as well go down to the tannery and bathe in a vat. It might take your hair off, but you would come out clean. Debt is not a disgrace nor is it a serious impediment. It has always been and always will be the forerunner or prosperity."

To the tune of "Marching Through Georgia." The Telegraph printed a song: "When we stroll at the riverfront upon a summer's day, the perfume that we must inhale is not like new-mown hay."

J. Horace McFarland, a nationally respected conservationist with a major printing business near 13th and Derry streets, was a genius at public relations. More importantly, he led his committee of 60 civic-minded leaders not to ignore Harrisburg's political realities. He pushed the idea that Harrisburg was the 77th largest city in the nation and should act like it. He insisted the project not be portrayed as a "Front Street Scheme."

It happened that 1902 was a rare golden epoch in Harrisburg politics, when enlightened patricians had the wit and the desire to take command. Usually the gentry play the role of the money-bags behind the scene, but Boss Simon Cameron was dead, his son J. Donald was retired, youthful Ed Beidleman was still three years away from going into the Legislature, and such neighborhood masters as Harve Taylor and Tom Nelley had not yet emerged to form an invincible Republican machine. There was no way for "zero voting," an old Harrisburg habit, to occur, because the aristocrats supported the Municipal League and not those who distributed the "street money."

So the bond issue won, 7,319 to 3,729, carrying 31 of 37 precincts though Front Street gave more support than Shipoke. McCormick was a bit behind, 7,066 to 4,503, and on Select and Common Councils, the Republicans held sway, 20 members to 10, and retained control of the School Board.

"The tide has changed for Harrisburg people are praising now instead of condemning, and the whole country is echoing with words of commendation for the Harrisburg Plan," the Telegraph editorialized. "There is no doubt about Harrisburg being awake and there is no doubt concerning the future of the city."

Harrisburgers voted to open their wallets, and indeed it was surprising. The Pittsburgh Post commented: "It is a credit to the intelligence of the average voter in Harrisburg that the loan received so amazing an endorsement."

Few before ever praised the intelligence of the average Harrisburg voter. And Vance McCormick became mayor on April 1, 1902.

10.

MAYOR MCCORMICK

AND THE

AWAKENING OF HARRISBURG

THE ROBUST MAYOR VANCE MCCORMICK was a glowing, if slightly stout, All-American who prided himself for being tidy, well-soaped and fastidious. No alcohol smelled on his breath, and there was no dirt under his fingernails.

McCormick's three years in City Hall, 1902-1905, had that scrubbed look, also. "The administration of Mayor McCormick was a revelation," acknowledged his friend, J. Horace McFarland. "The city was cleaned up, morally and physically, as fast as this active young man could bring it about."

In 1906 McFarland wrote a 20-page report, "The Awakening of Harrisburg," which he sold for 10 cents. He was especially pleased that the city had 22 miles of paved streets and they were "cleaned every day."

Mayor McCormick hired a corps of street sweepers—the last broom-and-cart man worked center city until the late 1950s, a jolly proletarian who would park his cart outside the restaurant he was taking a lady friend to lunch.

McCormick insisted the streets in the business district be sprinkled twice daily during the workweek. His public relations couldn't have been better. While often lax about their own cleanliness, Harrisburgers want the appearance of public neatness. The prevailing hypocrisy is to have a spruce-up campaign at least once during every City Hall administration. The City Beautiful reformers, like McCormick, heartily believed in cleanliness and they used it for good political effect in their bond-issue campaign.

McFarland advocated putting two comfort stations beneath Market Square, and the McCormick administration followed through. This was really avant-garde, for much of Shipoke was still using "outdoor plumbing." The comfort stations remained public until the late 1950s, and eventually in the mid-1960s were boarded up in the cause of public safety, not comfort.

The mayor was an automobile enthusiast; in fact in 1907 would be the founder of the Central Penn Motor Club, with headquarters at his Market Square newspaper office. The national AAA had been organized only five years before, and in 1906 Pennsylvania began issuing its first driver's licenses. McCormick's club threw its weight behind getting the River Road north of the city paved, and even threatened to take an obstinate Susquehanna Twp. to court if it didn't cooperate.

New fangled autos created controversy. One state senator ran for governor supporting a 24-mph speed limit, and as late as 1913, a year before World War I, Pennsylvania voters rejected a $50 million highway building referendum, to Editor McCormick's dismay.

Downtown Harrisburg and the Capitol are boxed in by what essentially is a peninsula—eight blocks wide bounded by the Susquehanna and Main Line and snipped at the south by the Shipoke steel mills of the time. Mayor McCormick used the bond issue to make access to center city a glistening-clean priority.

Old Camelback Bridge, one of the nation's most-famous covered bridges built by Theodore Burr in 1812 as Harrisburg became the capital, collapsed in the spring flood just weeks before McCormick took office. While the Walnut Street Bridge, or "Old Shaky," had opened after the 1889 flood, the Camerons, McCormicks and Haldemans formed a rival toll company and in 1904 opened the Market Street Bridge. Both it and Old Shaky had tolls until 1957 and for many years were generous profit-makers for their investors—5 cents for horse wagons and autos, 3 cents for horseback riders, and a penny for pedestrians or bicycle riders under 16. The tolls also served Harrisburg by discouraging West Shore development.

On the eastern access to center city, McCormick opened the Market and Herr Street subways—underpasses Harrisburgers insist upon calling "subways,' to the delight of New Yorkers and Philadelphians. Derry Street traffic was fed into center city with the Mulberry Street Viaduct, which in 1909 was the world's longest reinforced concrete span over railroad tracks.

McCormick emphasized street paving, and by the end of his administration had center city and most of Front and Cameron streets blacktopped—and this was a time when all of Cumberland County had only three miles of paved road.

Original plans called for a grass plot in the middle of Market Square, where the old butcher and produce sheds had been. The zest for street paving, however, was so high that the merchants like S.S. Pomeroy, J.H. Troup, W.J. Calder, Sam Kuhn, W.N. Knisely, and Fred Kelker prevailed upon City Hall to ignore McFarland's cries of desecration and asphalt the square.

11.

THE HARRISBURG IMPROVEMENT PLAN

During Harrisburg's Renaissance I after the turn of the century, impressive landmarks like the Capitol, St. Patrick Cathedral and the Rockville Bridge went up. They had stateliness, massiveness and grandeur, and would last for generations.

Permanence also is a quality of the three miles of river steps that were built as Harrisburg's shoreline for the Susquehanna—as remarkable a piece of construction as perhaps ever accomplished in Central Pennsylvania.

The river steps already have outlasted three major floods in 1936, 1972 and 1975, plus innumerable minor floods that drenched Shipokers. Winter after winter, ice floes punch at the steps, but to no avail. On the day of high water for the Hurricane Agnes flood of 1972, there was almost 30 times the normal river flow—or an incredible 650 billion gallons of water—in the nation's 16th largest river basin swirling, jabbing and pressuring the steps, but they held fast. A contemporary of the Capitol, St. Patrick, and the Rockville Bridge, they, too, are indomitable.

The steps were a minor $400,000 project in the $25 million or so spent on what was called "Harrisburg Improvement." Unfortunately, there is

The riverbank was once a catch-all for everything that floated down the river or that was thrown from the top of the bank.

no comparable river wall on the West Shore along the other banks of the Susquehanna.

They are a mere foot thick, made of concrete that was mixed one part cement, two parts sand, and four parts stone and then applied with an almost-dry mortar for solid binding. Henry McCormick Gross, the leading engineer on the project, inherited the recipe from his ancestors and personally supervised the construction like a top sergeant.

The spirited Pete Gross was old Harrisburg at its best, and appropriately he ended up being, literally, the last of the real Front Streeters. He was a younger cousin to Mayor Vance McCormick and was the son of McCormick's successor, Mayor Edward Z. Gross. Like them, he had a stocky Teddy Roosevelt frame, sense of command, and an alert mind that was always improvising another mission to be accomplished. After graduating from Yale, he served on the Mexican Border and in World War I, became a financier, a fine civic leader and, most illustriously, the brigadier general in charge of Pennsylvania's Selective Service for a quarter-century.

Gross' and Vance's mutual grandfather, J. Vance Criswell, built the 1862 reservoir at Reservoir Park so well that he went broke doing it, Pete Gross always maintained. His great-uncles, James and A.J. Dull, constructed the river piers for William H. Vanderbilt's South Pennsylvania Railroad in 1885, a bridge never completed for a line never opened because Andrew Carnegie backed out of the deal. Both the reservoir and the piers have lasted a century because Criswell and the Dulls used the concrete formula that their descendant Pete Gross followed.

The Harrisburg Improvement Plan was tripartite: esthetics and parks; street paving and access; and water, sewer and flood control. The latter were the most costly.

The $295,000 filtration plant at City Island was built by engineer James Fuertes as the most modern of its kind in the nation. Opened in 1907, it never failed unless it was flooded out. By 1948, however, Harrisburg had its gravity-fed DeHart Reservoir at Clarks Valley in full operation and stopped using the Susquehanna for other than emergencies. Finally the 1972 Flood knocked out the filtration plant completely. At its debut, the plant handled 10 million gallons daily.

With Fuertes' designs, the city also put up the Dock Street Dam, laid intercepting sewers, redid the Paxton Creek basin to increase its capacity

The construction of the walkway and steps transformed the city's rugged edge along the river, turning it into an elegant frame.

five times, and turned Wetzel's Swamp into the 140-acre Wildwood Lake with a spillway.

As most of the city streets were unpaved, it wasn't inconvenient to lay 95 miles of new water line, so vastly improving a system that went back to 1841 that citizens quickly tapped into spigot water and the city's water department was realizing a profit by 1906—politically a bad omen, because City Hall started its tradition of dipping into the water surpluses to balance its budgets.

The $641,000 Paxton Creek job was the only one oversold. It was to be a “controlled stream” guaranteed to stay “a harmless little stream never disturbed even in the highest flood periods.” Paxton Creek proved to be less amenable than that, and well into the 21st century it probably will remain a welterweight flooder with the Susquehanna as the heavy-weight in the always-threatening one-two punch.

12.

AN ACRE PER 80

OF ALL THEIR ACHIEVEMENTS, the reformers in the City Beautiful Movement were most enthusiastic about creating the Harrisburg Park System.

They almost reached their utopian dream of ringing the entire city with green space. They did make Harrisburg No.1 in the nation in park land per capita, just ahead of Decatur, Ill. With 1,087 acres of parks, Harrisburg had an acre per 80 residents.

Modern Pennsylvanians with their zest for camping, hiking and biking have yet to capture but a tincture of the obsession earlier Americans had for the outdoors.

William Penn wished his Pennsylvania communities would reserve one-fifth of their land for trees and parks. Harrisburg almost reached that ideal, with one-seventh of the city left free. And it wasn't easy to uphold that goal. There was always a developer or a politician with a scheme for "making use" of green space.

Unlike most of suburbia, Harrisburg virtually started with parks. John Harris II, the city founder, built his mansion on Front Street and deeded Capitol Hill to the commonwealth. Historian A. Boyd Hamilton said that had Harris not settled on the river bank, the early railroad barons would have laid track up the east side of the Susquehanna, as they did on the bluff of the West Shore.

With River Park in place, Harrisburg in 1876 set aside 88 acres for Reservoir Park. At the height of Renaissance I in 1906, conservationist J. Horace McFarland successfully fought a suggestion that a merry-go-round and toboggan destroy the serenity of that expanse.

Harrisburg's capitalists were enlightened enough never to permit their city to become a town of only "dark, satanic mills," as many other Pennsylvania cities became during the Industrial Revolution. Though they usually kept their money to themselves, they generously gave away land.

The Harrisburg Bridge Co. in 1904 donated the 20-acre City Island, though that year it was flooded at least twice. The next year James Cameron, the grandson of Simon and with the bridge company and Dauphin Deposit, gave the 75-acre Cameron Parkway. Between 1906 and 1915, the Hoffer, Cameron, Boyd, Dull, Alrick and Rutherford families contributed the 73-acre Paxtang Parkway, and finally in 1913 banker James McCormick, a cousin of Vance, added the 103 acres of McCormick Island. The last great gifts, the 12 acres of Italian Lake, were made by the Graham and Moeslein families in 1919 and 1926.

Wildwood Park, almost 969 acres of wilderness, was to be the gem of the park system. Landscaper Warren Manning, a student of Frederick Law Olmsted of Central Park fame, was agog at its possibilities, writing in a 1901 report:

"The opportunity for a great country park at Harrisburg lies to the north of the city in the tract known as Wetzel's Swamp, which includes about 500 acres of swampy and dry land, framed in with wooded bluffs on one side, and a line of fine old willows along the canal on the other. As it stands today it is a natural park with beautiful passages of landscapes, and fine vistas, even great stretches of meadow land to distant hills beyond. It is rare,

Wildwood Park was an improvement over Wetzel's Swamp, or at least a better name for the wetlands north of the city.

indeed, that a city can secure a property having all the elements of a park landscape, its border-planting of fine trees, splendid individual specimens, and woodlands carpeted in spring with numerous wild flowers."

The Camerons owned most of Wildwood and gave it to the city. Sen. J. Donald Cameron didn't have to lobby City Council very hard after that to have 11th street named for his cunning father.

Wildwood became one of the great might-have-beens, never fulfilling Manning's dreams. It was too expensive to develop and too far from city neighborhoods in a town with ample recreation space already.

Albright College in Reading briefly considered relocating to Wildwood. Messiah College, founded in Harrisburg in 1909 by the Brethren in Christ, went the following year to Grantham along the Yellow Breeches, not to Wildwood.

There was an American passion for zoos, and by 1910 there were 40 in cities. Harrisburgers between 1927 and 1945 did have their "Harrisburg Zoological Garden" at Wildwood. In its heyday it had four lions, four bears, a tiger, mountain lions, wolves, raccoons, seals, and a monkey house. Eventually, broken-down peddler horses from the streets were disposed there. A true zoological garden it wasn't, and Milton S. Hershey satisfied that demand with his own zoo at Hersheypark.

Finally Wildwood became the City Dump, and after 1950 a burning and smelly one—the dreadful reason Harrisburg decided to almost bankrupt itself with an incinerator at Don Cameron's old summer mansion by Lochiel. For $1, the Harrisburg Area Community College obtained the right to much of Wildwood and built its campus there in 1967—a dream the Renaissance II era of the community had to fulfill.

13.

A MADE-OVER TOWN

The coming of World War I put an end to the 15 years of the major implementations of the "Harrisburg Plan," or Renaissance I. That stretch of civic fervor was at least three times longer than most local reformers in the United States maintain their enthusiasm and aren't discouraged by the inertia of the old politics.

In fact, Harrisburg had enough stamina to have a second, less-robust 15-year period that lasted until the Great Depression. The campus high schools of John Harris and William Penn—themselves an innovation in urban beautification—were constructed during that era.

"No other city in all this broad land," wrote J. Horace McFarland, "has done all these things concurrently, harmoniously, and entirely upon the plans of experts so that a baker's dozen of years shows a made-over town with a degree of efficiency...much characteristic of the average German city." McFarland's remarks were penned just before World War I, when Harrisburgers still ate lots of sauerkraut, often worshipped in the German tongue, and were awed by Teutonic civic orderliness.

The Harrisburg Telegraph marked its 80th anniversary in 1911 by praising the renaissance and itself as a vibrant supporter:

"The improvements have largely paid for themselves through increased valuations of outlying properties and the erection of hundreds upon hundreds of additional houses and the rebuilding of many old structures in the business districts to meet growing demands. And all this without the suspicion of graft in the expenditure of the vast sums involved, without one item of shoddy work..."

That was true. If there was any stealing, it was either so minimal or so adroitly arranged that neither contemporaries nor historians discovered it. The Rev. Dr. George P. Donehoo liked to talk about the Harrisburg soul, and in that particular epoch it appeared to be pure.

Harrisburgers spent at least $10.5 million for their Renaissance I, plus another $15 million from increased tax assessments, according to Dr. George Lauman Laverty. This was at a time when few houses cost more than $2,500. Dr. Laverty, of Bellevue Park, was a third-generation physician who began his 55-year practice in 1912 and in his retirement wrote the definitive history of Dauphin County medicine.

The reformers—like Mira Lloyd Dock, Vance McCormick, Edward J. Stackpole Sr. and McFarland—were straight-forward about their plan's costliness, sometimes too much so. They estimated a 2-mill property tax increase would be needed, but only a half-mill was.

Private expert consultants played a role in designing the improvements, but otherwise there were no developers, planning offices nor urbanologists. There wasn't a single federal or state grant, either.

Amidst the bustle of improving itself to reap prosperity, Harrisburg grew like a teen-ager. In 1895 it expanded from Maclay Street—the fashionable Cottage Ridge neighborhood at Third and Maclay and Camp Curtin at Seventh Street—to Division Street. Houses started to be built near Reservoir Park, too. George A. Shreiner in 1906 started Shreinertown between State and Herr and 16th and 17th streets. William J. Calder laid out Cloverly Heights in 1908, opening up almost 200 acres of farmland south of Paxton between 13th and 20th streets. Bellevue Park began in 1910, just as the city line was extended from 18th to 29th Street. With the old Riverside community acquired in 1917, Uptown Harrisburg went to Vaughn Street.

Never again would so much growth take place, and never before had Harrisburg been so "awakened," a term the reformers relished and used appropriately. The good burghers were not remiss in giving thanks for all their bounty.

14.

A DIFFERENT SORT OF SELFLESSNESS

THE KEY TO HARRISBURG'S RENAISSANCE I was the leadership the city received. Bankers, lawyers, physicians, publishers and even businessmen "found time" to devote to public service.

The contrast to today is startling. Harrisburg hasn't had a mayor who was a physician in almost 20 years, or one who was a lawyer in almost a quarter-century. Few self-employed professionals try for City Council or the School Board, though they are eagerly available for judgeships and state senator sinecures.

A different sort of selflessness and patriotism existed at the turn of the century.

Dr. John A. Fritchey, a Democrat and the father of the future county coroner, was the mayor who preceded Vance McCormick. Fritchey had served a previous term, too, and then agreed to try to succeed McCormick and lost by fewer than 900 votes. Edward Z. Gross, a Republican and pharmacist, was related by marriage to the Cameron-McCormick clan, and he took City Hall after Vance. Dr. Ezra S. Meals, another Republican, then became mayor, followed by John K. Royal, an attorney and the last Democrat until Harold A. Swenson in the 1970s.

For almost 20 years, Harrisburg had highly educated, financially independent and modestly ambitious leaders in charge, men who had earned communitywide respect and were in a job they "didn't need" in the modern sense of career or self-esteem.

Dr. William H. Wilson, a professor in Texas, made a study of the Harrisburg City Beautiful Movement and was surprised at the quality of citizens involved. The beginning of the century was a time when fewer than 7 percent of Americans 17 or older had high school diplomas. Of the core of 21 persons who launched the Harrisburg Plan, one-third were college graduates. Wilson observed that their "sense of civic responsibility" and "grasp of political realities" were amazing.

Politics could be fun, at least to Vance McCormick. He reigned like a philosopher king, though not yet 33. The nagging annoyances of participatory democracy, due process, equal employment opportunity, union contracts, Civil Service and arbitration and red-ink budgets didn't exist. McCormick enjoyed inviting favored policemen and newspapermen to dine at his 301 N. Front St. mansion, with his man servants in livery doing their teetotaling boss' bidding by offering the boys a round of ice water.

McCormick deigned to serve a single three-year term. He balanced his $307,289 budget, said the volunteer boys in the fire department should be paid and claimed the city's chief problem is a "dearth of dwelling houses." He wrote the longest farewell address in Harrisburg history, taking 12 columns of newspaper type that Ed Stackpole wouldn't reprint in the rival Telegraph.

The Harrisburg gentry had public management to themselves, and that generation had the intelligence to take hold. The old bosses, like Simon Cameron, were dead, and the coming bosses, like Ed Beidleman and Harve Taylor, had not yet arrived. Marlin E. Olmsted in Congress was a wealthy Front Street corporation lawyer, concentrating his ambitions on becoming speaker of the House, an honor he almost achieved. Republican Olmsted died in 1913, and 12 years later McCormick walked down the street and married his widow.

The leadership of Renaissance I was shortsighted in only a few regards. Nothing was done for women, but they didn't get the vote until the 1920s. That nothing was done for blacks was in keeping with white Central Pennsylvania tradition, so another generation up from slavery was lost to oblivion in the longest-playing American tragedy there is.

A developed Wildwood Park never materialized. The gentry never considered establishing a college. Its feeling was that proper Harrisburgers could always be admitted to Yale—McCormick was on its board for 23 years—or Princeton, or Penn, or Dickinson, or even rural Penn state—where McCormick also was a trustee for 38 years. The result was that Harrisburg was Pennsylvania's last major city to get a college.

15.

BECOMING MODERN

A KEY PURPOSE of the Municipal League's "Harrisburg Plan" was to modernize public services to keep up with the growth of commerce. Seventy years later the Greater Harrisburg Movement devised the Haristown concept for the very opposite reason—to stimulate commerce in the dying center of what once had been an energetic Harrisburg.

Well before the $1.1 million bond issue and the mayoralty election of Vance McCormick in February 1902, Harrisburg made a stab at improving itself. Doubtlessly there were critics, but in 1889 after a flood exceeded only by those of 1936 and 1972, the city ripped down the produce and butcher sheds that had been on Market Square since 1790. The last two farmers markets that were razed were 82 years old, and in such poor condition that their lumber was sold for only $281.

The Chestnut Street Market, where Executive House is today, was built to replace the Square's markethouses.

With the unsightly shacks gone, Harrisburg could get busy with the task of becoming modern.

During the first five years of the 20th century, 2,500 buildings were erected in Harrisburg, or more than $6 million worth. That added one-fourth to the town's assessed valuation of $26 million. In addition, there was the new

$13 million Capitol and St. Patrick Cathedral, which cost $250,000 but by the congregation's 150th anniversary in 1976 was worth "either $12 million or is priceless," quipped its pastor, Monsignor William P. Bridy.

Where money is, bankers are sure to be. The banking capital in town doubled to $4.3 million in that period. By 1910 there were seven new banks—East End, Security Trust, Union Trust, Allison Hill Trust, Citizens Bank, Sixth Street Bank, and Peoples Savings Bank. Union Trust, next door to the present City Hall, in June of 1906 opened the first "skyscraper" of eight stories. The bank became one of about a dozen wiped out during the Great Depression, with depositors getting 20 cents on their dollar. The U.S. F&G took over, and Harve Taylor had his insurance offices there.

Market Square, after the vendors' sheds were removed, looked as spacious as a European plaza.

Dives, Pomeroy and Stewart—as Pomeroy's was known then—doubled its floor space in 1905 to compete with Bowman's and Schleisner's.

In 1904, Harrisburg Tech was built, and the next year the city got its first true apartment house, the five-story Donaldson Flats at Second and Locust streets. Nearby is what became known as the Hall Building, the YMCA opened. Harrisburg in 1854 started the fifth Y in the nation. Native-born Harris C. Fahnestock gave $25,000 toward the new building. His father, once a clerk at the Harrisburg Bank, became a major New York financier, perhaps the most illustrious go-getter the old town produced.

Local architect Charles Howard Lloyd, who did the Commercial Bank near the Broad Street Market, added the handsome Telegraph Building on Locust Street in 1909—with a clock for Harrisburgers who missed the old clock of the red brick Capitol when the new Capitol had no Big Ben. The current restored Kunkel Building, at Third and Market streets, resumes the tradition of Harrisburg's having a public timepiece.

Bell Telephone—which 70 years later would be a savior of Renaissance II's Harristown—was there also at the creation of Renaissance I.

H.C. Chute, of Western Union, in 1878 received the first consignment of telephones to Harrisburg. He wired a line from his home to the neighbor's. "Can you hear me?" he asked. "It's wonderful. I hear every word you say," the neighbor answered back. They were the official first words, but the mad genius of Eberly's Mill, Daniel Drawbaugh, as early as 1866 used a mustard can receiver and a teacup transmitter to talk across the Yellow Breeches. Carlisle's Hamilton Library has Drawbaugh's concoction.

Unfortunately, Alexander Graham Bell received the world's most valuable patent on March 7, 1876, Drawbaugh didn't get his worthless one until July 21, 1880, and the U.S. Supreme Court by a 4-3 vote favored Bell. While they argued, Southern Pennsylvania Telephone Co. opened at 3 N. Third St. in 1882, attracting 200 customers for a home price of $48 yearly and $60 for a business phone. Long distance arrived in 1890. What was then Pennsylvania Telephone moved to 210 Walnut St. in 1900 with 1,050 customers, and in 1901 United Telephone with 1,922 area-wide customers took an office across the street.

Bell of Pennsylvania was formed in 1907 and after acquiring Pennsylvania Telephone's 6,000 Harrisburg subscribers in 1911 opened a six-story office at 212 Locust St. Ever since, Harrisburg has been among the world's leaders in telephones per capita. That year Drawbaugh died, $350 from destitution.

16.

THE MERCHANT PRINCESS

AND THE

REAL ESTATE KING

ONE OF THE LEAST-HERALDED American migrations began in the 1880s and lasted through to World War I. This is when electric lights, high school diplomas, hospital medical care and streetcars came of age, and it is when at least 15 million Americans moved from the farms to the cities.

"I won't live in them cussed smothery houses," Huckleberry Finn proclaimed in that 1885 classic, but his master preferred otherwise for himself. Mark Twain lit out from provincial Hannibal, Mo., and was comfortably ensconced with all the urban amenities like indoor plumbing in Hartford, Conn.

Harrisburg's population between 1880 and 1920 more than doubled, or 147 percent, up yearly by 1,130 new faces. That growth rate of 3.7 percent annually over 40 years compares favorably with the 1960s' suburbanization of Lower Paxton Twp., 4.9 percent annually; Derry Twp., 3.0; Hampden Twp., 8.1, and Lower Allen Twp., 1.8.

Mary Sachs was the city's savviest and most civilized entrepreneur, shopping overseas for her clients.

Attaining the status of upward mobility meant becoming a city resident, especially for the children of immigrant peddlers and steelmill puddlers. The jobs were in the city, the living was better, and certainly the schools were the best—all the attractions that a half-century later suburbia would claim.

California professor Gunther Barth in 1980 said American cities at the turn of the century had six lures: apartment houses, the metropolitan press, department stores, vaudeville palaces, "the first urban spectator sport" in baseball, and marvelous mass transit. Had he added a thriving job market and the nation's best education his list would be complete.

Two Harrisburg legends were part of this migration, Mary Sachs the merchant princess and Josiah Kline the real estate king.

Miss Sachs arrived in Harrisburg in 1907 at 19, only two years after Old Home Week and she stayed 53 years. She came from an ethnic neighborhood in Baltimore, and after working briefly in a candy store on Steelton's West Side she clerked in Schleisner's on North Third Street. After William Schleisner's death, she was fired, so she went two blocks north, rented a shop at 210 N. Third St. from the Lowengard family, and opened her own retail business. She was single, in debt, and only 30. That first day in 1918 she sent herself flowers, signing her clothing manufacturers' names to the best-wishes cards—and for the next half-century her store had the flowers and glamour of New York's Fifth Avenue. When her rented quarters burned down in 1931, this 5-foot-2 unmarried Jewish woman rebuilt and reopened.

She bought a home along silk-stocking Front Street, entertained elegantly, and with her friend, Rabbi Philip David Bookstaber, a long-time widower and also childless, she did her duty to bridge the gap between the stalwart Harrisburg gentiles and the newly emerging, often professional Jewish community.

Like so many outstanding Harrisburgers of her day, however, she left no successors. She died at 72 in 1960, and her store was sold in 1968 and eventually closed in 1978.

Joe Kline, the son of a village store keeper at Lees Cross Roads in Cumberland County, came to Harrisburg when he was only 14. He was a pageboy in the 1899 Legislature and later in Congress, rode the Reading Line to Gettysburg as a "butcherboy" selling newspapers, read meters for the gas company, and eventually finished normal school at Shippensburg, took correspondence courses, attended the Wharton School and read law but never became a lawyer.

In 1909 he was a notary public, notarizing the original charter of Messiah College, and from 1914 to 1929 he was the state law librarian. But real estate was his game, and he began it in 1911. Eventually he built Harrisburg's first high-rise, the 117-unit Parkview Apartments, in 1941, then Thornwood Apartments, sold the houses for Wilson Park and the land for Bishop McDevitt and John Harris high schools, and when he was past 65 planned the area's first shopping center, Kline Village. "Why do you want to go in debt like that at your age?" his wife Bessie asked. "I've always been in debt and I always expect to be in debt," he replied. He told friends, "In everything I've done, I've tried to visualize it from five years ahead. To me, it has always been what I am going to do tomorrow."

Childless like Mary Sachs and Milton Hershey, he also became a philanthropist before his death at 79 in 1961. The Messiah Hall of Science was one of his gifts, and so was the Polyclinic's Kline Children's Hospital and Eye Clinic.

Harrisburg was the immediate future, and like a magnet it gathered the freshest blood. Once-independent towns like Rutherford, Paxtang, Penbrook, Camp Hill, Lemoyne, New Cumberland and Mechanicsburg became virtual colonies. Everyone expected this centralization would continue, that the "outskirts" would remain long-term and willing subordinates to the capital city.

17.

CLUB LIFE

The Dauphin County Bar Association—all male in those halcyon days—held its third annual dinner at the Harrisburg Club in 1902.

The barristers, many of ample girth, had their ices served in the shape of a law book lettered in gold, while the menu was presented as a miniature legal document. After the champagne punch, the entrees included raw oysters and asparagus tips. The "speeches were full of wisdom and wit," they reported, and hard rolls weren't thrown at honored guests at the head table—a low-brow tradition a less-august Dauphin Bar adopted in latter years.

Life in Harrisburg during Renaissance I, especially for those with the means, influence and imagination, was jolly. The "upper crust" liked to see and be seen. They hadn't settled in the capital city of Pennsylvania to be solitary and seclusive.

The Harrisburg Club at Front and Market streets (now the parking lot across from the courthouse) opened March 3, 1897, just four months before the Harrisburg Country Club. Respected aristocrats signed up for both—to eat and drink at the downtown club and to be the sportsman and family man at the country club.

"The debut of the Harrisburg Club was one of the dazzling moments in local history. Some 400 plutocrats assembled, to be served by attendants dressed in livery of dark blue and gold braid."

The debut of the Harrisburg Club was one of the dazzling moments in local history. Some 400 plutocrats assembled, to be served by attendants dressed in livery of dark blue and gold braid. The club had solid oak walls in every room and its electric lights were shaped like bell globes. The billiard room was on the first floor. There was a grand stairway and a balcony.

Sen. Boies Penrose and author John O'Hara were among the illustrious who liked to catch a drink, or two, or three, or four, at the Harrisburg Club, and in that era almost all the hard liquor was 100 proof or more. The club closed at the onset of World War II, and O'Hara used it for a model of his Fort Penn Club in his 1949 Harrisburg novel. He said the club created a new pattern in town, that of Front Streeters stopping by for businessmen luncheons instead of going home at noontime. The rule was that in the dining room on the second floor, a guest chose his company and uninvited table-hoppers were not encouraged. At the grill, anyone could sit at your table. This Harrisburg decorum later held true at the Penn Harris Hotel, until modern ill manners crushed it.

The country club stressed the outdoor life for the more robust gentry. It staged a baseball game its first day. John V.W. Reynders, a superintendent at the Steelton mill, brought his team up and he played shortstop. Vance McCormick pitched and captained the home team. W.O. "Wild Bill" Hickok played first base, coal dealer John Y. Boyd played second base, and brother Henry McCormick was in the outfield. It must have been the wealthiest per capita team ever assembled in Harrisburg, and club president, Marlin E. Olmsted, the congressman, was pleased to see his boys win.

McCormick kept his team for almost 20 years, adding cousin Henry "Pete" Gross to the roster, a few Patriot editors, and any industrialists, financiers, physicians and lawyers who could field and hit. The McCormick club was not to be laughed at. Vance and Wild Bill had been All-American football players at Yale. Dr. Harvey Smith once played third base for Washington in the big leagues, and his brother Paul, later the judge, was a superb athlete and coach.

Club life, both dry and wet, flourished during this sociable era.

The Harrisburg Republican Club, off Market Square, and the West End Republican Club, near the Broad Street Market, opened about 1902. Both were hangouts for M. Harvey Taylor. In 1904 the Elks Club at 216 N. Second St. opened. Meade D. Detweiler was the two-term national exalted ruler, having unified Elkdom coast to coast. For this, he was honored with a statue of an elk in Reservoir Park. The Harrisburg Elks, with 1,700 members, did a yearly $200,000 food and bar business, and their steak dinners were $1. The golden days of this club lasted through 1930, and by 1963 its center-city home was demolished.

The Zembo Temple was founded in 1904, and six years later its building opened at State and Third streets. The University Club, two doors up Front Street from the Harrisburg Club, opened in 1916, and had such dinner speakers as Lowell Thomas, Count Von Luckner and H. V. Kaltenborn. That same year the Fleming Mansion on the riverbank became the home of the Civic Club. The Engineers Club was at Front and Chestnut streets, across from the Harrisburg Hospital.

There was even a Harrisburg Academy of Music, which Professor E. J. Decevee started in 1896 on Second Street. Decevee's alumni not only played in major orchestras but also in Harrisburg's proud Commonwealth Band that lasted from 1888 until 1943. It was the professor's daughter, Mrs. Alice Decevee Mitchell Morgan, who in 1931 organized the Harrisburg Symphony.

18.

A LIBRARY, BOOKSTORES, AND A NEW HOSPITAL

"AHEAD OF ITS TIME, compared with other cities of equal size, Fort Penn went in for a metropolitan social life," John O'Hara observed about early 20th-century Harrisburg in his *A Rage To Live*.

There were "finer things" the new Harrisburgers sought, beyond paved streets and filtered water. Among them were a library, bookstores and a new hospital.

The Harrisburg Library—now the Dauphin County Library System—was a prominent part of Renaissance I. It began as a library company in 1794, with such sponsors as William Maclay, but it wasn't until 1889 that it became a public association, first with a library room on Market Square and then on Locust Street.

Mrs. Sara Jane Haldeman Haley lived on Front Street in the Gov. John Andrew Shulze house, with her garden facing Walnut Street. She was one of the town's grand dames, the daughter of ironmaster Jacob M. Haldeman, the founder of New Cumberland in 1814 and an owner of the old

Camelback Bridge. Her brother Jacob S. was once ambassador to Sweden, while her other brother Richard was The Patriot editor and son-in-law of Simon Cameron. She was a long-time widow of a Philadelphia attorney and had had her portraits done by the great Thomas Sully and Harrisburg's most famous artist, J. Augustus Beck.

Mrs. Haldeman Haley died at 84 in 1896 and bequeathed her garden and $80,000 to the Harrisburg Library for local architect Charles Howard Lloyd to build its handsome colonial limestone structure that opened in 1914 with 10,000 books on its shelves, or more than many college libraries had in those days. The town's illustrious were the guardians of the treasure: Casper Dull, president; banker James McCormick Jr., who lived across the street, treasurer, and such trustees as Judge George Kunkel who presided over the Capitol graft scandal in 1908, George Gorgas, William M. Donaldson and A. Boyd Hamilton Jr.

The librarian hired in 1913 was Alice Rhea Eaton, and she stayed 40 years. The gracious Miss Eaton was a schoolteacher from Titusville, educated at Drexel Institute and at Cambridge in England. She had been a librarian in Buffalo, Philadelphia, and Utica, N.Y., before coming to Harrisburg, where at her death in 1968 she was 95.

Harrisburg has never supported many bookstores, but in 1908 it got its most famous, Aurand's, at Third and Forster streets. The father and son, A. Monroe Aurand, had the same name and both died in 1956, when their store closed. The father, a Lutheran Huguenot, had published a weekly magazine in Snyder County before joining the migration to Harrisburg with his "new, old and rare books," a collection that eventually overflowed the shop with 150,000 volumes.

Aurand Jr. was a printer, pamphlet historian and folklorist as well as a bookseller. He translated his friend Edwin Markhams's "The Man With the Hoe" and Lincoln's "Gettysburg Address" into Pennsylvania Dutch.

The Harrisburg Library had one of the choicest corners downtown, the former garden of Sara Jane Haldeman. The building was designed by Charles Lloyd, whose buildings are still admired.

His local best-seller of 1938, *The Witches in Our Hair,* included his finding that a high percentage of history's beheaded women were redheads. And his research on bundling, which he carefully differentiated from "bungling," resulted in five little books, such as his minor classic, *Is It Indecent to Court in Bed?*

Katherine Comstock, a Red Cross ambulance driver in World War I, opened the second store, The Book Shop, on Second Street in 1927. She was succeeded by her niece, Julie Comstock, and then by Priscilla Harrington, and finally for many years, Alice Louise "Lee" Yeager. The shop's final location was on Third Street facing the Capitol before it closed in the mid-1970s.

The Penn Book Shop on South Third Street, lasted a few years longer. It was started in 1935 by Sam Levin, a native of Steelton who took used books from the Aurands to launch his business.

The new hospital, the Polyclinic, was chartered in 1909, evolving from Dr. E.L. Shope's private hospital at 1700 N. Second St. He was the first president and Dr. William Tyler Douglass Sr. the vice president. In 1914 they moved their "poly-clinic" into the old Gov. David Rittenhouse Porter Mansion at Front and Harris streets, just in time for the 1916 ice cream epidemic which resulted from faulty pasteurization at nearby dairy farms and caused 33 local deaths. The 1918 influenza epidemic followed, and an estimated 475 lives were lost in the community. The devoted hospital superintendent from 1916 to 1946 was Katherine Elizabeth Landis, a bulky 5-foot-8, 190-pounder from Union Deposit who lived in the hospital.

The Polyclinic from the start was an earnest rival of Harrisburg Hospital, and both remained stubbornly individualistic institutions. In the mid-1920s the Polyclinic moved to its permanent site on North Third Street. Director George McFarland had his brother J. Horace plan a dazzling rose garden for the entrance to the new hospital.

19.

THE FIRST SUBURBIA

THE YEAR 1905 OF OLD HOME WEEK in Harrisburg, a 26-year-old theoretical physicist named Albert Einstein at the University of Bern presented his paper on his concepts of time, velocity and space. His first inkling about relativity, Einstein said, came when he rode the streetcar and observed the Bern town clock hands move faster as he approached it.

Had Einstein been an urbanologist aboard the Derry Street Trolley to the end of the line in Derry Twp., his genius might have discerned a social relativity in the making—the first suburbia to threaten the privileged domain of the new Harrisburg

Derry Street had been the wagoners' trail, east to Philadelphia and west to Pittsburgh. A fountain for the horses to drink after their heavy pull is still at 13th and Derry.

With the opening of the Mulberry Street Viaduct in 1909, Harrisburg's eastern province was free to be settled. The Roman term "viaduct" was indicative of Harrisburg's minor empire complex.

Mount Pleasant, as the 13th Street section of Allison Hill was known, soon was filled with "Philadelphia houses," those row houses costing a maximum of $2,500 and popular with railroading and steel mill families.

Business concentrated on the Hill. J. Horace McFarland had his publishing house near the viaduct. Banks, restaurants, cabinetmakers and a few machine shops and mills opened. By 1918, Charles F. Still came down from Halifax to start a shoe-repair shop. His descendants carry on the trade into the 1980s, the last of the neighborhood's original family businesses.

Farther out at 19th Street, the Pennsylvania Thresherman's and Farmer's Protective Association opened in 1919. It was one that stayed put, and by 1983, as the Pennsylvania National Insurance Group, is the city's fifth largest employer with more than 500 employees.

It was at the distant end of the line, however, that the not-too-distant future was being made. A Mennonite bishop's grandson in 1903 started the Hershey Chocolate Co. as "an industrial utopia where things of modern progress all center in a town that has no poverty, no nuisances, and no evil."

Milton Snavely Hershey wasn't an emotional man, but like Harrisburg's city-beautiful romanticists, he was caught up in the spirit of his time. In latter years he was more of a Dutchman and usually replied to questions, "I have no comment to make."

Though twice bankrupted and now at age 46 hardly a fledgling, Hershey was resettling from Lancaster to his native homestead with dreams of building more than just a fortune. He became so optimistic he advised that Derry Twp. should never need taxes higher than 16 mills.

The childless Chocolate King did so well that by Nov. 15, 1909, he and his wife drew up the deed for the 10,000-acre Hershey School, and the first four boys were admitted Sept.1, 1910. In 1951 the school dropped "Industrial" from its name, and by the mid-1960s it admitted black boys and then in 1977 girls. It has produced almost 6,000 alumni, including many executives of Hershey Foods.

A community like Hershey, in 1903 or 1983, is so singular as to be an exception to any rule: A propitious and prophetic suburban success from the beginning. In its first 80 years it passed the halfway mark to Harrisburg's appraised property valuation of $350 million. Hershey Foods' worldwide net sales soared five-fold beyond to $1.6 billion, with its future prospects as limitless as humankind's sweet tooth.

The uneducated Milton Hershey proved to be light years ahead of the more-advantaged Harrisburg aristocrats.

His contemporary Front Streeters retained their mansions as permanent residencies. A few more gracious estates would be built until the Depression of the 1930s, though the Harrisburg wealthy were far more modest about conspicuous consumption than the coal, railroad and steel barons elsewhere in Pennsylvania.

To escape the summer's heat, many of these affluent had country farms. Col. Henry McCormick, the father of Vance, started his clan off in Cumberland County by buying Rosegarden in Upper Allen Twp. as early as 1880. Eventually the McCormicks owned almost 600 acres on the West Shore. Marlin Olmsted, the congressman, bought the 69 acres of Cedar Cliff in 1903. Vance had been in his wedding party and married his widow. When the McCormick males were gone, a native Shipoker, William Lynch Murray, in 1954 bought Cedar Cliff and four years later with the new high school the name became the popular designation for the area.

Milton Hershey, in contrast to the McCormicks, Olmsteds and others, had no summer home. He built his modest mansion across the railroad siding from his factory, and the cocoa aroma wafted in his front door.

20.

A CONFEDERACY OF TERRITORIES

By World War I, Harrisburg was riding the wave of its Renaissance and had undisputed sovereignty over the entire community. At least 35 percent of Dauphin and Cumberland County—as compared to 13 percent in 1980—lived within the city limits.

Harrisburg simply enveloped Central Pennsylvania, much as the new Capitol dominated the skyline.

In 1910 the Rotunda could have held the combined populations of Camp Hill, Lemoyne and Lower Allen Twp., or just under 3,900. The new, $250,000 St. Patrick Cathedral, with its 29 stained-glass windows from Munich and a dome that soars 200 feet, had seating for 1,500, or more than the population of either New Cumberland or Penbrook. The Edison Junior High School auditorium, opened in 1919, had more seats than there was population in any West Shore town but Mechanicsburg.

As the locale of state and county government, Harrisburg was the political and financial hub almost to Carlisle.

When one wanted to hang up a shingle to practice, Harrisburg was the place. There were lawyer and doctor rows, and office clusters for architects, insurance men, real estate dealers and stockbrokers. The Episcopal Church joined the Catholics in making the city its diocesan headquarters. This was the center for the Masonic Order, most statewide associations, the hospitals and, of course, the major banks. It also was Sin City with bawdy houses on Dewberry Alley, Mulberry Street, Verbeke, State, North Sixth and North Seventh streets. Cameron Street became automobile row.

There was an agreeable, extended-family familiarity to this city life of the early 20th century that neither the latter-day affluent suburbia nor the city itself after the 1950s was able to preserve or duplicate.

Professor Wilbur Zelinsky of Penn State, once a street kid from Chicago, in 1977 published a geographical study, "Pennsylvania Town." He isolated factors that applied to Gettysburg, Steelton, Middletown, Carlisle and that early Harrisburg. There was "sheer compactness" that produced a "crowded neighborliness"—a point Scranton-born urbanologist Jane Jacobs says is essential to sustaining city life. There were town squares for a sense of center-ness. There were trees. There was brick duplex housing—old Harrisburgers called them "half a double"—that engendered human warmth that can't be matched at modern townhouse apartment complexes with swimming pools and paved parking.

Harrisburg copied Philadelphia with its numbered streets and its alleys for convenience and backyard privacy.

What Zelinsky praised as a "mixture of functions" old Harrisburg had.

Growing up in that Harrisburg was almost a social affair, an involvement that took in the entire neighborhood. It was not accidental that most children, especially the boys, acquired nicknames—just as their Indian counterparts of two centuries before carried the names of tribal, environmental or character predispositional connotations. Harrisburg had hundreds of "Hap" and "Haps" for happy-tempered boys.

The city was a federation of neighborhoods, like old New York, Philadelphia or Steelton. It wasn't a republic—some neighborhoods were more equal than others in wealth and influence—but more of a confederacy of territories: Shipoke, Schreinertown, Goattown, Front Street, Hardscrabble, Allison Hill, Midtown, Ridge Avenue, Schuddemageville, Riverside, Sibletown, and Bellevue Park.

Many neighborhoods were self-contained. If they declined, so did their businesses, churches and grammar schools. But most were remarkably permanent, and if they dissolved it usually took more than a generation or two.

Cottage Ridge at Third and Maclay streets, begun in 1890 when that was city line, was one of the exceptions. It thrived only a generation and a half. Former Mayor Maurice C. Eby and future Mayor Howard Milliken lived there, as did merchants J. William Bowman, W.M. Donaldson, and Benjamin F. Burns. Manufacturer David E. Tracy and publisher E.J. Stackpole Sr. lived next to each other in fancy row houses until they departed for nearby Front Street.

Cottage Ridge became under-priced for the aristocracy after World War I. As upper-mobile Catholics and Jews moved in, the name disappeared. By 1968 when the new Governor's mansion opened a block away, only old-timers remembered.

Steelton at the turn of the century also had its cottage Hill for steel executives. Yet Steelton was able to retain its better-priced homes for more than a half-century, even though the Steamrollers' football field was placed in its midst.

21.

SHIPOKE, ONCE THE PUDDLERS' HOVEL

WHERE ONCE THE STENCH of sauerkraut permeated the premises, mixed with the odors from the river, the soot from the passing coal-burning locomotives and the reddish-brown effluvium from the steel mills, today the fetor of broccoli wafts. In old Shipoke, broccoli would have been considered punishment. Now it is a delicacy, and people dress up to eat it and dishes like quiche, spinach salad, avocados, and creamed asparagus—groceries unheard of in the early 1900s.

Sunday supper used to be "what was left over from Friday night," according to one native-born son. Now Sunday dinner—note the upward touch in status terminology—is apt to start off with Bloody Marys and hors-d'oeuvres and advance to vichyssoise. Gone is "coffee soup," that Shipoke concoction of coffee, sugar and bread that was the elixir for virility and longevity. Where once Old Highspire Rye was swigged, vintage wine is now sipped.

After the last forkful of gateau fromage avec amaretto, a modern Shipoker isn't likely to march south to combat a Steelton West Sider, battling for the honor of being the tougher neighborhood. It took a few "boiler makers" of Old Highspire and Graupner's beer to inspire those confrontations. And, besides, Shipoke after the 1972 Flood was gentrified and Steelton's West Side leveled.

Gentrification is the influx of the upper middle class with their peppermills into a neighborhood that not only the working class, but also the sociologists, abandoned. Few places in the United States had such a radical transformation as Shipoke, once the puddlers' hovel.

In its iron age, Shipoke from the 1870s to the 1920s was a neighborhood of 350 people. It stretched north from what was the Chesapeake Nail Works and Central Iron and Steel to Mulberry Street, bounded by the Susquehanna and Cameron Street. Much of it was noisily contained between the railroad and the river, a geography that erased pretentions.

In its sterling-silver age, 1962 to the present, Shipoke is only two blocks wide, to Race Street, and covers the domain of what used to be old Harris Park Elementary School territory. There was a decade of modest pioneering gentrification, then came the flood, and after that the advent of enthusiastic resettlement.

Modern Shipoke has about 225 people, most of whom know what sirloin is but not fatback. A number of new Shipokers have jobs with titles like "consultant," "adviser," or "administrative assistant," occupations unheard of at the old mills.

Lying as it does between the Susquehanna and Paxton Creek, all of Shipoke is floodplain. At least 42 times in 200 years, it has been drenched—which is not quite as many times, even after the baths of 1972 and 1975 and the near-deluge of 1979, that its citizens tenaciously have rejected proposals for a flood-prevention wall, as Sunbury erected after the 1936 Flood.

Its name is unduplicated in the annals of American urban history. The probable meaning comes from "poke," as in a small place or container, and "shi," with its obvious Anglo-Saxon implications. Albert M. Hamer Jr., for years the county law librarian, insisted however:

"There was a bird, somewhat like a small crane but smaller, like a pigeon with long legs, which came in on the marshes in the vicinity of Paxton Creek. They remained on the river or in the marshes all day, and in the evening their favorite roosting spot was the rocks and trees along Cameron Street. . . They had large wings and flew with their long legs tight together. They flew slowly in the form of an 'S' and were very shy. . . From their shyness and their slow motion in flying, i.e., they 'poked' through the sky, the word 'shi-poke' is said to have been formed. No one in Shipoke has ever been found who knew the correct ornithological term for this bird, and it is now said to be extinct."

If London's Berkeley Square could have its nightingale, South Harrisburg had its shipoke. The more logical, if less exotic, name should have been "Harris Park," after its famous elementary school.

Shipoke went up in 1873, replacing the White Horse tavern, but in April of 1962 it was replaced by the Nationwide Inn. School Principal Samuel P. Stambaugh and such teachers as Miss Mark Pikley, whose father was school superintendent, and Miss Genevieve Fritchey, whose brother was mayor, helped make this grammar school outstanding. It was M. Harvey Taylor's only alma mater, and among its other scholars were Judge Karl Richards, architect William Lynch Murray, accountant Walter F. Kuhn, merchant Russell J. Charles, radio celebrity Edward J. "Red" McCarthy, Harrisburg Dairies co-founder Ben Wolfe, ex-Postmaster Wilmer E. King, football greats Tony and Frank Wilsbach, and the firefighting family that produced state Fire Marshal Chet Henry and city Fire Chief Ed Henry. The school was named after Rep. Robert Harris, son of the city founder, who owned and laid out Shipoke's property lots in 1842.

22.

MARIS HARVEY TAYLOR

AND

OTHER SHIPOKERS

MARIS HARVEY TAYLOR WAS REARED at Conoy and Showers Alley, married a Shipoke girl, lived there 48 years, and for the rest of his 58 years talked about Shipoke.

With proud, moderate hyperbole, he told about a life that included homes—at best $1,500 wooden structures, and if rented, $8 monthly—that were heated by kitchen coal stoves and had outdoor plumbing, and of 66 hours work in the mill for a $10 weekly paycheck.

Taylor came from what in Shipoke was advantage. He was born in 1876 on Bailey's Row, just south of the Dock Street Bridge, and his father Morris did well enough at the Chesapeake Nail Works (it later became Central Iron) to move his family of six children to better circumstances north of the bridge. Taylor at 12 went to work with his father at No. 2 mill, and spent 24 years there, mostly as a clerk.

The Baileys of the Harrisburg National Bank were the principal landowners, mill proprietors, and Republican bosses in that First Ward. They made Morris a school director and then in 1907 his son Harvey the city councilman from Shipoke for eight years. Edward Bailey at election time gave Taylor silver dollars for street money. Harve once slipped one to a retarded friend. As the man cast his ballot, the dollar piece fell from a hole in his pocket and rolled across the polling room. He ran out the door, while Harve scurried in to retrieve the silver dollar.

Taylor didn't exaggerate by much how poor Shipoke was. The 1900 property assessment list showed the mean house value in Shipoke to be $930.50, or less than a fourth of what houses were on the Bailey's Front Street.

Harry F. Sheesley, born in 1872, was one of Taylor's long-time compatriots. He stayed his entire 90 years on South Ninth Street, 12 of them as a councilman. Sheesley, too, had stories about Shipoke's boiled chicken pot pie Sunday dinners, King Oscar cigars two for a nickel, plugs of Polar Bear chewing tobacco in the jaw, the "black wagon" picking up smallpox victims for the Harrisburg Hospital's pest house, hand-me-down clothes, fetching of coal from the railroad tracks, shad coming up river, torchlight political parades, and using the Susquehanna as the community bathtub. There were so many Sheesleys below Dock Street where the coal yards and mills were that the place was called Sheesleytown.

Taylor's lifespan overlapped Shipoke's iron age and its sterling silver age. He remembered Gen. Joseph F. Knipe, who lived at 329 S. Vine St. Knipe was a Mexican War veteran from Mount Joy who came to Harrisburg in 1848 to work on the railroad. He subsequently opened a shoe and boot store and reared a family of five daughters and four sons.

During the Civil War, Knipe organized a volunteer cavalry unit, saw action at Antietam, and returned to Harrisburg to nurse his wounds. He is credited with naming Camp Curtin for the distinguished governor. With the Gettysburg invasion, he commanded the Harrisburg defense, using a Mexican war cannon to lob shells on the West Shore. That cannon later stood for decades in front of the old State Museum. Knipe, before his death in 1901, was postmaster. In 1870 he was the unsuccessful Republican candidate for mayor, losing to William K. Verbeke.

Taylor also could recall the Trullingers and Pancakes, who from 1870 to 1890 owned the lumber yard and planning mill at 500 Race St. and built many properties to make old Shipoke.

The P.G. Leidich Drugstore opened in the 1890s at S. Front and Vine streets and lasted until 1965. Miss Helen R. Mowery taught elocution for decades in the Knipe house, down the street from Councilman DeWitt Fry's brownstone stoop—Shipoke's first restoration before World War I.

Shipoke slipped in the early 1950s. Phoenix Steel, the successor to Central Iron, closed in the late 1950s. The $6.4 million South Bridge octopus of concrete opened for traffic on Jan. 22, 1960, taking space and the quiet isolation away from the neighborhood.

It was in 1962 that the father-son lawyer team, Paul and Henry Rhoads of Paxtang, invested in Shipoke. Urban pioneers, including the suburban disenchanted, followed. For as little as $15,000 the new immigrants could take something of 100-year vintage and by re-wiring, re-roofing, re-kitchening, re-painting, re-heating and refurbishing have a gem worth $80,000 at re-sale. After the 1972 Flood, the townhouse developers arrived, seeking their fortunes.

What established gentrification after the flood was a French café named Au Jour Le Jour, or "from day to day," with proprietor and maitre d' Robert Straub, son of Mayor Albert Straub. "Cuisine," a word old Shipokers never heard of, became fashionable, and the namesake dirty bird was replaced by dining on "le noisettes de canard" sprinkled with garlic and cloves.

23.

BLACK NEIGHBORHOODS

THE LIFE OF THE AVERAGE HARRISBURG BLACK of the early 1900s remains as obscure as the lives of his more-distant parents or grandparents. All shared the "short and simple annals of the poor."

Harrisburg's traditionally placid ostracism prevailed since the 1740s, when pioneer John Harris was rescued from the Indians by his good man Hercules. The City Beautiful Movement, for all its civic achievements, ignored this racial group. Blacks continued to live in segregation, be educated in segregation, and be buried in segregation. Black emergence wouldn't come until the 1960s.

There were five black neighborhoods: Harrisburg's "Bloody Eighth" Ward, Sibletown and Springdale, Adams Street in Steelton, and Edgemont in Susquehanna Twp. None was fashionable, but all were rich culturally.

Steelton had the most vibrant black community, because job opportunities were better at the mill and because of Steelton's amazing history of ethnic balance—rare for any place in the world even to this day.

As early as 1904 Steelton had the first black councilman, a distinction that 80 years later remains unheard of on the West Shore and most of the East Shore. Peter Blackwell was a genuine hero, though the historical record on him is scant. A college graduate, he came to the mill town in

The Wesley Union African Methodist Episcopal Zion Church was located in the southern half of the Old Eighth Ward, close to its black parishioners.

the 1880s and stayed at least until after World War I. In politics he was a Republican, and he insisted the GOP make room for fellow blacks in its patronage. He founded the black Steelton Press weekly and ran a restaurant on Adams Street famous for its baked beans.

Steelton had three black churches, including the First Baptist Church that marked its 100th anniversary in 1981. By 1910 almost 40 blacks had graduated from Steelton High School, coming up through the Hygienic Grammar School under Professor Charles F. Howard, who was principal from 1886 to 1936. Harrisburg, in contrast, might have had 20, if that many, black high school graduates by 1910.

The "Bloody Eighth" was the ward behind the Capitol that ran north from Walnut Street. Well into the 1920s it was a mixed neighborhood, with much of the early Jewish community settling there. It is doubtful if much blood did flow in its alleys. During Prohibition certainly, there was more available white-lightning booze at its speakeasies than blood. "There is not a night passes but arrests are made for disorderly conduct and many citizens deem it unsafe to go into that neighborhood after dark," reported The Patriot—not in 1983, not in 1903, but in 1866. The Eighth Ward, in short, probably had a livelier reputation than the facts warrant.

At least three major figures came out of the old Eighth.

William Howard Day, of Briggs Street, might have been the first black state employee. Though a college graduate who had worked in Canada for the Underground Railroad before the Civil War, he became a mere clerk for the auditor general when he came to town in 1872. Day was secretary of the General Conference of the AME Zion Church, was elected to the Harrisburg School Board in 1878 and in 1891-93 was school board president, possibly the first such black man in the north.

Isaiah Parson in 1903 became Harrisburg's first black policeman. Another Parson, H. Edwin, was the first black druggist, and it is his daughter, Mrs. Sara-Alyce Parson Wright, who in 1974 became the executive director of the national YWCA. Dr. Charles H. Crampton began his medical practice on Forster Street in 1906, and in later years was the vice chairman of the Dauphin County Republican Committee and the athletic trainer at William Penn High.

Edgemont, northeast of Harrisburg State Hospital, was the first "suburb" the black Eighth Warders moved to. The Hodges family had been in Harrisburg since the 1840s, and between 1906 and 1910 Robert Hodges helped develop Edgemont. Isolated yet nearby, Edgemont soon was a community of 260 families. Its Glenwood School, opened in 1917, became well known.

The blacks in that era had to be survivors, and they must have been incredible ones. John Bodnar, the ethnologist, in his study of the Steelton mill reported that few black fathers and sons in their lifetimes before 1940 ever advanced on the job. In fact, until after World War II, a minuscule minority of blacks had lifetime jobs or careers. Most blacks were day laborers on whatever job they could find all their lives.

One scholar recently poured over courthouse records and discovered that as late as 1925 only 13 percent of the Harrisburg and Steelton blacks owned their own homes. There were black neighborhoods, but whites had the deeds to the property.

24.

THE HIDDEN HISTORY OF SIBLETOWN

SIBLETOWN AND SPRINGDALE are Harrisburg black communities well into their second century. Sibletown, in particular, has a hidden history that awaits discovery by a black Edward Gibbon or a novelist like David Bradley.

Not only is Sibletown one of the oldest black neighborhoods in Pennsylvania, but it also has a national distinction for its stalwart black Republican politics. It earned notoriety in The Wall Street Journal as the "Sixth of the Seventh" precinct, the only black one nationwide voting for Barry Goldwater in 1964. It did that by a 378-303 count because its leaders, the late Charles A. "Nibs" Franklin, a city sanitation inspector, and Marshall S. Waters, a courthouse employee, didn't want to see Sen. Hugh Scott cut on the ticket.

The neighborhood goes from 13th to Cameron and from Boas to Maclay Streets, and it has been the home of some of Harrisburg's most exciting characters.

The incomparable Pearl Bailey once lived in Sibletown, sang and danced at Pete and Mike's jazz joint on Cumberland Street, and found her first husband there, a drummer named Lester Miller. Oscar Charleston, now in baseball's Hall of Fame, lived there, and his widow remained in the neighborhood.

William McDonald Felton, virtually unknown today, was one of the most unusual blacks to have lived in Sibletown. He became an expert mechanic and in the early days of aviation staged air shows in Cloverly Heights, on what had been the Calder Farm and today's site of the Foose Elementary School. After World War I, Mac Felton opened his Auto and Aeroplane Mechanical School at 25 N. Cameron St. On the side, he also ran a dance hall.

Sibletown was founded in 1870 by W.H. Sible, a white—and the community has been only predominantly black, not totally black. Sible bought property on what was 11 ½ Street, next to 11th Street which is today's Cameron Street. He obtained old wooden freight cars from the Pennsylvania and Reading railroads made in the Cameron Street shops, and used the lumber to build houses, which he rented for $5 monthly. He and his son were highly regarded landlords, often accepting potatoes for the rent and never booting out tenants. Jonus Reis in 1907 succeeded Sible Jr. as the principal landlord, and then in 1922 came grocery store proprietor David J. Hurwitz, the uncle of Harrisburg's brilliant attorney, for the next three decades.

Marshall Waters' father, Robert, a courthouse custodian, arrived as a tenant in 1871 and produced 15 children, of whom 11 lived to adulthood. Marshall, born in 1913 and for 42 years a Republican at the courthouse, added eight more children, eight grandchildren, and eight great-grandchildren. The Waters family, numbering at least 200, became Harrisburg's largest clan. "I can't stand on Market Street for 15 minutes and not meet a relative," Marshall liked to say. One of them, attorney Nathan Waters, a nephew of Marshall, in the 1970s became the first Harrisburg black to run for the state Legislature. He lost, but he was one of the few Democrats ever to carry Sibletown.

For decades Sibletown had a population of more than 2,000, but after Hurricane Agnes in 1972 engulfed it, the community dropped to about

350. It had been the most complete of the Harrisburg black enclaves, with two churches, including Bethel A.M.E. where Vance McCormick often was a guest worshiper, the Downey Elementary School, a grocery, a funeral home, a playground, bars and restaurants that included the latter-day Yellow Front saloon for the politicians, and such nearby employers as Harrisburg Glass, Harrisburg Steel, W.O. Hickok Manufacturing, Stanley Spring Works, Harrisburg Railways, Telegraph Press, Ritter Brothers, and in early days, the Harrisburg Mattress Factory.

Springdale is the neighborhood from 13th to 20th streets between Market and State. It was founded by Turner Cooper, a freed slave who arrived in 1868 and went into carpentry after working on the reservoir in Reservoir Park. Ephraim Slaughter lived there, the city's last Civil War veteran who died in 1942. Professor John Paul Scott, an 1883 Harrisburg High black graduate, started the Scott clan there, teaching in Harrisburg for 47 years including at the Lincoln School that opened in 1904.

25.

J. HORACE MCFARLAND

AND

BELLEVUE PARK

"No matter how big Harrisburg grows, it will always be a country town. It has country-town ideals," J. Horace McFarland once huffed. Even so, in 1909 he began construction of Bellevue Park, a 300-lot venture that defied all his complaints about Harrisburg's being backward.

Bellevue Park was Central Pennsylvania's first, and has remained, its most enduring and noble experiment in land-use planning and city residential living. Its imaginative vision as a commercial undertaking is still evident. There are suburban Versailles and compounds that have far outspent Bellevue Park, but they self-consciously lack its urban-residential component and can be too exclusive or too isolated, or both.

As McFarland and his partner, Herman P. Miller, first advertised: "Permanent views, assured surroundings," and "city homes with country advantages...within 15 minutes of Market Square."

The property started at the end of the Market Street trolley line at 21st Street, and, as plotted by landscaper Warren Manning, was 134 acres

J. Horace McFarland's impressive Breeze Hill mansion in Bellevue Park was carefully and happily restored in 2010.

with irregular-shaped lots, two ponds, underground wiring, private trees and gardens, and "a series of deed covenants" for zoning protections against unsightly fences, billboards, smoke, unnecessary structures, poles and businesses of any kind, including physician and dentist offices.

Such intelligent use of land was not accepted by all. There were early court battles for underground wiring against the protesting utilities, and in the late 1940s Bellevue Park went as far as the Pennsylvania Supreme Court in an unsuccessful bid to block the $948,000 Thornwood Apartments on Hale Avenue. Builder Josiah Kline and associates won that battle, but in the end the Thornwood Apartments, with at least some esthetic pretensions ignored by most subsequent suburban complexes, added to the neighborhood tranquility.

The Bellevue Park Association was established on June 8, 1914, the oldest community organization in the Harrisburg area. What it adamantly refused to do is probably its greatest achievement—it never built a swimming pool.

McFarland was a rose gardener of international fame with the feverish temperament of his hero, Teddy Roosevelt. His father, Col. George F. McFarland, the son of a canal boatman, fought at the Battle of Gettysburg, losing one leg and having the other shattered. The colonel was from McAlisterville, and came to Harrisburg to head the soldiers' orphanage schools and publish the Temperance Vindicator. He also dabbled in real estate and had a nursery and greenhouse business. His son George became one of Harrisburg's first auto dealers and a promoter of Polyclinic Hospital, while Horace established the McFarland Press on Crescent Street by the Mulberry Street Viaduct. Horace developed one of the nation's first multi-color printeries, and his rose publications were widely read.

With friends like President Roosevelt and John Muir, McFarland was president of the American Civic Association, fought for the national park system, led the crusade to save Niagara Falls, wrote a dozen books, and was a relentless foe against billboards, overhead wiring and commercial blight. Without him, the City Beautiful Movement in Harrisburg either wouldn't have begun or it wouldn't have lasted long.

26.

FRONT STREET, THE BEST ADDRESS

IF THE REFORMERS of the City Beautiful Movement could have transformed every city neighborhood into other Front streets, their New Jerusalem would have been realized and they could have rested.

Front Street was the best address in the entire area for 180 years, or from 1766 when the city founder, John Harris II, built his mansion, until 1946 when the post-war emigration to suburbia commenced. That span of splendor might even be stretched to 1977, when the last authentic Front Streeter of the Cameron-McCormick clan, Brig. Gen. Henry McCormick Gross, died.

Gross, like the last of the old Romans, lived to be 92—the longest-living male of his tribe, by two years over the illustrious founder, Simon Cameron. He was the son of a mayor and married to a Bailey, but he also was a capitalist, a military man, and a civic leader. He was the father of five children and the grandfather of 12, but after him none lived on Front Street anymore.

Front Street hit its prime between 1900 and 1930. There was a nine-part picture album, Art Work of Harrisburg, published in 1914 by Gravure Illustration Co. of Chicago, and almost every other photograph was of Front Street. It was as if just living there were an esthetic experience.

There are 32 blocks between the Harris Mansion and Division Street. In its apotheosis, the neighborhood harbored 12 politicians, including the governor; the congressman; the Republican state chairman and a former mayor; 10 lawyers, including four who were or would be judges; three bankers; three newspaper executives; two clergymen; two manufacturers, and many of the community's outstanding physicians.

The roll call of names were the most respected in town: Kunkel, Haldeman, Brady, Metzger, Kelker, McCreath, Herr, Hoffer, Gross, McCormick, Wharton, Hickok, Gilbert, Fox, Royal, Dull, Reily, Cameron, Bailey, Boas, Mitchell, Baker, Wickersham, Cunningham, Doutrich, Stackpole, Tracy, Payne, Bergner, Schuddemage, Herman, Knisely, Wallower, Hamilton and Weiss.

It was a street of white gentiles for decades—Weiss was John Fox Weiss, a successful prosecutor in the 1908 Capitol Graft scandal. The first outlander to move in was the Jewish community, and it did so in style—laying the cornerstone of Reform Temple Ohev Sholom on March 18, 1920, at Front and Seneca streets. Ohev Sholom—"Love of Peace"—had been established as a congregation in 1855. By 1928, Temple Beth El built on Front Street, too.

The boulevard had the major clubs, including the fancy Harrisburg Club. Two generations later, only the Civic Club and the newer headquarters in the Myers-Boas Mansion of the Dauphin County Bar Association remain.

In its prime, Front Street was without gasoline stations or glass-box office buildings with macadam parking lots in front. Victorianism was in full flourish—towers, porticos, steeples, gingerbread, decorative porches, mansard and gambrel roofs, and flower gardens. Even Simon Cameron, though his tastes were always those of a farm boy, transformed the Harris Mansion after he bought it during the Civil War from a Colonial into a Victorian mansion.

SUNKEN GARDENS ALONG RIVER FRONT. HARRISBURG, PA.
116882

The Hardscrabble neighborhood on the west side of Front Street above Forster, where the "unruly river rats" lived, was condemned by parks superintendent Harve Taylor in 1914. It was replaced by the Sunken Gardens by 1922.

Front Street was the type of thoroughfare people like to stroll down. For many of them, it was a walk around the neighborhood. When the 1890 Fleming Mansion became the Civic Club in 1916, at least 62 of its ladies lived on Front Street, of course.

The one botch was Hardscrabble, three blocks of shacks owned by whites and blacks on the west bank north of Forster Street between Herr and Calder. Here the unruly "river rats" lived with their coal dredgers. In good years the boatmen would scoop out as much as 500,000 tons of coal and culm and sell it to the power companies for $2 to $4 a ton. In 1914, Shipoke Councilman Harve Taylor, as superintendent of parks and public properties, got a condemnation ordinance through council and the courts. By 1922, slovenly Hardscrabble was replaced by the Sunken Gardens.

Harrisburgers and visitors alike remember Front Street embowered in trees. It was Taylor, who didn't know an oak from a maple, who began the planting of most of the 550 American elms along the drive. They grew to form a leafy arcade, adorning the already sumptuous river front. Taylor said his Front Street project was his finest achievement in his eight years in city government. Unfortunately, the Dutch Elm disease began its attack in 1952, and during a 20-year period denuded what had been the glen-like, lambented shady roadway.

27.

LOSING FRONT STREET

FRONT STREETERS, for well past the World War I era, presumed their neighborhood would endure as quality residential property as long as Harrisburg lasted. Novelists James Boyd and John O'Hara used Front Street in their novels for a setting as stable as their characters could be unstable.

That Front Street declined to commercial status is not so surprising, however, as its lasting so long as a first-class residential neighborhood. Few of its high-mortgage suburban successors retain their family occupants past one generation.

As late as 1980, Evan Miller, a native Front Streeter, told the Dauphin County Historical Society that of the original 90 single-family structures of 1900 between Paxton and North streets, there remained 40 standing, though many after eight decades were non-residential in use. During the early 1920s, there were 231 families from the Harris Mansion to Lewis Street. Within 60 years, all were gone except, appropriately, the doctors' offices of the town's oldest family, the Kunkels.

Front Street faced at least 40 years of catastrophic urban challenges. The 1930 Depression and World War II affected its family wealth and ties, as did subsequent inflation, high taxation, and the lure of selling off fashionable real estate with a respectable ZIP Code. Too many Front Streeters stopped marrying one another—the middle and surnames of males on the street between 1890 and 1950 were almost repetitive. Too many Front Streeters also left their local businesses, or went from college to other communities to practice their professions.

The servant problem accelerated the flight to suburbia. Where can a sleep-in nanny be had for $20 weekly anymore? Mary Sachs, who died in 1960, had a butler, and she might have been the last Front Street chatelaine who needed a butler, enjoyed having one, and could afford to have one.

The newer generation, too, was not comfortable with Front Street's neighborliness and its visibility. The old capitalists liked that. The emerging managerial class preferred to re-colonize its own gentry ghettoes off an interstate exit surrounded by acres of protective privacy.

Front Street became a one-way thoroughfare in 1956, because the River Relief Route north of the city, planned in 1941, wasn't opened until the mid-1970s. Tractor-trailers barreled south on Front Street, and by 1961 the once-proud boulevard was 45 percent commercial. When the green-bucks blight hit, there was no stopping it. And too much of this commercialism was simply bad commercialism. The Harrisburg Planning Commission in 1970 calculated that 40 percent of the Front Street owners—undoubtedly the new ones who rented office space and didn't live there—were violating zoning ordinances. The old aristocrats, fastidious as to their property, would have never understood the tax-write-off mercenaries stealing value from themselves.

There were a few, inconsequential attempts to halt the despoliation. Mayor Paul E. Doutrich in 1980 proposed that Front Street be renamed "Susquehanna River Drive," an idea almost unanimously rejected. Susquehanna Twp., as indifferent to the rapacity of buyers and sellers as Harrisburg, did strike a blow for a modicum of modesty on Front Street in 1982 by rejecting a request for a zoning variance that would have permitted the first massage parlor.

The real end to old Front Street, as in all sagas, came from the inside, the upstairs and downstairs at the aristocrats' finest lodgings. Once, for example, the Cameron-McCormick clan dotted the street: 101, Donald McCormick, president of Dauphin Deposit; 105, the Olmsteds, of whom the Widow Olmsted married Vance McCormick; 301, Vance and his maiden sister Anne; 305, older brother Henry B. McCormick; and 407, Miss Mary Cameron and her sister, Mrs. Elizabeth C. Bradley, and their brother, James, the grandchildren of Simon Cameron. All eight of the third-generation McCormicks and the lone third-generation Cameron male died without issue, six of them never marrying.

They just didn't lose Front Street and their family line, they also lost continued ownership in the mills, the bridges, the traction company, the banks and the newspaper. They left estates, but they weren't empire-building Rockefellers or Mellons.

The bloodlines thinned. A neighborhood that produced senators, generals, physicians, authors, bankers, clergymen and industrialists, as well as a slew of assertive women—Mrs. Rachel Fox, Mrs. Gertrude Olmsted Nauman and Mrs. Henderson Gilbert, to cite three—brought forth a generation that fled town, or went childless, or didn't relish the discipline of being hard-working entrepreneurs. They opted instead to be either payroll careerists or parlor-sitting coupon clippers. When these offspring settled for salaries and suburbia, the speculators infiltrated.

28.

FRONT STREET PATRICIANS

WHEN THE POLICE IN 1917 investigated a burglary at 1901 N. Front St. and asked to speak to the help, Mrs. Frank Payne exclaimed: "I'd rather lose the $2,000 worth of jewelry than have my servants subjected to such indignity." At that time, if a steelworker saved every penny, he would accumulate $2,000 in two years.

Front Street might have thought of itself as aristocratic, but it was more patrician or superbourgeois. It had the tastes of go-getters, amply fortified by old money and position.

Its political and religious views often were narrow and defensive, while in behavior it followed the social conventions, not the sophistications, of its day. So controlled were its proprieties that no scandalous debauchery or even any notorious wastrels emerged. An occasional alcoholic was about as far as old Front Street deviated.

The street never achieved the hauteur of Philadelphia's Main Line. It lacked a nasal whine and a dismissive laugh, and didn't even have a cotillion to fuss about. There was a surplus of wealthy daughters, but no debutantes. This upper crust was too visible, and with its absence of remoteness came responsibility. For all their security and style, the chubby paters familias and their grayed matriarchs were sentimentally middle class.

Harrisburg's "our crowd" was not overly ambitious as financiers and industrialists, but most were quite properly concerned that their offspring attend a nice preparatory school before going off to Yale, Princeton, Penn, or a finishing school. The products of this nurturing slipped from being owners to being physicians, attorneys and bankers. Vance McCormick with pride listed his occupation as "Capitalist." The succeeding generation scaled down its status to "professional."

Front Streeters lacked the luxury to disassociate themselves from the real world. It was, after all, only a block away, and the slums just a few blocks farther.

Many were Victorian enough to be eager humanitarians, satisfying their self-esteem and upholding their family's reputation by performing social service. But it was the plutocrats' proximity to real life that fueled Front Street's outstanding leadership record—from buttressing the City Beautiful Movement to providing basic charity to the poor.

John O'Hara described such a Pennsylvania neighborhood as having "the proprietary tradition of the resident gentry who knew their people."

These patricians were involved. The early rosters of the Choral Society, Symphony, Community Theater and sports teams—not just the bank boards, Republican Party and country club—were filled with their names.

Working-class Harrisburg rubbed shoulders with these entrepreneurs and their ladies, and often was fond of them. The proprietary class of that Harrisburg of 1910 and 1920 probably was far less deliberately arrogant than the more-smiling, insecure managerial class of the 1980s. "I was secretary to Mr. Henry B. McCormick for two years, to Mr. Vance McCormick for 27 years and to Miss Anne McCormick for 16 years," wrote a woman 15 years after the last had died. "They were a wonderful family and I am proud to have been associated with them."

The Archibald Knisely residence and the Edwin Herman residence to its right in this postcard once epitomized upper Front Street elegance. They were demolished in the early 1960s to make room for the new Governor's Home.

While these Front Street patricians were as blind to Tanner's Alley or the backside of Sibletown as a modern-day suburbanite, they did have the skill not to so polarize their community that there would be irreparable hostility between the haves and the have-nots. Harrisburg's social and economic status demarcations were kept in place, but contempt and rudeness were regarded as bad taste.

It was the Alricks, Calders, Bombergers, McPhersons, Camerons, McCormicks and Kunkels who founded what is today the United Way. These same patricians were there in 1909 to charter Family and Children's Service, the Methodist Mission in 1910 as the predecessor of today's Uptown Neighborhood Center, and Bethesda Mission in 1914 as a "Christian workshop and a workingman's hotel." Their names were associated with the Children's Industrial Home at 19th and Swatara streets, the Home for the Friendless at Fifth and Muench, the Harrisburg Nursing Home at State and Filbert, the Messiah Home Orphanage at Bailey and 12th, and the Sylvan Heights Home for Orphan Girls.

The Front Street squires and duchesses seemed as comfortable at giving commands as they were with their principles of noblesse oblige. To them it was poor taste to be oblivious about their community's needs. For most, their family's prosperity was dependent upon the town's well-being. Their wealth, and that from their ancestors, was invested where they lived.

And so they lived in their city and were concerned with it, and in their parlors as the sun set over the Susquehanna they discussed their city. When they were no longer there, the change was noticed.

29.

UNWASHED HARRISBURG

BEFORE THE 1920S, Harrisburg was a tough blue-collar town. A bureaucrat was almost as scarce as a duckbill platypus, and half as respected. The middle class was the minority, with few gentlemen in vests and even fewer career women in tailored suits.

Once there were 15,000 lunch-bucket railroaders in the area, and 8,000 steelworkers in Steelton and another 3,000 in Harrisburg—a 26,000 count almost matching the number of modern-day federal and state employees. Contemporary Harrisburg is shamed by a notorious reputation—myth though it is—that the town is about as exciting as green fettuccini. Was there a Harrisburg three or four generations ago where people lived in row houses, ate boiled cabbage, drank rotgut, frequented red-light districts, bet on the prize fights, disdained haute culture, desired no learning beyond high school, and in schoolboy football repeatedly battered the meanest brats from Pennsylvania's most forsaken coal pits and mill towns?

Are the anthropologists cheating again? Was Carlisle, or even Pottsville, ever more socially acceptable than Harrisburg? How could Scranton think of Harrisburg as backwater? And why would Dutchmen who ended up in Pennsylvania's capital city say they came "down from Reading," as if they were descending from a champagne town to a beer town?

Is it possible that the white-collar, dinner-party Harrisburg of today, underwritten by the state pension plan, expense accounts and other niceties, evolved from a blue-collar, dirty-fingernail burg?

Could it have been that Harrisburg Tech, so prominent academically, could kick the football tar out of everybody because it had hungry, hard-muscled puddler and railroader sons of the same gashouse-gang breed as the louts, bullies and swaggering jocks from Mount Carmel and Monessen? For every smooth Jacques Barzun with a "million-dollar mind and five-cent body" there was a coarse Clarence Beck with a "million-dollar body and five-cent mind."

In the pre-1920s era, much of Harrisburg had little sophistication, and didn't want any. That is the reason the City Beautiful reformers got busy in the first place, and why Renaissance I was such a success. Had Harrisburg basked in couth, it wouldn't have needed prophets. Had cologned businessmen been ensconced in sheltered suburbs and not been forced to live by the sweaty working class, they would have never interested themselves in civic improvement.

Once bureaucracy and its middle-class platitudes arrived in Harrisburg, social placidity was enthroned. The urgencies of the blue-collar tumult could be pushed aside, just as racial questions were. A new leadership arose that assumed, "It's hard to get things done in Harrisburg."

Proletarian low-life dominated old Harrisburg.

The newspapers had daily accounts of the latest killed and maimed on the railroad or in the mills, or who drowned while taking Saturday baths in the river—it was an exceptional year when Harrisburg had fewer than 30 drownings in the Susquehanna.

This was one of the leading railroad centers in the world. In 1910 there were 13 million railroad passengers going through Harrisburg. In March of 1910, there were 177,952 railroad cars behind steam locomotives rumbling through town. The noise must have been deafening.

That same year, Harrisburg manufactured 40 million King Oscar, Sweet Girl and Owl cigars. And since Harrisburg and Steelton were second only to Pittsburgh in Pennsylvania steelmaking, the combination of train soot, cigar smoke and noxious mill fumes was almost enough to coat gleaming Miss Penn on the Capitol Dome in a film of grime.

Such a world wasn't one for legislators and bureaucrats. As the 20th century dawned, the commonwealth had only a $12 million biennial budget, which in the 1980s would last state government barely four hours. There were but 300 state employees, not all of whom were in Harrisburg. The Legislature never actually met in 1900. It had adjourned on April 20, 1899, resumed for the first six months of 1901, and then was off all of 1902.

Government was so minute that it literally operated out of the new Capitol and the Old State Museum. That lucrative modern industry—leasing state office space—didn't exist. There were lobbyists—called "borers," appropriately—but they lived in dank hotels and rooming houses, not split-levels.

And then in the 1920s, the South and North Office buildings were opened, a Capitol Complex established. The migration of the "washed" to Harrisburg began, as the "unwashed" stepped back, no longer of prime economic significance. Fewer blue collars hung on backyard clotheslines, and laundresses saw a dramatic increase in their white-collar trade.

30.

POWER, STEEL, AND DREAMS

THE RAILROADS WERE THE FIRST major industry to come to Harrisburg. This was good flat land for track, the state capital, and Midstate transit hub, and there was a labor force of docile Dutchmen who with loving care could baby the great steam engines, perhaps the finest and most endearing pieces of American machinery ever built.

The railroads were power, steel and dreams, as masculine as "railroaders coffee"—a brew so strong it supposedly could cut through a throat full of dust, eat the bottom out of a tin cup, and retain its viscosity of gravel even after being diluted with spring water. With a whistle and a road, the railroads didn't need the ad-agency hype of the modern airplanes. Conductors were figures of authority, not founts of bubbling pleasantries like flight attendants.

The smoke-belching iron horses went through the center of Harrisburg until 1935. The Pennsy had 2,490 of them as late as 1949. These handbombers would load at coaling stations, wharfs as high as the 100-footer at Verbeke Street—35 tons to get east to Manhattan Transfer, or 60 tons to go a mile a minute pulling 150 gondolas to Altoona.

Running like great black cats, the locomotives went off into the night. Tight-lipped Dutchmen at the throttle would ease them across the Rockville Bridge, puffing their grayish clouds into a cinder-color sky in a sight of almost unimaginable beauty. And then at the Cove, just north of Summerdale, the engineers would floor the old girls and they'd purr in rapid rhythms up to 100 mph—anticipating the thrill of their grandsons, the hot-rodders.

In a panoramic view from above, glistening steel rail radiated from Harrisburg in all directions like a galaxy. Main lines, sidings, and classification yards were designed into an orderly pattern, not the pandemonium of the modern highway sprawl. The railroads were Euclidean geometry combined with the might of Vulcan. Sensible, conservative people understood the railroads.

The railroad barons conquered Harrisburg, and the railroad employees acculturated it. A major part of the political genius of Harve Taylor was that he understood what each had done, and he never got on the wrong side of either the barons or the trainmen. This town listened, because rattling freights and brightly lit Pullmans meant paychecks.

The Cumberland Valley Railroad was the first line into Harrisburg in 1837, and it lasted until 1919. It not only erected the first railroad bridge in these parts, but also it premiered the first sleeping car for American railroading. Sending as many as 40 trains daily into Harrisburg, the CV roared through Carlisle and Mechanicsburg, carrying goods from 152 grist mills, 80 small distilleries, nine iron furnaces and three paper mills.

The great Pennsylvania Railroad was chartered April 13, 1846, and was using Harrisburg by 1849. In December of 1852, the first Pennsy steam engines sped from Philadelphia to Pittsburgh, a $9 trip that took 16 ½ hours. Conveniently, Pennsy lobbyists de-trained at Harrisburg with enough money and influence to almost "own" the Legislature for at least a half-century. A Republican pro tem of the State Senate is supposed to have exclaimed, "The Pennsylvania Railroad having no more business in this chamber, we stand adjourned."

The Pennsy in its prime was said to be the best-run corporation in the world. It might have been the richest, and certainly it was worth more than all of state government. At one time it had more employees than the Army had soldiers.

Beside the CV and the Pennsy, Harrisburg had three other railroads. The Camerons in 1854 were behind the founding of the Northern Central, which made a fortune during the Civil War and in 1911 became a subsidiary of the Pennsy. The Philadelphia and Reading began passenger service to Harrisburg for the 1858 inaugural. And in that same era, the Dauphin, Schuylkill and Susquehanna launched its runs north to Pottsville and the coalfields.

In the early 1900s, there were as many as 400 daily trains—150 of them in passenger service—coming through Harrisburg. The known record occurred in March of 1910, when there were four railroad cars a minute through town. Often there were second sections—or a train running right behind the scheduled one—to handle the heavy westward business from New York and Philadelphia.

A Harrisburger could get virtually anywhere in continental U.S.A. from center city by train. As the Board of trade stated in 1911, Harrisburg had railroad "lines unsurpassed by any other city of its size." Not one soul, not even the manic-depressive, imagined that the glorious Pennsy, as the Penn Central, would be bankrupt by the spring of 1970.

31.

THE PENNSY AND THE MASTERPIECE

HARRISBURG HAS NO EIGHTH STREET because the Pennsylvania Railroad took it for its Main Line. Nothing stood in the way of the railroad. The Blizzard of 1888, the floods of 1889 and 1902, and the Cleveland and Cincinnati Express colliding with a disabled freight at Lochiel in 1905—only unforeseen mishaps could stop the railroad, and then temporarily.

At the turn of the century in Harrisburg, the railroad called the shots. And with a local payroll more than $7 million, or at least five times that of all state government, the railroad was nigh invincible.

The Pennsy, in particular, marched forward like a behemoth. No one disputed its right of way.

What once were burial grounds for the German Reform, Lutheran, Presbyterian and African churches were taken before 1850 for its Pennsylvania Station and parking lot. Atop of part of that cemetery, the railroaders' restaurant, the Alva, opened in 1916. The Pennsylvania Canal was acquired by the Pennsy in 1901, and in due time three of its competing railroads in Harrisburg, all but the Reading.

Between 1902 and 1925, taxpayers spent almost a half-million dollars to go under and over the tracks, so they would be safe from the iron horses and so the railroad wouldn't be inconvenienced or lose a minute on its time schedule.

The Market and Herr Street subways went under the tracks. The Mulberry Street Viaduct, 13th Street Bridge and Soldiers and Sailors Memorial Bridge—always called the State Street Bridge—went over the tracks.

Good as their getting was, the railroads were generous partners in the Harrisburg area's prosperity.

The Pennsy laid 161 miles of Steelton steel rail for its Harrisburg Yards from Dock Street to Rockville, employing 3,000 plus another 1,500 who manned the trains in this division. In 1905 the Pennsy opened its $6 million Enola yards, with 76 miles of track and 700 employees, as one of the nation's busiest freight-classification centers.

The Reading developed the Rutherford Yards with 57 miles of rail at a cost of $2 million. It employed 1,925 on its 31 daily trains, at its yards and in its new Reading Terminal, a marble, Gilded-Age depot that was the finest of them all but lasted only from 1904 to 1957 until it was replaced by the Harrisburg Post Office [on Market Street]. At Rutherford, yardmen "rode the hump" to switch as many as 7,000 freight cars a day. On a grading in the holding yard, railroaders would steer free-rolling freights at 15 mph, an exciting day's work that lasted until 1952 and which its veterans said was more dangerous than working at the steel mill.

The future was so bright that the railroads rebuilt what they lost. The Cumberland Valley had its first timber bridge across the Susquehanna go up in flames, its iron bridge collapse in a flood, and in 1916 built the masonry span south of Harrisburg Hospital. The Northern Central at the Dauphin Narrows lost a timber and then an iron bridge before putting up the famous Rockville Bridge.

The Rockville Bridge remains the masterpiece of when the Pennsy was the king of the road.

The bridge has the strength of six bridges and is composed of 220,000 tons of stone—or 21/2 times the weight of the Washington Monument. It is 3,830 feet wide and its 48 arches make it the world's longest stone-arch railroad span. George Nauman, the brother-in-law of Front Street's Gertrude Olmsted Nauman, was its engineer, and he built his bridge to challenge the next Ice Age. Certainly the 1972 Flood with is 650 billion gallons of water at its crest didn't brother the Rockville Bridge at all.

The bridge cost $800,000, and it opened on Easter Day of 1902. Two months later, that June 15, the first Broadway Limited, exhaling its acrid smoke, made its maiden crossing. In the cab of Engine 395 were four Harrisburgers, Calvin C. Miller at the throttle, and A. Wilson Black, J.R. Bartly and H.W. Campbell. Engineer Miller waved to crowds as he rolled across, and then reaching the West Shore he had four miles to Duncannon and he let Old 395 burn—a 91-second sprint.

"So fast, indeed, did it go that the road-crossing whistle seemed to come from the rear of the train instead of from the engine," wrote a passenger. "The rush of air against the steam as it came from the whistle squeezed the sound and the noise resembled a wild, unearthly shriek that seemed to linger among the trees."

32.

RAILROAD LIFESTYLE

WITH 15,000 RAILROADERS for more than a generation, the Harrisburg area developed a lifestyle that emphasized traits like thriftiness, punctuality, regimentation and close-knit neighborhoods.

Railroader families congregated on Allison Hill, along Ridge Avenue, or Sixth Street, and in such train towns as Rutherford, Middletown, Enola, West Fairview and Marysville. Even rural Perry County had its railroaders, though its train service lasted only from 1889 to 1928.

Many trainmen were early risers, so the sidewalks "rolled up at 9 o'clock" and Harrisburg nightlife never thrived. Yardmen and brakemen weren't much for café society.

In those days trains ran on time—a rather critical matter when there were 400 going through Harrisburg a day. Ruddy-faced Dutchmen once had been the canal boatmen, and many of them and their sons—and grandsons, as railroading was a family tradition—went to work on the iron horses. The Pennsylvania Dutch are punctual by necessity. The combination made Harrisburg railroaders' descendants who became state employees.

To this day, Harrisburg has some odd behaviors involving the importance of time. It is as if a train dispatcher set 8:15 p.m. as the starting time, not 8 or 8:30, for concerts at the Forum. There's the popularity of breakfast

The Pennsylvania Railroad Station was a destination for hundreds of trains arriving each day when Harrisburg was defined by railroading.

meetings for business persons, a throwback to the days when railroaders gathered at dawn for eggs and scrapple.. The habit of hurrying home after work—unusual for a capital city—might stem from the fact that railroaders, unlike coal miners or puddlers, seldom thirsted for a shot and a beer after a day's toil.

Railroader families were clannish and supportive. In their neighborhoods they had their churches, like the Fifth Street and Ridge Avenue Methodist churches or the Augsburg Lutheran.

The Rev. Silas Comfort Swallow was a railroaders' parson at Ridge Avenue from 1886 to 1892 and then a founder of the Epworth Church at 21st and Derry streets, and finally a visiting minister back at Ridge Avenue until his death in 1930. As "The Fighting Parson," he preached old-time religion and warned his railroaders not to "pickle" their vital organs in alcohol. "No-Swallow" he was called when he stepped into politics as a prohibitionist, running for governor in 1898 and 1902 and finally for president, no less, in 1904. Professional politicians disdained the man, but his railroaders loved him and gave him 132,931 votes statewide, the second highest tally a third-party candidate in Pennsylvania has ever received.

Railroaders were fond of athletics. The Fifth Street Church had top basketball teams, the Harrisburg Athletic Club, with Harve Taylor as its southpaw pitcher, was filled with railroaders. The Pennsylvania Railroad had its railroaders' YMCA from 1889 to 1933 where Bethesda Mission is today, installing the town's first swimming pool for $13,000 in 1924. The Reading Railroad Y was at Rutherford.

For years the Pennsy Family Club Sports Night Dinner was one of the town's gala events, promoted by Walter F. Bashore. He was the son of a railroader from Enola and worked for the Pennsy himself for 46 years, eight of them as the Harrisburg stationmaster. Bashore had a fleeting career as an outfielder for the Philadelphia Phillies, getting all of two hits in 10 times at bat. His distant relative was heavyweight Freddy Bashore, an amiable boxer and the only pug to be knocked out by Joe Louis, Rocky Marciano and Ezzard Charles.

As railroading for decades was one of America's most segregated industries, few jobs or neighborhoods in Harrisburg were integrated. It is ironical that the local railroaders, though a tolerant folk, contributed to the long, dismal history of race relations in the Harrisburg area with their preference for racial separatism.

Railroad politics in Harrisburg meant Republicanism from top management to laborer. Harrisburg's GOP chieftains, like Lt. Gov. Ed Beidleman and Sen. Harve Taylor, kept in touch with the Pennsy brass at Broad

Street in Philadelphia, and it wasn't a coincidence that both cities until the 1950s voted in a similar fashion. Beidleman, boss from 1912 to 1929, was a brilliant lawyer who worked both sides of the track. For labor he pushed through full-crew complement, the streetcar motorman law and workmen's compensation, which in 1916 provided weekly benefits of $5 to $10 but saved the railroads millions from compassionate juries in death and injury cases. For management, Beidleman had an enviable practice with Arthur H. Hull and Thomas D. Caldwell as counsel for railroad and traction companies.

33.

FACTORY TOWN

"THE CITY OFFERS EVERY INDUCEMENT to the manufacturer, and anybody in search of a mill or factory location cannot afford to overlook Harrisburg," the Harrisburg Telegraph reported in 1911.

Harrisburg was at its peak as one of the most productive factory towns in America—steel, engines, boilers, silk, cigar, typewriters, wheelbarrows, seamless cylinders, nails and more. The Panama Canal was built with Jackson Manufacturing's wheelbarrows and steel from Steelton, and so was the Burma Road. Central Iron and Steel's products went into battleships and bridges.

Factory smoke meant paychecks, and those in turn made Harrisburg a magnet for new residents. They swarmed in off the farms and over from Europe as new citizens of a new world to take a job.

"Infant industries aplenty," Telegraph publisher Edward J. Stackpole Sr. said of Harrisburg. That was true, but no one foresaw how short-lived this industrial boom would be.

The famous Fleming stationary steam engines, of up to 2,500 horsepower, were made by 450 employees at the Harrisburg Foundry and Machine Works in south Harrisburg, and were billed as "high speed machines, generally desired for direct connection with electric generators or rotary pumps, are not excelled by any make for similar service." The company was started by William R. Fleming in 1857, the same Fleming whose mansion in 1916 became the Civic Club.

Will Fleming's cousin Sam became the two-term Republican mayor in the 1880s, and his son, Col. Samuel Wilson Fleming, married Sarah Hastings, the governor's daughter, and was co-founder in 1915 of Gannett, Fleming, Corddry and Carpenter, the area's largest engineering firm. The Foundry eventually was merged into the steel plant, and both were defunct within a century.

The Harrisburg Boiler Works at 19th and Derry streets was another prominent industry that all too soon disappeared. When the Harrisburg Fire Department in 1914 bought its first apparatus, a Morton hose wagon, to replace horses, the new equipment was built at the boiler works.

Elliott-Fisher opened in 1896 on South Cameron Street and was soon producing 100,000 typewriters a year. By 1911 it was ready with "a marvel of mechanical ingenuity...not duplicated anywhere," the mechanical bookkeeper. "This machine seems destined to spread still further the fame of this city to all quarters of the globe," reported The Telegraph. Yet by 1930 Elliot-Fisher was sold out to Underwood typewriters, and in 1976 its empty buildings were razed.

Harrisburg expected to be a center for cotton and silk until at least the millennium. The cotton mill, at Front and North streets, opened before the Civil War and by the turn of the century was a silk mill employing 450 persons producing 1.5 million yards of broad silk and 3 million yards of ribbon a year. The mill closed in the 1920s, and the $488,000 Central YMCA opened on its site in 1933.

Two anthracite strikes in the mid-1920s led the way to homes being heated by oil, and Harrisburg declined as a hard-coal distribution center, a business that made a fortune for John Y. Boyd among others. Hummelstown

Brownstone Co., from 1860 to 1929, was another enterprise lost to history, and so was the 500-employee Harrisburg Shoe Manufacturing Co. on Vernon Street. Cigars—King Oscar, Sweet Girls and Owls—became another forgotten industry. Once Harrisburg Cigar Co. had 900 workers producing 900,000 stogies a week plus two more cigar factories in Steelton. Even before the Depression, this business faltered. The Harrisburg Art Association in 1927 had its first studio in an abandoned cigar factory.

Only two of the early manufacturers lasted.

W. O. Hickok Manufacturing Co., now in its fifth generation, was started in 1866. William Orville Hickok I came up from Chambersburg in 1839, and after one business failure devised machinery for making "pen rulings," or straight lines for bookkeeping. He also served as president of Harrisburg Common Council for six years. His son and grandson, Hickok II and III, were All-Americans at Yale.

Caleb Jackson started Jackson Manufacturing in 1876 in Kennett Square, but investors Sen. J. Donald Cameron and his brother-in-law Wayne MacVeath brought the business to Harrisburg so it could use their Central Steel and Northern Central Railroad. The wheelbarrow plant eventually settled at Lochiel, down the hill from Don Cameron's mansion, now the site of the city incinerator. The company was sold in 1964 to a Baltimore conglomerate, but maintains its Harrisburg operation. The Hambay Foundation was established by its bachelor president from 1907 to 1941, James T. Hambay.

34.

FROM SIZZLING TO COLD

IRON AND STEEL were made in Harrisburg for 190 years. With Steelton, this area once had as many as 12,000 steel workers and was second only to Pittsburgh as the largest steelmaker in Pennsylvania.

The setting was perfect for steel: Iron ore from Cornwall and Pine Grove Furnace, ample supplies of coal and water, convenient transportation with the Pennsylvania Canal and the railroads, nearby markets for sales, and an abundance of reliable immigrant labor.

Between 1880 and 1910, reports historian John Bodnar, steel profits in Steelton doubled, but average wages went up by a mere penny an hour. Occasionally pay raises were a mill or two, or one-tenth of a cent. In 1908 a man working a "hunky banjo," or large ore shovel, received $1.44 for a 12-hour day.

No one in that era ever dreamt that someday the Pennsylvania Railroad would go bankrupt. Neither did anyone think there would be a time in Harrisburg when a heat of sunburst-yellow molten steel wouldn't be tapped hissing into ladles.

Henry Fulton began making wrought iron nails in 1785, the year John Harris founded Harrisburg. The first rolling mill by the canal at Mulberry Street was started in the 1830s, and two decades later former Gov. David

Rittenhouse Porter built an iron furnace at Cameron and State streets. Simon Cameron, Jacob Haldeman and Andrew Carnegie—the latter with the Lochiel Iron Co.—were among early investors.

The McCormicks and Baileys put together Central Iron and Steel in Shipoke in 1853, adding the Chesapeake Nail Works in 1866 and taking over the Paxton Rolling Mill. After Central Iron rebuilt its mill in 1892, Carnegie borrowed the designs for upgrading his famous Homestead mill.

Down in Steelton, Pennsylvania Steel Co. was formed in 1865 with an investment of $200,000, and the Camerons, Hickoks, Calders, Kelkers, Haldemans, Boyds, Kunkels and others raised $24,577 to buy 97 acres for the company. On May 25, 1867, steel was produced—the first steel in the United States from a plant built specifically for that purpose. The Golden Gate and George Washington bridges have Steelton steel that sparkles in the sunlight yet.

Earlier in 1853, within a year of the Pennsylvania Railroad's historic cross-state run from Philadelphia to Pittsburgh, eight Harrisburgers invested $25,000 in Harrisburg Car Manufacturing Co. to make rolling stock for the Pennsy. The first eight-wheel passenger car came out of the Allison Hill plant. At the turn of the century, the company dropped out of railroad manufacturing, moving to Governor Porter's iron furnace on Cameron Street, and with $1.15 million of recapitalization, became Harrisburg Pipe and Pipe Bending. Elias Z. Wallower, who would go on to build the Penn Harris Hotel, was the financier who masterminded this expansion to a 23-acre, seven-block-long site, the nation's largest.

By 1905 the company—it became Harrisburg Steel in 1935 and Harsco Inc. in 1956—had 800 employees and was producing $1.5 million of durable goods, including the nation's first 22,000 seamless cylinders a year for such buyers as Budweiser beer. Built in "muck heaps and mud holes...a repulsive and dreary marsh," the plant had three open hearths and an

The Harrisburg Steel Company plant was part of the local steel-making complex that once employed up to 12,000 men, second only to Pittsburgh.

annual capacity of 60,000 tons of ingots. David E. Tracy was president for six years. His mansion on Front Street became the first Osteopathic Hospital, and Tracy Hall at Bishop McDevitt High School is named for him.

Between the two world wars, the engine, boiler and nail factories in Harrisburg closed. Wartime is good for steelmaking and fabrication, but post-war often brings shutdowns. In 1955, Phoenix Steel bought old Central Iron, and in December of 1960 it closed the Shipoke mill forever. Employment had declined from 1,700 to 50.

Steelton remains on the map, however, because in 1916 Bethlehem Steel bought the plant and it had the management, resources and incentive to challenge a tough market. In the early 1960s, Bethlehem closed its last blast furnaces, but in 1970 it replaced its 10 open hearths which once did two heats a day with three huge electric furnaces. Employment had once been 8,000. It would never again, in all likelihood, reach half of that, but Steelton kept going. Now in 1983 Bethlehem is investing $84 million in a continuous caster process, eliminating the old rough-drawn ingot method of making steel as the plant becomes internationally competitive once more.

Harrisburg Steel of Harsco, now a conglomerate in East Pennsboro Twp., faced foreign competition it couldn't buck. Rather than invest $13 million for electric furnaces, it ended steelmaking in 1975. Once its ladles poured sizzling steel at 3,000 degrees, but by September of 1982 the old mill was cold. An industrial no man's land, the factory was stripped, put into mothballs and left to rust. Ten generations of Harrisburg steelmaking were over, and likely never to return.

35.

THE TROLLEY ERA

By the early 1920s, it was possible to get from New York to Newville, of all places, by streetcar. Had the trolley line been built to Shippensburg, the dream of linking Manhattan to Maryland would have been realized.

This was the golden age of American hometown public transportation, and it is even more appreciated in retrospect than it was in its own day—because in contemporary hard times it is impossible to get from Downtown Harrisburg to the Harrisburg International Airport on steel wheels.

In 1923 there were 4,625 miles of trolley line in Pennsylvania, about 400 of which made direct and indirect connections with Harrisburg. In Philadelphia and Harrisburg, they were called "trolleys," and in Pittsburgh and the coal region, "streetcars."

The fare was a bargain: until World War I a 5-cent fare zone to Camp Hill over the Walnut Street Bridge or to Steelton, after the war 7 cents, then 8 cents and eventually 10 cents, with rates of 21 cents to Rockville, 50 cents to Hersheypark and $1 for a weekly West shore pass.

The service was often incredibly good. There were about 130 trolleys on the East and West Shores, on regular and frequent schedules. Motormen could get their trolleys going 40 mph on a straight-away, as passengers in the comfortable straw seats listened to the musical whine of steel hitting steel—and the Steelton mill at one time was making 80 percent of the trolley rail in the United States.

Passengers indeed could "dodge life's stress and its strains," as Don Marquis' verse put it, though occasionally wayward motorists and pedestrians didn't dodge the clacking trolleys quickly enough. Amputations of arms and legs were the common result of youngsters' collisions.

Motormen and conductors, though they worked a 60-hour week in their white-segregated industry, made a jolly crew. Harvey A. Boxer Sr. for 20 years was a conductor on the Market Street trolley with extravagant courtesy. Happy Boyer would usher ladies to their seats. As a singer for the Zion Lutheran Church Choir, he often would break out in song, such as "On the Road to Mandalay." And so customers wouldn't miss their stops, he would call out "Millionaires Row" as the trolley went from 19th to 21st streets where the Aughinbaughs, Haehnlens, and Josiah Kline lived. Happy had a rabbit foot for throwing over goal posts at Harrisburg Tech and John Harris games. He was such a trolley man that he never got a driver's license for a personal automobile.

The trolley era lasted 80 years, or from the city's first horse-drawn trolleys of July 4, 1865, until 1946 when the Hershey line closed. Horses were used for 23 years. Then came the fabulous electric era for a half-century, from July 4, 1888, until July 16, 1939, when Henderson Gilbert, the lawyer and president of Harrisburg Railways, donned a straw hat and rode the last car, No. 815, from Market Square to Middletown.

Only Richmond, Va., was ahead of Harrisburg in getting electrified city trolleys. Harrisburg pioneered because it was in the forefront of adopting electricity. A carbon-arc-light experiment was tried on Market Square on May 11, 1883, or two months before Thomas Edison at Sunbury set up the world's first central generating station for overhead wiring on the

Trolleys were Harrisburg's effective system of mass transportation between 1865 and 1946. Steelton made the rails.

world's first double-voltage, three-wire system. That August, St. Edward's in Shamokin became the world's first lighted church, and on Nov. 12, 1883, Edison was in the capital city to witness Harrisburg Electric Co. pull the switch.

The first lighted room in Harrisburg was the men's bar of Pat Russ's European Hotel by the railroad depo0t on Nov. 20, 1883. Irish Pat stood on a chair to screw in the light bulb and his finger must have touched an exposed wire. He was knocked to the floor, and for a minute his railroader customers thought he was a goner. But Pat lived to see, within five years, the electric trolleys running outside his door. Central Pennsylvania Traction Co., to be Harrisburg Railways in 1913, soon had a 70-mile line to Hummelstown, Middletown and Rockville.

Cumberland Valley Electric Railway Co., established in 1895, had lines from Harrisburg to Carlisle by 1904. That same year Milton Hershey opened his routes to Hummelstown and Lebanon, trolleys that sometimes had freight cars to bring milk to the chocolate factory. And then there was a 10-mile line through Lykens from 1899 to 1924. Harrisburg Foundry and Machine Co. built many of the early motors and generators for these systems.

Chester senator and future governor William C. Sproul was instrumental in 1912 in joining seven companies to form the Valley Railways, with a 44-mile system that included Carlisle and Marysville. The trip from Harrisburg to Carlisle took 90 minutes and cost 60 cents, and ended in 1936.

The bus and auto replaced the trolley, but have never replaced its poetic splendor and innocence.

36.

THE FINEST PUBLIC SCHOOL SYSTEM IN PENNSYLVANIA

AT THE TURN OF THE 20TH CENTURY, Harrisburg developed what is regarded as the finest public school system in Pennsylvania. The schools certainly were a powerful attraction for families to move into the city, and hundreds of non-residents were tuition-paying pupils until the late 1940s.

Such was an emphasis on education that by the fall of 1919 there was a pupil strike—to go to school, not to stay out.

The new Edison and Camp Curtin junior high schools—the original Camp Curtin at Sixth and Woodbine streets—opened that fall. They were part of the 30-year program that cost at least $10 million and gave the city a magnificent neighborhood school system of 26 buildings for more than 15,000 pupils. Few cities in the nation could top Harrisburg for its extensive building program, backed by concerned school directors and taxpayers.

With Edison and Camp Curtin opening in 1919, the district's enrollment hit a record 14,000, up by 1,300. Though Edison was built to accommodate 1,400 pupils, there were 538 more seventh-, eighth- and ninth-graders than Superintendent F.E. Downes expected. Downes, the school chief from 1905 to 1923, announced the junior high pupils in the center city would remain at their grammar schools.

Willard School pupils didn't accept Downes' plan. They wanted to be admitted to Edison, so they went on strike. The Willard grammar school as far back as 1869 had been Girls High and it was on State Street, where the Harrisburg Moose Club is today. Its youthful strikers wished to be at Edison because it offered Latin. Parents agreed that was a good reason, and after a week Downes and the school board relented.

A leader in the strike was 12-year-old David L. Silver, son of Rabbi Eliezer Silver at Kesher Israel Synagogue at Capitol and Briggs streets. The rabbi supported his son, who in 1933 would return to Kesher Israel himself as a rabbi for a half century.

Harrisburg education in that era generated excitement like this. Before Renaissance I, local education often had been perfunctory. After Renaissance I, it could be perditious. But during the golden epoch, education was prestigious.

After Philadelphia and Lancaster, Harrisburg was Pennsylvania's third school district, established April 11, 1827. But a strong anti-education sentiment prevailed for decades. In the momentous 1834 fight for public education in Pennsylvania, led by Gettysburg's sardonic Rep. Thaddeus Stevens and his biting harangue before the Legislature ("Even voluntary fools require our compassion, as well as natural idiots"), Dauphin County voted 11-3 against free education, outdone only by Berks County's 30-3 negative vote. When compulsory education for children ages 8 to 13 took effect in 1895, many Dauphin countians again were opposed.

As Dr. William Franklin Rutherford penned in his memoirs before his death in 1904, too many locals were "broad-bottomed, hard-headed Dutchmen of the drowsy, Sleepy-Hollow type, who believed in ghosts and hard work, were fond of playing ball and pitching horseshoes on Sunday... and who were bitterly opposed to education, fearing that thereby the children would be rendered proud and lazy."

The drop-out rate was horrendous. In its first half-century of public education, Harrisburg produced only 685 public high school graduates, and 477 of them were girls. The bloc of graduates going on to post-high school education was less than 30 percent until at least Sputnik in 1957. Harve Taylor was the rule, not the exception. He left school at age 12 and never again over 94 remaining years bothered about formal education, nor did he ever champion education as a politician.

Harrisburg didn't get its first black male high school graduate until 1883. There were 10 segregated black grammar schools, and they were considered all the black pupils needed. Steelton, with its long tradition for ethnic consciousness, was much fairer to blacks.

Any suggestion there is a correlation between Harrisburg's finest education and when it had its strongest Jewish community risks the charge of reverse discrimination. No historical data exists, because ethnicists have yet to study the question and educators consider it too touchy, but the suspicion is strong. Concerned Jewish parents between 1910 and 1970 contributed to making their sons and daughters the student leaders. Racial disturbances and the 1972 flood sent the Jewish community scurrying to the suburbs, and with them seemed to go much of the indefatigable social omnivorousness for academic excellence and achievement.

37.

THE ZENITH OF LOCAL EDUCATION

WHEN A FRENCH DIPLOMAT ON THE STAFF of Lehigh University asked a friend, the Pennsylvania education secretary, to recommend a public high school for his brilliant son, the educator looked across Walnut Street and suggested Harrisburg Technical School.

Jacques Barzun was enrolled and though nominally in the Class of 1924, he blazed through in three years and was on his way to Columbia University. "I had the good fortune to come in contact with a fine group of high school teachers," he wrote in his most famous book, *Teacher in America.*

Prof. William D. Meikle perhaps was the most renowned. He taught for 55 years, knew 16 languages and gave Paris-born Barzun straight A's. On one occasion when Meikle was drama coach, he used Barzun as a prompter. The lean, willowy lad startled him by disposing of the script after he easily memorized all the lines. Meikle later taught at William Penn High, the Harrisburg Academy, Messiah College and the University Center, was a translator, and was equally respected as an outdoorsman, hiker and tennis coach.

"It was a fine experience," Barzun noted about his brief Harrisburg years, "during which I made half-a-dozen life-long friends." One was Wendell Hertig Taylor, son of physician Dr. Louise H. Taylor at Third and Kelker

The monumental Central High was opened in 1893 as a consolidated, coeducational school at Capitol and Forster Streets. It became an all-girls school in 1920.

streets. Barzun and Taylor in the 1970s collaborated on the definitive critique of detective stories, A Catalogue of Crime.

The quality of Harrisburg schools was unquestionably high, perhaps the zenith local education ever has reached in the city or suburbs.

It was inexpensive education, too. Superintendent F. E. Downes in 1908 wrote that the average family with five children living in an assessed home of $5,000 paid less for schooling than for its milk bill, or $31.50 yearly.

Harrisburg played politics with its education, also. The statewide system of partisan school director elections encourages that, though until the 1970s Harrisburg kept its schools firmly in the hands of Republicans. Segregated grammar schools were part of the politics, popular with the white mill and railroading families. While Harrisburg was getting even more Jim Crow, its congressman, Marlin E. Olmsted, was in Washington making national headlines by trying to federally guarantee the voting rights of southern black Republicans. Ironically, six decades later a southern senator broadcast the degree of segregation in Harrisburg area schools to prove his own Mississippi had more integration.

The oddest local politics was the way Harrisburg for years divided itself into two wards for Downtown and Uptown educational districts. It once supported four high schools, one for boys and one for girls in each of the two wards. The opening of Central High in 1893 at Capitol and Forster streets as a consolidated, coeducational school was Harrisburg's great step forward.

The $125,000 Central High was launched with 21 teachers and 650 pupils. It had four curriculums: Classical, Latin-Scientific, English-Scientific, and Commercial, with Household Economy soon added for girls. Its first principal, Dr. Charles B. Fager, maintained that if a pupil lasted only a year at Central before dropping out, the education gained would be worthwhile.

As a football power, the blue and gray Capitolians were state champions eight times and, better than that, defeated the famed Harrisburg Tech 11 times and tied it twice in their 15 games.

Among Central's early teachers were judges Karl Richards and Paul G. Smith and Mayor John A. F. Hall. Its alumni included Smith and his equally athletic brother Dr. Harvey Smith, Mayor William K. McBride, Col. John B. Warden, Carl B. Stoner Sr., and after it became an all-girls school in 1920, Pauline Frederick, the first woman national television newscaster. Almost 45 years later, apple-cheeked Doc McBride deeded Wildwood Park to the Community College and his classmate, similarly rotund Carl Stoner, a lawyer, was the school board president who helped establish HACC.

Central got off to roaring start. In its first graduating class of 98, Fager reported 13 went to college and nearly all the rest took jobs.

But having Central wasn't enough for Harrisburg. In 1904 it opened Tech two blocks away, on the site where Boys Union High had been from 1867-1886 and where City Hall would be from 1929-1982. Tech became one of the greatest high schools in Pennsylvania history—with its "Golden Legionnaire" alumni to this day proclaiming it so.

38.

LEARNING SPREE

THERE MIGHT NOT BE ANOTHER HIGH SCHOOL in the entire United States where the alumni, like the Harrisburg Tech Golden Legion, gather annually and shout praises almost 60 years after the school's demise.

Old Tech was one of the monuments of Harrisburg's Renaissance I. Its name was a misnomer, as it had more academic than technical education for its all-male student body, but it served as a beacon for all to move into the city and enroll their sons.

Dr. Charles B. Fager came over from Central to be its principal. He was a small, dignified physician with thick spectacles, a gray mustache, and the presence to silence even the toughest mill and railroading kids who played on its victorious football teams. Another equally petite but powerful figure, Paul G. Smith, also came from Central to be football coach. Smith, once a reporter for The Patriot and later county judge, guided the 1917, 1918, and 1919 teams that earned national ranking.

Tech opened just as Harrisburg began a $1.1 million program for seven new grammar schools in seven years. The city had the commitment to match economic growth with educational excellence. By 1924 it had the area's first public kindergarten, and population was going up so fast the school board considered a third junior high to join Edison and Camp Curtin opened in 1919.

The learning spree was in evidence elsewhere, too. The Catholic Diocese started secondary education in 1918 with Cathedral High on North Street. In 1930 it was replaced by the twin-towered Catholic High on Market Street, and renamed in 1957 for its founder, Bishop Philip R. McDevitt.

Harrisburg Academy had a historic change in the midst of this era. The Academy, founded in 1784 as the 10th oldest boys' school west of the Philadelphia area, was at the Maclay Mansion on Front Street from 1827 to 1908, where Vance McCormick, its most enthusiastic alumnus, could keep an eye on it. In 1907 Headmaster Jacob Fridley Seiler died. He had come from Yale, took the post at age 28, and stayed a half-century. Prof. Seiler had no duplicates: a mathematician, linguist, historian, trout fisherman, Democrat like McCormick, and for 49 years a Sunday school teacher at McCormick's Pine Street Presbyterian Church and for 44 years as an elder there. Seiler's unmarried daughters, Martha and Susan, opened the Seiler School for girls in 1898, and a half-century later it merged back into the academy.

Harrisburg Academy moved up to Riverside on Front Street, near the home of Vance's cousin Henry Gross. It slipped into receivership in 1942 after McCormick's death, and the Army Air Corps took over its buildings to train actors Bruce Cabot and Robert Preston, director Joshua Logan and other celebrities for combat they would never see. Meanwhile, the academy ended up at Vance's brother Henry's place at 305 N. Front Street and in 1949 graduated its first coed class. A decade later it joined the exodus, becoming Harrisburg Academy on the West Shore.

To compete with the football glories of Tech and Central, Vance McCormick as a trustee at Penn State recruited James "Mother" Dunn, the Nittany Lions' first all-American and still its greatest legendary lineman, to be the Academy's coach for the 1908 season. Dunn's team lost all six games and never scored a point. He packed off to medical school and eventually became a famous surgeon in Hawaii.

Harrisburg didn't fail to get a college because it never attempted to get one, though Messiah College was founded here in 1909. There was Beckley College near Market Square, a business school from 1918 to 1933 operated by a 280-pound salesman, Charles R. Beckley. That school produced Albert Williams of Plymouth, later president of IBM. Mechanicsburg had Irving Female College, 1857 to 1929, a successor to a short-lived female college at the John Harris Mansion.

The most outstanding development was the opening of the Harrisburg Hospital Nursing School in 1905, followed by the Polyclinic's in 1911. Before these three-year diploma schools closed in 1974 and 1976, they graduated 4,828 registered nurses.

Harrisburg had such zest for education that in 1926 it opened the $1.67 million William Penn High at Italian Lake and the $1.21 million John Harris High on a 35-acre campus, financed with 30-year mortgages.

Original plans had been for a 3,000-student high school at the William Penn campus, but the rival residents of Allison Hill were enraged. Political boss Ed Beidleman agreed with his Hill constituents there be two schools. Beidleman unfortunately lacked the vision to recommend annexation, but there didn't seem to be a need—pupils from Susquehanna Twp., Penbrook and Paxtang used William Penn and John Harris until the later 1940s. It was only in the 1950s when sensitivities heightened that Harrisburg found itself in a boundary noose.

39.

AN OBSESSION FOR SPORTS

LIKE MOST PENNSYLVANIA mill and railroad towns, early Harrisburg took to sports and it excelled. Some of its area teams remain among the greatest in the annals of American sports. Jim Thorpe, the Carlisle Indian, is regarded as the supreme American athlete, and the unsung Carl Beck of Harrisburg was but a step behind.

The first quarter of the 20th century was both the dawn and the twilight—appropriately, Harrisburg had its Twilight Baseball League—of American hometown amateur sports. This was the heroic era of true sportsmanship, the generation ahead of the professional's "Golden Age of Sports."

Why such grit and glory? Historian Lewis Mumford on the founding of the Olympic Games in 776 B.C. reasoned that the newly citified Greeks established the "pastimes and vigorous bodily occupation" to "bring back these rural virtues as part of daily urban routine." That is at least a partial explanation of why as Harrisburg rapidly grew into being a city it also had an obsession for sports. Completing the trend, congested suburbia today produces marathon runners.

The football records, in wins, ties and losses, show that powerhouses used to reign:

Central High Capitolians (1889-1917) 137-91-18, .602; Harrisburg Tech Maroons (1904-25) 131-53-11, .712; Carlisle Indians (1893-1917) 169-87-13, .660; Steelton Rollers (1894-1981) 297-112-30, .726, and William Penn Tigers (1926-70) 200-196-40, .505.

Central won eight state championships, and Tech won four plus a national title in 1919. Overall, their combined winning mark was.650, and Harris and Penn followed with a combined record of .609 for 45 years. The percentages accumulated as Central played Tech and Harris played Penn, and all four went up against Steelton. The Harrisburg-Steelton football rivalry by now is one of the nation's oldest, continuous sporting events. Steelton is one of but a handful of American high schools to have won more than 500 football games, and its percentage would be over .700 if it didn't have to mash bones with Harrisburg.

Baseball started first, but unfortunately most of the baseball records are lost in the dustbin of history. Organized baseball here goes back to as early as 1884, when The Patriot began printing box scores.

As a game of swift, quick-thinking specialists, baseball appealed to the Harrisburg temperament. The Patriot in the 1940s reprinted a 1911 rotogravure photograph of the Harrisburg Country Club nine that included Vance McCormick, pitcher; his cousin Henry Gross, left field; Dr. Harvey F. Smith, third base; his brother and future judge, Paul G. Smith, shortstop; Councilman Harve Taylor, second base; and the governor, no less, John K. Tener, first base.

That team was as accomplished as it was wealthy.

McCormick had been an All-American quarterback at Yale and such a madcap ballplayer that when he was 47 and at the Versailles peace treaty he wrote his mother that if he had time he would organize a ball club for the Parisians.

Doc Smith, though only 5-foot-8 and 160 pounds, hit .275 in 1896 in the big leagues for Washington. He taught Latin at Central High, became a surgeon and founded the Tumor Clinic at the Harrisburg Hospital, while his wife Blanche was a suffragette, a founder of the University Women, Great Books and League of Women Voters organizations, and was an actress and president of the Community Theater in 1933. Brother Paul Smith quarterbacked at Central and Bucknell, and his 97-26-7 (.789) coaching record at Central and Tech ranks him with such Pennsylvania football mentors as Pop Warner, Jock Sutherland and Joe Paterno. His teams scored an eye-opening average of 34 points a game.

Big John Tener not only pitched in the National League but as president of it while he was also governor. Taylor was on the YMCA's first basketball team, was a sandlot football halfback, and for the Harrisburg Athletic Club once outpitched Gettysburg's Eddie Plank, who was a year older. Connie Mack invited both southpaws to camp. Plank seized the opportunity and ended up in the Hall of Fame.

Doc Smith, who died at 91 in 1962, was president of the Harrisburg A.C. in 1901-04. He wanted to build an athletic complex, but a Henley Regatta on the Susquehanna, start statewide tennis tournaments and introduce the game of cricket to the mill boys. The ebullient Doc thought nobody in the world could lick his Harrisburgers at sports.

40.

THORPE, BECK, AND KITZMILLER SCORE

THERE WERE MANY SUNNY AFTERNOONS of thrilling football at Island Park, but perhaps the most memorable were:

1912—Jim Thorpe for the Carlisle Indians scored three touchdowns in 20 minutes and went to the bench. 1919—the national schoolboy title game and Harrisburg Tech defeated Portland Ore., by 56—0 as Carl Beck tallied five times. 1925—Tech's closing season and another title game, a 27—0 shutout of Cedar Rapids, Iowa, with John Kitzmiller scoring 21 points including a record 48-yard field goal.

Thorpe and Beck were living legends. A teammate said Beck had "a million-dollar body and a 10-cent mind." That probably also held true for "The Horse," as Harrisburgers called James Frances Thorpe.

The two were carefree, roughhouse types for whom much of life was a puzzle except when they were in athletic competition. "Flying Dutchman" Kitzmiller, now almost forgotten, was different. The sensible son of a railroader, Big John earned 16 letters at Tech, made All-American at Oregon, played pro football briefly, and became a trucking manufacturer on the West Coast.

Fans said Thorpe, Beck, and Kitzmiller could have starred just as spectacularly in modern athletics. "When I played at Carlisle," Thorpe said 30 years later, "I was as fast as any of them, but oddly enough they always stressed my strength more than my speed. I twice ran the 100 in 9.4. I could do it any day in 10 flat. In football togs, I could step off the 100 in 11 flat. Having had speed, the modern game would have been made to order for me, so when I hear someone say Thorpe would have been no great shakes at this kind of football, it kind of gets under my skin."

Had there never been a Thorpe, Pop Warner still would have had great teams with Joe Gayon, Gus Welch, Isaac Seneca, Bemus Pierce, Shinbone, Wounded Eye, Asa Sweetcorn, Bull Frog and the gang. In six tries against the Indians, Penn State won only once. The serious Nittany Lions scored a total of only 27 points against the madcap Indians' 97.

Thorpe, of course, excelled at track, but he never defeated Lafayette College all by himself. The fact is Warner took seven other Indians to Easton, though Thorpe did take five first places.

Another myth is that for an Island Park meet, Thorpe arrived by running all the way from Carlisle. He was capable of that, but Lazy Jim hated practice and never ran when he could walk, ride or sit. It was his Olympic colleague, Louis Tewanima the little Hopi, who ran the 18 miles in 110 minutes and, without breaking stride, joined the intercollegiate two-mile event and won it. Nobody knows if Tewanima then ran back to Carlisle.

Thorpe was hardly a giant. He and Jack Dempsey were 6-foot-1 and 185 pounds. What Thorpe possessed, besides an untroubled mind, was a perfect athletic body—a 16-inch neck, a 32-inch waist, a 40-inch chest and a 72.5-inch reach.

No athlete ever had a year comparable to Thorpe's 1912. At the Olympics in Stockholm, he won four of the five Pentathlon events and scored 8,412 of a possible 10,000 points in the Decathlon. Carlisle threw him a parade when he returned with $50,000 worth of trophies. That fall he scored 25 touchdowns in the Indians' 12-1-1 season. The following year he married Iva Margaret Miller in Carlisle's St. Patrick's Church and signed a baseball contract with John J. McGraw's New York Giants.

Hitting a curve ball was almost as tough for Thorpe as mastering basic arithmetic, so he ended up on the Harrisburg Indians in 1915, where he batted .298 and stole 21 bases. He made his debut on July 25 in a doubleheader against Providence, belting a homer that 5,822 fans swear landed in Wormleysburg. Babe Ruth in 1928 sent one toward the Lemoyne Bottleneck and Willie Mays with Trenton in 1950 clouted a pitch to Pennsboro Manor.

Al Schacht, the "Crown Prince of Baseball," was Thorpe's teammate and might have influenced Jim, after a bit of firewater, to one day hang by his toes from a top-floor window of the Warner Hotel and scream war cries to startled palefaces on the sidewalk below.

Carl Beck from Allison Hill was as wild and cocky. On a dare he tried all of Thorpe's 1912 Olympic events, excelling in the broad jump, shot put, discus and all the running times but behind Thorpe only in the javelin and high jump. For Tech in 1919, he finished with 34 touchdowns and in six straight games scored the first time he had the ball.

Beck, after flunking college, played with the Pottsville Maroons and was with the Massillon (Ohio) Tigers when Thorpe was on the Canton (Ohio) Bulldogs. After that, Tech teammate Tony Wilsbach got Beck a job at his beer warehouse, and Carl drank as much as he stocked until he "got religion." In 1962 and 1963, Thorpe and Beck died within eight months of each other.

41.

TECH, CHAMPION OF AMERICA

WALTER CAMP HAILED the 1919 Harrisburg Tech football team as "Champion of America," but the late Professor Ed Knauss, a scholar of early Harrisburg athletics, claimed the 1918 team was better.

In those two years, under Coach Paul G. Smith, Tech was undefeated in 21 games and surrendered only one touchdown and a field goal. Nothing like that happened again around here until 40 years later when John Harris, under coaches George Chaump and Mickey Minnich, rattled off undefeated strings of 28 and 39 games, respectively.

Knauss favored 1918 Tech with a 9–0 record, because against tougher competition it gave up only 10 points. The 1919 team, however, had a 12–0 record and shut out everybody, including Wilkes-Barre, Chester, Baltimore Poly, Bethlehem Prep, Greensburg, and undefeated Erie. The great Carl Beck was sidelined with an injury, but the Maroons still whipped Steelton, 70–0. Then in the national championship against Portland, Ore., on City Island on Dec. 6, Tech won 56–0.

For a city completing one of the nation's most impressive urban-improvement plans, Tech was a vivid source of local pride.

The Maroons suited only 19 players for its games. The starting line-up was: RE, Zip Malick, later a prominent local teacher. RT, John Arnold. RG,

On the gridiron at Island Park, Harrisburg Tech defeated Portland, Oregon, 56-0, for the purported national high school football championship in 1919.

Fats Ellinger. C. Phog Smith. LG, Bill Pleam. LT, Carl Hoffsomer. LE, Vic "Snaps" Emanuel, who later captained Gettysburg College, played pro with the Pottsville Maroons and Massillon (Ohio) Tigers and coached at William Penn. QB, Buddy Lingle. RH, Carl Beck, who in three years scored a record 445 points. LH, Paul Garrett. FB, Tony Wilsbach, bruising younger brother of Frank Wilsbach, and the two set a brother's mark of 830 points at Tech. Team captain Calvin "Hap" Frank was injured most of the season. He went on to be a great Penn State halfback and became a National Guard general and popular Harrisburg politician.

Before Tech's games on City Island, trolley conductor Harvey A. Boyer Sr. would throw his rabbit foot over the goal post. Happy Boyer continued this tradition for the John Harris games from 1926 to 1960. When Bishop McDevitt played arch-rival Steelton, Coach Ralph Farina would invite Boyer to the Crusader's field for luck. Sometimes Boyer dropped his snowshoe rabbit's foot, weighted with keys, but then he would toss it over the goalpost a second time as the crowd cheered. Boyer was a farm boy from where the West Shore YMCA is today. He ended his years an elevator operator in Harrisburg Hospital, while his son, Haps Jr., a railroader, organized local midget baseball.

The Penn State Nittany Lions between 1892 and 1905 won one of three games they played on City Island and lost a fourth in Steelton. The Harrisburg Area sent great talent to State College: Eugene E. Miller, Glenn Killinger, Carl Beck's older brother Clarence, Dick Rauch, Joe Lightner, Hap Frank, Manny Weaver, and in later years Tony Orsini, Tony Rados, Donny Caum, Glenn Ressler, Mickey Shuler, and Scott Fitzkee.

Miller was only 5-foot-6 and 145 pounds, and the gatekeeper at Beaver Stadium once wouldn't let him in. He went from Central High to quarterback the Nittany Lions' 1912 undefeated season, setting a game-rushing mark of 250 yards that later big horses like Franco Harris, Lydell Mitchell, Lenny Moore and John Cappelletti couldn't break. Miller became principal at Edison Junior High and would delight students by walking on his hands across the auditorium stage. In his last years, he was a Harve Taylor city councilman.

Rauch became an amateur poet, respected ornithologist, head of the Harrisburg Zoo, and coach of the NFL champion Pottsville Maroons, but his most flattering kudo was that John O'Hara called him the handsomest man in America.

Killinger became Penn State's greatest all-around athlete, though he was only 5-foot-10 out of Tech. With him, the Nittany Lions went 24 games undefeated in football and had 30 straight wins in baseball and a 37–5 record in basketball. He went on to play with the New York football Giants, coach at Dickinson, Penn State, Rensselaer Poly, Moravian, West Chester State and Navy, and managed the Harrisburg Senators to the 1928 Eastern League pennant.

42.

THE DIAMOND AT ISLAND PARK

HARRISBURG RATES A FOOTNOTE in the history of professional baseball—Senators on June 22, 1952, signed the first female.

It was a crusty male Harrisburg, of all towns, which tried to unisex the national pastime with a brunette at second base.

"She can hit the ball a lot better than some of the fellows on the club," remarked general manager Dave Kohn, still a prominent Harrisburg attorney.

"Like hell," retorted manager Buck Etchison. After photographers took her picture warming up, Etchison sent her to sit in the press box. Unlike Bill Veeck's midget on the St. Louis Browns, Ms. Engle never got a time at bat.

It was only two months before pro baseball closed forever at Island Park. Eleanor was a recent beauty queen from Shiremanstown and a stenographer at the Public Utilities Commission. She would have made a perfect Ring Lardner story, except she was too shy for any snappy comments to cynical sportswriters.

Ms. Engle had the pulchritude, but not much power. It is doubtful 30 years later she could have made the town's most noted baseball team, the non-male, fast-pitch softball Her-icanes in the State Employees Recreational League, which garnered statewide press clippings for its 1981 undefeated season. The Her-icanes, not in business for 14 years, have had genuine sluggers like Sandy Wilson, Darla Harbold and Linda Kreiser.

Actually, Eleanor Engle couldn't have made the 1952 Harrisburg Senators any more pitiful. The team played its final games at Island Park that Sept. 1, splitting a doubleheader with Sunbury before a mere 301 paid fans. Hometown boy Maynard Snyder hurled the nightcap 2–1 victory. Then on Sept. 7, the Senators bowed out of history with a loss at York. They sank with an inglorious 46–94 record, and the Inter-State League itself folded.

Baseball was the one activity that cheered up Harrisburgers enough to dispel their notorious solemnity. The diamond at Island Park provided more laughs than politics, the theater or a day's job ever could.

It was here that pitcher Al Schacht began his routines as the "Crown Prince of Baseball," succeeded by another zany, Maxie Pitkin, also a Harrisburg twirler. Loud-mouth Arthur "The Great" Shires, called "The Superfool of Baseball," was another Harrisburg ballplayer. Centerfielder Jim Thorpe could be a joke too, as baseball didn't matter to him and he never used his full athletic talents to master the game.

Harrisburg had minor league ball for 34 years, compared to 31 for Lancaster and 27 for York.

Harvey L. Ensminger, the photographer, was the last club president, with such investors as Judge J. Paul Rupp, Clarence S. Shenk, Walter E. Burns, Harry G. Banzhoff Sr., Dr. Ben Gainsburg, Hap Frank, Bob Mumma Sr., V.D. Leisure and Ben Wolfe helping to swallow the losses. The only winners in the last years were the batboys—Floyd Batarin, John Krafsig and Norm Yoffee all became lawyers and Andy Musser ascended to national television fame as a sports announcer.

Baseball's greatest pitching talent came from nearby and played here, but never on a Harrisburg pro team—Christy Mathewson of Bucknell, Eddie Plank of Gettysburg, Chief Bender of the Carlisle Indians and Stanley Coveleski from Shamokin.

Shortstop Hughie Jennings, another Hall of Famer from Pittston, played on an early Harrisburg team in the 1880s. Harrisburg won the Tri-State pennants in 1912 and 1914, but though Joe Chabek had a 28-3 pitching record he never made the big leagues. Billy Cox from Newport and pitcher Jimmy Brooklyn Deshong out of Tech and William Penn highs were Senators before going to the big time. Les Bell, the Cardinals' third baseman from Harrisburg, had a lifetime average of .290 and later managed the Senators to a 1941 flag. Ray Mueller, the iron-man catcher, played here, married a Harrisburg nurse and resettled in Steelton after 14 years in the majors.

Harrisburg's Twilight League produced some major leaguers: Russ Wrightstone from Bowmansdale with a lifetime .297 average, George Staller from Rutherford, and Billy and Lin Myers, the slick infielders from Enola.

The Harrisburg Indians, Orphans and Senators, as they were variously known, won six pennants. The Harrisburg Black Giants, sharing Island Park and owned by the American Alley pool room proprietor Col. Charles W. Strothers, had Rap Dixon of Steelton and the "Black Joe DiMaggio," or Oscar Charleston.

43.

SHOW-BIZ CROSSROADS

THOUGH THE OLD VAUDEVILLIANS in baggy pants loved using the name Scranton in their routines to prove they played the sticks, Harrisburg probably saw more of their shticks. For at least a half-century, from 1880 to 1930, the capital city was a show-biz crossroads.

Harrisburg was the convenient stopover between Philadelphia and Pittsburgh on the Pennsylvania Railroad's Main Line. Edwin Booth did "Hamlet" in the Grand Opera House on May 9, 1887. Al Jolson sang in blackface in the Majestic Theater during the World War I era.

The biggest names in theater detrained from their Pullmans to strut their stuff in the Opera House, the Chestnut Street Auditorium, or the Majestic, Colonial, Orpheum-State and Hippodrome theaters.

Harrisburgers enjoyed the celebrities, sometimes too much. In a Christmas story for 1901, The Patriot reported:

"The manager of our Grand Opera House has been caused no end of annoyance by depraved men and boys who seemingly go to any lengths to peep into the rooms occupied by actresses. Partitions were bored through, bricks knocked out of solid walls a foot thick, and metal perforated. At length this nuisance became so intolerable that a detective was employed and an arrest made. Even this failed to stop the evil. At one time the trouble was so bad that an inspection of the dressing rooms was made daily and patches of tin placed on every suspicious crevice or hole. Some of the rooms are so marked in this way that they look as though they had passed through a siege."

Theater was popular until World War I. A typical 1900 billing at the Opera House included a matinee of "The Fatal Cord" for reserved seats of 20 and 30 cents, and 10 cents in the second tier or peanut gallery. The price went up to 50 cents for the evening show of "The Innocent Sinner." As often as three times yearly, "Uncle Tom's Cabin" played Harrisburg. When "Ben Hur" was here, the traveling company put eight horses and two chariots on stage.

Mindless Harrisburgers, expecting the bright lights forever, kept no records, nor many playbills, of this pageantry of talent. Yet such figures came to town: Sir Henry Irving, Richard Mansfield, John Drew, James O'Neill who was the father of the playwright and had his traveling show "Count of Monte Cristo," Lillian Russell, Will Rogers, Ethel Barrymore, Eddie Cantor, Albert Hole the boy soprano from England, Ellen Terry, Harry Houdini, Maude Adams, Otis Skinner, Helena Modjeska, whose son founded the Harrisburg engineering firm, and possibly Rose Coghlan the famous mother of Charles Coghlan of Gretna Playhouse.

W. C. Fields was here the week of March 14, 1910, because The Patriot noted about this 30-year-old Philadelphian: "Anybody who misses an opportunity to see W. C. Fields, America's foremost comedy juggler...is missing a whole lot. As a comedy juggler, Fields stands in a class by himself and certainly there has never been a juggler on the Orpheum stage who would compare with him either as a manipulator or a comedian. Incidentally, it is an actual fact that Mr. Fields commands the highest salary that was ever paid an individual artist that appeared at the Orpheum."

W. C. needed the money. That week the notorious tightwad, using stationary from the Columbus Hotel, wrote his estranged wife Hattie in Philadelphia that he was short of cash to help support their son, Claude Jr., who he abandoned.

Vaudeville outlasted theater because its performances could be coupled with featured movie films. George W. Gekas, as a Harrisburg youngster and ardent fan of vaudeville and movies and today the congressmen, in a 1979 lecture to the Historical Society said vaudeville didn't die until 1936.

The old Orpheum in 1914 had two daily vaudeville shows, the new Colonial Theater had three, and the Majestic had legitimate drama. Yet the dour Dutch audiences gave Harrisburg a reputation as a tough town that rationed its applause. "If you can play Harrisburg, you can play anywhere," was the word on the theatrical circuit.

Yet it is not true that Harrisburg "killed" Joe Jefferson. Joe Sr., a great touring actor, did die here in 1832 and is buried in Harrisburg Cemetery, but his son, Joe Jr., famous as "Rip Van Winkle," returned here often before his death in 1905.

Supreme Court Chief Justice John Bannister Gibson, of Carlisle, so loved Joe Sr. that he donated the marble grave slab and wrote the actor's epitaph. On the high court for 35 years, Gibson wrote 1,200 opinions, tuned pianos, played the violin, read French and Italian, practiced medicine and dentistry on the side, including making partial plates, and fathered eight children.

44.

THE GRAND OPERA HOUSE

THE GRAND OPERA HOUSE was at Third and Walnut Streets, later the site of the Penn Harris Hotel where Strawberry Square is today, and it was the pride of Harrisburg.

Built for $130,000, the opera house—a misnomer, because no serious, large-scale operas ever were performed there—opened Oct. 13 in the midst of the 1873 recession. With an orchestra, family circle and peanut gallery, it seated 1,324, or about 8 percent of the city's adult population in 1880.

Harrisburg Rep. Andrew Jackson Herr spoke at the dedication: "A widespread feeling of indifference among the people had to be overcome, a general suspicion that it was a mere money-making scheme had to be allayed, a conviction that it would end in a failure as disastrous as many other speculations had ended had to be removed. Some...imagined... it would never rise about the foundation stones, others that the sheriff would sell it as soon as the roof should be placed upon it."

Herr's ironic remarks were re-quoted 103 years later when Harristown broke ground for Strawberry Square.

The Grand Opera House lasted 33 years until it burned down Feb. 1, 1907. Though it was beginning to look shabby and unstylish, this "Tem-

The Grand Opera House opened in 1873, thrived, and burned down in 1907. The site was taken over by the Penn Harris Hotel during World War I; today it's Strawberry Square.

ple of Amusement," as The Patriot called it, only a week before it went up in flames staged the wedding of two Harrisburgers following a matinee.

Beyond its theater and occasional concerts, the Opera House was the favorite convention spot of the Republicans and Democrats. Until 1914 and the primary system, the two parties selected statewide candidates at conventions.

The Republicans had eight conventions at the Opera House, and six of their candidates became governor. One of the Democrats from their four conventions made it all the way.

The conventions could be rowdy, hard-drinking affairs. Liberal Republicans claimed Henry Hoyt's nomination in 1878 was set up by Simon Cameron at the Lochiel Hotel. The 1890 nominee supposedly paid the party $100,000 for the privilege to lose in November. When Matt Quay was selected party chairman in 1895, so many backers, most of whom weren't delegates, crowded the second-floor hall that the floor almost gave way. At a Democratic convention, Dan McCleary of Schuylkill County was stopped because he lacked a ticket. "Are you a delegate?" the doorkeeper asked. "Well, partially so," said Dan. "I have a friend inside who is a delegate over whom I have great influence." And in slipped Dan to politick.

The Opera House was built by the Masonic Hall Association, which took the fifth top floor. Soon creditors took over, and Col. W. W. Jennings, Lane S. Hart, David Mayer, Spencer Gilbert, William Lamberton Jr., the Kunkels and others formed the Opera House Association.

Druggist George H. Markley on the first floor joined with newsstand dealer William B. Till to bring in theater and pay the association a per diem rental. Nathan Apell, Harrisburger, and Moses Reis, a New Yorker, succeeded Markley and Till. Those two doubled business by opening the Lyceum Theater on Locust Street in 1903. The Lyceum in 1908 became the Orpheum, which in 1925 was plushly rebuilt as the State Theater. And when the Opera House burned down, Appell and Reis built the fireproof Majestic up the street at 323 Walnut.

An early morning explosion in the Opera House cellar created one of Harrisburg's worst fires. There were six inches of snow on the ground, but the flames spread to 10 buildings. Jeweler E. G. Hoover got his gems quickly out of his store, as the Park Hotel, next to the Opera House, collapsed. Six firemen were hurt as $500,000 worth of property went up in smoke. The Opera House had a listed replacement value of $350,000, but was on the tax rolls as worth $101,139.

Within a week of the fire, civic leader J. Horace McFarland, calling for a civic center with a hotel, library and theater, issued a statement to the Municipal League:

"The pride that all of us take in the beauty of the Capitol and its surroundings should be strong enough to induce us to see that such buildings hereafter erected shall have the effect of enhancing the beauty of the magnificent statehouse and grounds. We owe it to the people of the state, whose confidence in us was shown by their willingness that the new Capitol should be erected here, to see that we do nothing which will in any degree detract from the beauty of the Capitol."

45.

THEATERS IN A TOUGH TOWN

SUBURBIA, NATIONAL AIRLINES AND TELEVISION combined to collapse nightlife in Harrisburg, as they did in many other American towns. When the big stars, no longer riding trains on the circuit, could be seen on a video tube from an easy chair, the theater marquees went dark.

For 50 years Harrisburg had as good a run at show-biz as anybody.

Yet it is puzzling. Penurious and church-going Harrisburgers didn't throng to the theaters, nor were they enthusiastic audiences. It was, as performers said, "a tough town."

Similarly, with theater all around them, Harrisburgers themselves made minimal contribution to the American stage. Its only resident writer was Helen Reimensynder Martin, who lived on Front Street and wrote 35 novels. A native of Lancaster, she called Harrisburg "a provincial town." She is remembered today for "Tillie: A Mennonite Maid," which became melodramatic theater, and "The Snob," which became a film starring John Gilbert and Norma Shearer.

Donald M. Oenslager was the lone native-born genius. Son of a doctor, he was born in 1902 where the State Museum is today. He grew up to be the ultra-sophisticated set designer for "The Emperor Jones," "Of Mice and Men," "The Man Who Came to Dinner," "Born Yesterday," "Sabrina Fair," and many other Broadway hits.

Actresses, not actors, came out of this male-dominated community.

Marie Doro, or Marie Katharine Stewart, was born in Duncannon in 1882 and played in "The Admirable Crichton," "Oliver Twist," and "Diplomacy," the latter as the first American actress to give a command performance in London. As a leading lady of films in 1920, she earned more than President Wilson.

Pauline Moore Watkins, a William Penn High graduate, co-starred with Henry Fonda in "Young Mr. Lincoln." Isabel Bishop McEneny, who died earlier this year, did "The Iceman Cometh." Nancy Wickwire, a John Harris graduate, did "Saint Joan" and "Under Milkwood," but had an untimely death at age 48. And Nancy Kulp, of Mifflintown, made it big in the 1970s in television's "The Beverly Hillbillies."

The record is slim, and it traces back to Harrisburgers preferring to import rather than nurture their own talent. The Orpheum once advertised it needed "six pretty girls" for vaudeville. Nobody showed up. Then it advertised it needed just "six local girls." Fifty appeared at the stage door.

Yet there was an immense amount of show-biz. Here are theater openings: 1903, Lyceum at 212 Locust; 1908, Majestic at 323 Walnut, the Hippodrome at 333 Market, and the Bijou at 34 N. Third; 1909, the Lyric, Victoria and Photoplay on Market; 1910, Regent at 410 Market, and 1912, the Colonial.

Once there were as many as 27 theaters, most of them motion picture houses, in Harrisburg.

The Majestic could seat 2,000. The State Theater, the fanciest Harrisburg ever had, replaced the Lyceum and Orpheum and could seat 2,600 when it opened in 1926. The Colonial, where the Lochiel Hotel had been from 1874 to 1912, was so classy that when it showed "The Birth of a Nation," it had a 30-piece pit orchestra.

The Chestnut Street Market went up the year after the Grand Opera House, and in 1888 its upstairs auditorium was finished. The hall, larger than today's Zembo Mosque, was turned into the Madrid Ballroom in 1926 by Gene and Henry Otto of Lancaster.

Big names—Strangler Lewis to Anna Pavlova and Ignace Paderewski—played the Madrid, as well as the big bands of Paul Whiteman, Rudy Vallee, Glen Gray, Duke Ellington, Cab Calloway and the coal region's fighting Dorseys. After one Madrid engagement, Jimmy and Tommy Dorsey adjourned to the middle of Chestnut Street to slug it out, and fraternal peace had to be restored by the Harrisburg police. The local bands of Red McCarthy, Dan Gregory, C. Lloyd Major, Don Peebles and Howard Gale also played there.

The Madrid had basketball and boxing. Harrisburg was a fair fight town, drawing on the great brawlers Pennsylvania produced in the first 40 years of this century. Billy Gray was one of the cleverest from Harrisburg, and up from Steelton's Standard Theater came Johnny Gill, Demo Atanasoff, Marlin "Ivory" Eshelman and Indian Julius Russell. Dr. Israel Oscar Silver often was the ringside doctor, and in 1973 his B'nai B'rith Apartment was built on the same site where he had once swabbed puffed eyebrows.

Among the referees to work the Madrid were Jack Dempsey, Gene Tunney, Maxie Baer, Jim Braddock, Tommy Loughran, Primo Carnera and Joe Louis. On one occasion, Gov. George H. Earle, a diehard amateur athlete, impulsively climbed into the Madrid ring to referee.

The Chestnut Street Auditorium, well past its prime, suffered a severe fire in 1951, and four years later was razed for a parking lot. Along with it went center city's show-biz and nightlife.

46.

THE LOCAL PRESS

"NEWS ARE SCARCE IN THIS VILLAGE," Sally Harris with her quaint grammar complained for 42 years in her social columns in the Patriot, Telegraph, and Sunday Patriot-News.

Sally wore feathered hats, had a career back to World War I and was an exuberant character, but she was wrong about Harrisburg news. Rather than a dearth, the glad and the sad tidings gushed prodigiously, almost promiscuously, for more than 170 years. Harrisburg, like Washington and New York, is drenched in news, as floods of handout releases are generated daily. Intelligently construing the significance of all this news is something else.

As the capital city, Harrisburg is a percolating Three Mile Island with two separate news nuclear chain reactions. The Capitol press corps, on the tails of the governor and Legislature, doesn't know where Naudine Street is, while the local press seldom can identify the House and Senate whips. This bifocal vision of the news gives Harrisburg a press that is unusually varied and quite different from any other community's in Pennsylvania.

For such a dogmatic institution, the Harrisburg press is strangely mysterious and uninformed about itself. There have been at least 25 local newspapers in Harrisburg, but no one has a complete count or even a copy of all of them.

The first paper, The Harrisburg Advertiser, was started by Eli Lewis of Lewisberry soon after Harrisburg, population about 500, became a borough on April 13, 1791. That paper, typically, is lost to history. John Wyeth absorbed the Advertiser on Oct. 20, 1792, into The Oracle of Dauphin County and the Harrisburg Advertiser. He published his four-page weekly on Mondays from his print shop on Mulberry Street.

Wyeth became assistant burgess—making him the first Harrisburg newspaperman to mess in politics—and his family was involved with the paper for 40 years. His sons, John and Francis, built Shakespeare Hall, which became the Bijou Theater and eventually in 1909 the Telegraph Bldg., in 1822 at Locust Street and Raspberry Alley.

The Patriot-News quixotically has no official history. Vance McCormick's eruditic editor, Dean M. Hoffman, in a 1922 letter complained "early historians did faulty work" and that is why no one knows "the date of the very first issue" of the Patriot. Hoffman guessed the founding date might be June 7, 1843, when The State Capital Gazette merged with The Pennsylvania Reporter and The Keystone under the name The Democratic Union. Future Gov. William F. Packer of Clearfield and silent-partner Simon Cameron were part of that deal.

Later editors, trying to choose among at least 15 progenitors—Harrisburg in 1830, for example had 11 newspapers for a population of 4,000—selected a birthdate of March 4, 1854, when the Pennsylvania Patriot was published. That date is the origin of "Patriot" for Harrisburg, and it remains a distinct newspaper name in America. Two evening papers, the Quincy Patriot Ledger in Massachusetts and the Jackson Citizen Patriot in Michigan, use "Patriot" as only part of their name.

Yet the Patriot-News shortchanges itself. Its earliest ancestor was likely the Dauphin Guardian of 1805, founded by Jacob Elder, the grandson of the "Fighting Parson" John Elder, to be a rival of Wyeth's Oracle.

It was Wyeth, however, who set the tradition for a heavy emphasis on local incidental news. Here is the story of June 2, 1809: "A man to be shot for the benefit of his wife and children—$1 a shot, 100 yards distance, with rifles, on Wednesday, the 13th instance; at Govanstown, at 3 p.m. The above mentioned man is in a very low state of health, and wishes to leave his family smug."

Such hometown-flavored reporting was the staple for generations. John O'Hara in *A Rage to Live* has his fictional Harrisburg Sentinel columnist, Arthur James Hollister, expound: "If the telegraph wire said 1,000 people had been killed in an earthquake in Chile, the important news in Fort Penn would still be that a rich and beautiful young girl was going to go to bed with a handsome, more or less unknown city slicker. It's regrettable, out of proportion, but it's true. Or, is it regrettable? Come to think of it, if the people of Fort Penn were more interested, morbidly interested in this earthquake and a 1,000 people killed, I'd quit the newspaper business, or at any rate I'd get out of Fort Penn."

Hollister was commenting about rich and beautiful girls of 1920. Sixty years later such behavior isn't considered so aberrant as to make news, or even gossip, in Harrisburg.

47.

THE CAPITOL PRESS CORPS

THE ANTAGONISM BETWEEN the "esteemed bummers," or legislators, and the "jackals," or Capitol press corps, must go back to 1812 when Harrisburg became the capital. "Boobies" and "skunks," respectively, also have been longstanding terms of endearment.

Certainly by March 4, 1820, the mutual hostility was well seasoned. On that date the first statewide Democratic convention, with 132 delegates, was held at the Dauphin County Courthouse, which served as the Capitol until the red brick statehouse went up two years later. At the convention the press was seated up front within the brass rail, "which from the known modesty of the tribe was very necessary," sneered a politician.

The Pennsylvania Legislative Correspondents Association was formed in 1895 as the nation's oldest statehouse press corps. Thus an experienced crew of newsmen had been so developed that by 1906, when the Capitol was dedicated, the modern telegraph lines could carry their shocking stories of the Capitol Graft Scandal.

The besieged governor, former judge and scholar Samuel W. Pennypacker, no sooner was in office in 1903 than he was referred to in print as the "ugly little dwarf." This angry veteran of the Civil War retaliated with a stringent, possibly unconstitutional, libel law that lasted four years.

Beneath their walrus mustaches and bowler hats, most of the early legislative correspondents were of the rough-hewn sort with little formal education. The commonwealth provided a newsroom on the E. Floor—for entresol, or mezzanine—where these petulant scribes smoked their cigars, spilled their coffee, scattered their papers, occasionally took a snort from a bottle, and played cards in their spare time when they weren't typing out dispatches. Their newspaper contemporaries like Mark Twain, Stephen Crane, Ring Lardner, Theodore Dreiser, Ernest Hemingway and William Faulkner gravitated into literature, but none of them did.

The top newspaper of the era, perhaps of all time in the state, was the Philadelphia North American, of which later speaker of the House, Hi Andrews of Johnstown, was a staffer. Editor Edwin A. Van Valkenburg, a native of Wellsboro, orchestrated the vituperative coverage of the Capitol Graft Scandal, making it into an early-day Watergate. At Sen. Matt Quay's death in 1904, Van Valkenburg wrote: "A shadow has passed from Pennsylvania." He called Sen. Boies Penrose "only an unwholesome memory." For such candor, Teddy Roosevelt praised Van Valkenburg as "the most useful American citizen now alive," and Lincoln Steffens on his 1916 Christmas card jotted: "You have shown that when the press represents the public, the government must."

Pennypacker considered the North American "a worthless sheet." In his delightful memoirs, the governor recalled giving an interview to one of its reporters:

"He took out his pencil and memorandum book and made ready, and I proceeded: 'Celerity ought to be contempered with cunctation. 'Won't you please repeat what you said?' 'Certainly, Celerity ought to be contempered with cunctation.' 'Would you object to spelling that last word for me? 'Not at all. C-u-n-c-t-a-t-i-o-n.' He went back to the city, hunted up his dictionary and wrote two or three columns and the paper has not yet entirely recovered from the shock."

The politician-press spats periodically become news in themselves. One of the most humorous occasions in the 1880s was when legislators turned a water hose on a Patriot reporter they claimed was drunk. Not so funny was the illegal imprisonment for 16 days in 1862 of four Patriot editors after they charged Telegraph editor and city postmaster George Bergner had "purloined" state money and stolen letters. Bergner was a shill for War Secretary Simon Cameron, who surreptitiously permitted federal agents to shanghai the four editors to Washington. What the Patriot really had done that incensed Cameron and Bergner was maliciously encourage blacks to join the Union Army, thus discouraging Harrisburg white enlistments.

Like dogs chasing cats, the press hounds politicos. The 1970s were particularly horrendous. "So many of you in the profession have the attitude that if government does something with which you don't agree, it is wrong," House Speaker H. Jack Seltzer, of Lebanon, mused before he retired in 1980.

He blamed press coverage for making "public image of the legislature lower than whale manure." A wit in the newsroom said that was so much bologna, a reference to Seltzer's family enterprise.

48.

THE PATRIOT

AND

THE TELEGRAPH

The City Beautiful's Renaissance I flourished in conjunction with, and because of, the sudden blossoming of Harrisburg newspapering.

In December of 1900, Edward J. Stackpole Sr., 39, bought the Harrisburg Telegraph and reduced its price from 2 cents to 1. On Aug. 1, 1902, Vance C. McCormick, only 30 but mayor of the city, purchased The Patriot. For the next 34 years the two Front Streeters, who truly disliked each other—and one was Republican and the other Democrat—would brawl with all the intensity of two rock-ribbed Presbyterians.

The spat actually began before McCormick was a publisher. In the February mayoralty election, Stackpole opposed him. The Orr family owned The Patriot and counterpunched Stackpole's Telegraph.

Stackpole was a true-blue Republican who never forgot that Republican boys won the Battle of Gettysburg two years after he was born. His newspaper so disdained Democrats that it never supported one. McCormick's father was a colonel in the Civil War, but Vance never encouraged any form of veterans' patriotism. For much of his life, Vance regarded most Republicans as a bunch of privileged Tories, and he doubted their ethics and sometimes their morality.

Their rivalry was so raw that it created modern Harrisburg newspapering.

The Telegraph was founded in September of 1831 and went daily on Oct. 7, 1856. Its likely predecessor was the 1813 weekly, The Chronicle, published by the A. Boyd Hamilton family, a clan that went into the 20th century and remained friendly with the Stackpoles.

The Patriot's ancestry went back to 1865, but it noted its birth year as 1843, the adoption of its name Patriot in 1854, and its first daily as the Daily Patriot and Union in 1858.

Through the 19th century, both papers were little more than "organs" for their political parties.

The Bergner family—for whom the Bergner Building at Third and Market streets was named—ran the Telegraph from 1856 to 1882 as a propaganda sheet for Simon Cameron after he switched from the Democratic to the Republican party.

The Barretts, Haldemans, Meyers, Orrs and others kept The Patriot in the Democratic camp. It was Richard Haldeman, who happened to be the son-in-law of Simon Cameron, who probably penned the infamous editorial about Lincoln's Gettysburg Address. It was Haldeman's brother-in law, Wayne MacVeagh, who as Republican state chairman sought to praise the president for the remarks and Honest Abe replied, "You are the only person who has such a misconception of what I said." Before MacVeagh became U.S. Attorney General for President Garfield, he founded the Nauman, Smith, Shissler and Hall law firm, the city's oldest, in the Bergner Building, where the Telegraph then was published.

Though the early Patriot appears to have been more "serious" than the Telegraph, often its news judgment was just as bad. The day it slighted the Gettysburg Address, it emphasized that coal prices rose to $11 a ton, that Mr. Durkee punched his friend Mrs. Prudence Hatfield, and that James Cowden, Charles Sanford and George Newman got drunk in Harrisburg—all while Lincoln was giving the finest speech in the English language just 33 miles away. Yet it must have known its readership. A year later in his re-election, Lincoln lost Adams County by 404 votes, lost Cumberland County by 732 votes, and only through the machinations of Cameron carried Dauphin County by 1,775 votes.

The Telegraph was more stable. McCormick purchased a paper that had been located at 214 N. Second, then at Third and Strawberry, and finally at Market and Dewberry in what would be the Doutrich Store. McCormick moved it to 11 N. Market Square on St. Patrick's Day of 1906. The shop probably was archaic the day it opened. Its presses were in the basement, the editorial staff on the third floor, the engravers on the fourth floor and the compositors on the fifth.

It was there in 1917 that McCormick founded The Evening News, the success he needed to win the circulation war against the Telegraph. Yet while McCormick as mayor could launch a $25 million Harrisburg improvement plan, he did little to modernize his own newspaper plant and 40 years later it was in shambles at his death.

49.

THE BEST DRAMA IN TOWN

WHEN VANCE MCCORMICK of the Patriot-News and Edward J. Stackpole Sr. of the Telegraph passed in the street they might have nodded politely, but there is no confirmation they ever spoke pleasantly to each other.

McCormick, 11 years the junior, lived at 301 N. Front St. and Stackpole at 1825 N. Front, or 104 doors apart. Their newspapers were three blocks apart. Their churches, McCormick's Pine Street Presbyterian and Stackpole's Market Square Presbyterian, also were three blocks apart, though the Stackpole sons became Episcopalians.

For 34 years the two gentlemen—and that they were, every inch—provided the best drama in town.

The 5-foot-6, pugnacious McCormick had the wealthier pedigree. He probably considered the lanky Stackpole nouveau riche. After all, McCormick's grandfather was president of Dauphin Deposit as far back as 1840 when the Stackpoles were Upstate farmers.

McCormick came from advantage, educated at Yale where he was the All-American quarterback for the 1892 undefeated Bulldogs. He later briefly coached the Carlisle Indians, virtually ran the Harrisburg Academy and was an active trustee at Yale and Penn State.

Edward J. Stackpole, Sr., sent out this picture of himself as a Christmas card in 1896, inscribed on the back with the words "Much Joy and Happy New Year." He was 35 at the time and bought the Telegraph four years later.

Stackpole was the self-made man, down from McVeytown and Orbisonia. He started as a printer at the Telegraph in 1881 when he was 20, and, saving his money, he was able to buy the paper in 1900.

McCormick prudently waited until he was 52 to marry the Front Street widow of his friend, Republican Congressman Marlin E. Olmsted, and she had more money than he had.

Stackpole married Kate Hummel and had three children. His two sons went to Yale, served in both world wars, and each became a lieutenant general. The boys, tall, lean and patrician, were courteous, respected gentlemen of the old school. Ed Jr. became a recognized Civil War historian, never mentioning he had been wounded three times in World War I combat. Albert H., known as Bill, was the more sociable brother as editor of the Telegraph, a commentator on the family's WHP radio, a founder of the Pennsylvania National Horse Show and, for a short period, an editorial writer for the Patriot-News. Bill Stackpole was so gentle and gallant that he insisted his WHP radio not play vocalists after 11 p.m., because he thought lyrics and sopranos disturbed Harrisburgers' slumber.

Neither McCormick nor Stackpole had children or in-laws who had the passion to succeed them in newspapering. Both patriarchs had printer's ink in their blood, though it was the uneducated Ed Sr. who wrote a book about his career while the learned Vance never did.

Each hungered to run the town, immerse himself in politics and, quite frankly, manage the news as only aristocrats can. They were men of probity, and that made their editorial tyranny less objectionable. Each tried to outdo the other in espousing the City Beautiful Movement, a good cause that would have floundered had these two publishers been negative, nit-picking Neanderthals. Yet they had such a firm hand on their papers that controversial public alternative views seldom were aired.

Though Simon Cameron was in his family tree, McCormick was the Democrat. He was mayor, the 1914 losing gubernatorial candidate, Woodrow Wilson's 1916 national party chairman, and an adviser at the Versailles peace deliberations in Paris in 1919. All the Democratic presidential candidates, except whiskey-wet Al Smith in 1928, received McCormick's blessings. Twice he came out for Franklin D. Roosevelt, but then his basic conservative susceptibilities surfaced and he rejected the New Deal. On the front pages of his newspapers in 1940 he itemized 26 reasons for his political apostasy, as self-conscious an old-time Protestant expiation as an honest but troubled man can make.

There is no record of the Stackpole clan's ever backing a Democrat. Ed Sr. not only profited from his close ties with the GOP with state printing contracts, but he was the three-term patronage postmaster of Harrisburg, made the expected endorsements and sang the praises of such local bosses as Ed Beidleman, Harve Taylor and the ward leaders. Ed Sr. even put a few Republican pals on his payroll. As FDR bothered McCormick, the liberal Gov. Gifford Pinchot annoyed Stackpole.

It wasn't political conviction alone that made McCormick and Stackpole such vibrant men. Without families wishing to follow in their footsteps, they wanted to make the present count more than the future. They brawled intensely because it was their way to aggrandize their mutual aversions and stir excitement while they could.

50.

NEWSPAPER RIVALRY

UP AT THE HARRISBURG COUNTRY CLUB, where Vance McCormick was majordomo, or out at the Colonial Country Club, where Edward J. Stackpole Sr. was president, the patio patter often included laughter about which publisher was eviscerating the other at any given moment, and what the pretense was this time.

In hometown newspaper rivalry, as in love and war, all is fair.

McCormick was at his priggish best in 1907 when he hired New York auditors and headlined in his Patriot the state printing contracts The Telegraph Press received. Later, on Nov. 4, 1912, The Patriot used a front-page, four-column-wide cartoon of The Telegraph Press as a hog in a bib slopping down bowls of printing-contract porridge—$1.3 million worth in 12 years from the state Republican machine, or so McCormick contended.

Stackpole was a gentleman in not criticizing McCormick as mayor—and also correct, because McCormick was one of the greatest mayors in Pennsylvania history. The job was three years then and Vance did not wish re-election, so Stackpole did his best to have his Republican pal, Edward Z. Gross, an in-law of the McCormicks no less, succeed Vance.

Gross won and Stackpole rejoiced to see the McCormick Democrats tossed out of office in 1905. With humor seldom seen in Harrisburg newspapering, Stackpole printed "Goat Tickets." These provided the bearer with a "Salt River Excursion" on "The Old Reliable Democratic Schooner," to be boarded at the river steps. "Up the Salt River" was the old Harrisburg euphemism for voter rejection.

In 1914 McCormick ran for governor against the amiable, cigar-chomping Dr. Martin G. Brumbaugh, president of Juniata College. Stackpole swung his Telegraph against McCormick and was thrilled to see Vance receive only 41 percent of the state-wide vote.

That election was the low point of McCormick's career. The once-great mayor and public benefactor lost his own city by 2,136 votes and the rest of the county by 2,073. All his popularity in Cumberland County amounted to only a 227-vote majority. McCormick lost all 11 precincts in Steelton and 47 of the 52 in Harrisburg. Strange places like Halifax, Millersburg, Paxtang, and Williamstown did come through for him.

The most ruthless Republican cad of all was Ed Stackpole Sr., who said McCormick spent $30,000 of his own money in "desperation" to get on the "Mule ticket," money that could have provided relief for Harrisburg's 300 unemployed. He also charged that teetotaler Vance hustled after liquor money. McCormick, more accurately, said the booze interests and "cohorts of money kings" were behind Brumbaugh, the Boies Penrose candidate.

The dirtiest Stackpole editorial was that McCormick was "no friend of the workingman," because as treasurer of his family's coal mine near Portage he had settled for $400 per man after five miners were killed. If that were true, McCormick was generous. For mine fatalities in those days, most coal barons simply sent flowers to the funeral.

The day after his defeat when McCormick knew he wouldn't be President Wilson's governor in Pennsylvania, he picked up Stackpole's Telegraph and saw a front-page cartoon. He was caricatured as a despondent Napoleon, right arm inside his field jacked, riding a "donkey-moose" in retreat from Waterloo. The honorable Ed Stackpole had his fitting revenge for The Patriot's having pictured The Telegraph Press two years earlier as a hog wallowing in the state trough.

Each publisher had his obsession, and Harrisburg readers expected them daily as they did train derailments.

McCormick's Patriot headquarters was located at 3rd and Walnut streets. Stackpole's Telegraph was three blocks away on Locust Street. McCormick never put up a building for his newspaper, but Stackpole built a "skyscraper" for his.

McCormick's bete noire was liquor. He instructed his editors to give full play to every booze bust during Prohibition in saintly Harrisburg awash with bootleg moonshine. It was almost five years after McCormick's death that The Patriot-News finally ran its first liquor ad.

Stackpole's fixation was vice, especially slot machines—though every club in town, including the favorite veterans' posts, had them. When state trooper axes finally fell on the one-armed bandits in a statewide permanent end to slot machines, The Telegraph had been dead for three years and its spiritually uplifting editorials forgotten.

McCormick never put up a building for his newspaper, but the poorer Stackpole hired architect Charles Howard Lloyd and on April 28, 1910, opened his 101-room, seven-story Telegraph Building on Locust Street. It had two elevators, an unusual central vacuum-cleaning system, a brownstone front from the Hummelstown quarries, and on top was a five-foot, 500-pound Seth Thomas clock to replace the old state Capitol clock of 1897. For all his class, McCormick was outclassed by Stackpole with his "skyscraper."

51.

THE EVENING NEWS

IT TOOK SEVEN YEARS after rival Ed Stackpole Sr. opened his fancy Telegraph Building for the competitive Vance McCormick to come up with a scheme for winning the newspaper war. The answer was The Evening News.

The Telegraph with its easy style outsold McCormick's more-serious morning Patriot. The mellow-tempered Stackpoles encouraged more localism in sports and columning. Even before them, The Telegraph emphasized chit-chat. For example, while it never knocked the Gettysburg Address as The Patriot did, it didn't regard Lincoln's remarks as significant.

The Telegraph was ultra-provincial. On Sep. 2, 1918, it had Lenin dead by an assassin, but played the story on page 3—and the Soviet revolutionist lived five more years.

During the 1930s, The Telegraph campaigned for Daylight Saving Time, only to have readers reject that hog-wild idea. In its fashion, The Telegraph acquiesced like a contrite husband:

"The Daylight Saving vote conducted by The Telegraph reveals the fact that Harrisburg is still a very conservative community. Old-fashioned time arrangements are good enough for a majority of our people. Well, perhaps, after all, there is some virtue in conservatism at a time when half the world is flying off at a tangent in pursuit of what our old friend J. Caesar used to call 'new things.' It is just as well, maybe, that we are a trifle 'sort in our ways.' But just the same, personally, we sure are going to miss that extra hour of daylight."

Chekhov didn't give better lines to Uncle Gayev in "The Cherry Orchard."

Unlike the wealthier McCormick, Ed Stackpole lived off his publishing income. The Telegraph furthermore had to fight a competitor in the evening market, The Star-Independent at the Keystone Building that E. Z. Wallower founded in 1876.

McCormick as mayor had advocated river festivals and from 1907 to 1915 there were gala boat parades. In the summer of 1916, Stackpole stole the idea and created the first Kipona, with city councilman and parks director Harve Taylor as the planner and banker George W. Reily as admiral. Stackpole even swiped the name Kipona from the old Delaware Indians, meaning "bright, sparkling water."

Wallower also owned the Walnut Street Bridge and was busy building the Penn Harris Hotel, so as he planned Kipona with Stackpole he agreed to sell him The Star-Independent for, as Stackpole described, "the general good of the newspaper industry." Stackpole bought it in early February of 1917, shut it, and raised the price of the Telegraph to 2 cents.

When McCormick heard of the Stackpole purchase, he became so angry he broke his riding crop over his knee. Then he summoned his general manager, Richard Wharton, and his editor, Dean Hoffman, to his Cedar Cliff farm, and there almost overnight they put together what would be The Evening News.

The Telegraph's destiny was decided 30 years before its demise. As of Thursday, Feb. 15, 1917, McCormick was the publisher of a morning-and-afternoon newspaper cycle. "Now we never sleep," he put in one of the two "ears" on the masthead, and in his editorial he vowed the new paper would be "an unflinching enemy… of sham and hypocrisy in politics, of pretense and form everywhere." Best of all, it cost 1 cent.

McCormick crowded 21 local stories on its first front page and, anticipating journalism of 60 years hence, instituted a "Daily Magazine" page. Most importantly, he stressed reporting. He sent Charles G. Miller to Capitol Hill for 32 years. In 1950 John Scotzin, "the man who interviewed William Penn," as Gov. Dick Thornburgh once quipped, succeeded Miller, a record of continuity unduplicated in the annals of Pennsylvania newspapering. For local politics, Al Hamman of Royalton, a dapper, courteous little man, knew everybody's business in Harrisburg for 43 years.

In head-to-head competition, McCormick within seven years had a p.m. paper outselling a rival that been around for 93 years. Just before his death in 1936, Ed Sr. tried a Morning Telegraph tabloid that failed within four years.

The Evening News roared out to circulation of 24,841 in its first full year. The Patriot was a bit above that and The Telegraph was near 40,000. The Patriot then slipped to under 20,000 from 1929 through 1944, and The Telegraph hit an all-time high of 51,026 in 1930.

52.

NEWSPAPER MEN AND WOMEN

VANCE McCORMICK SPENT 45 YEARS in the Harrisburg limelight, and he loved it.

"He had many irons in the fire and he kept them all in use," The Patriot's obituary editorial said on June 18, 1946. "A dated tablet on his desk, on which he kept a list of meetings and conferences to which he gave time and attention, would read like a directory of agencies and organizations devoted to school, church, welfare and kindred service." He lived to be 74, but never retired, and was at his newspaper office the week of his death.

Busy being Vance McCormick, advocating clean politics, temperance and sportsmanship, working for Harrisburg Hospital and the YMCA, and escorting the likes of Pablo Casals to perform in Harrisburg—such a man didn't share the glory on his newspapers with anybody else.

The Stackpoles, pere and fils, were gentler souls and not the advertisements for themselves that McCormick was. So they developed newsprint and airwave celebrities, and they diversified their business as McCormick never cared to do.

Edward J. Stackpole Sr. was a lifelong printer at heart. In 1925 he opened his new Telegraph Press Building at Cameron and Kelker streets, making it into a respected publishing house that turned out Gideon Bibles, the American issue of Hitler's *Mein Kampf, The New York Times Index,* stamp catalogues, magazines and a large title list of military and outdoor publications.

Stackpole also got into early radio in 1924 with the prized WHP station on a frequency of 580 kilocycles for CBS. The station became the first permanent one in Harrisburg with television on April 15, 1953, though Lancaster's WGAL Channel 8 was beamed into the area four years earlier. By the time Ed Sr. died in 1936, his other enterprises were more sure of success than his newspaper.

Unlike outspoken McCormick, the Stackpoles stayed in the background and nurtured three Harrisburg media household names: Mrs. Lillie Hench "Sally Harris," Paul Walker, and Ronald Francis Drake.

Mrs. Hench took the pen name Sally Harris, but she wasn't the Sallie Harris of South Front Street, the last-named Harris descendant in town of John Harris. That Sallie died Christmas Day of 1928, and news hen Sally covered the dismantling of her house by Harrisburg Hospital. Sally was from Cumberland County, graduated from Vassar, and in 1913 started with The Patriot. She then became social editor of The Telegraph, a picturesque figure with a pince-nez and bird feathers in her hats. The lady was indefatigable. She was a world traveler, a soloist and director of Market Square Presbyterian Church choir, a teacher at Seiler School for 41 years, and a Wednesday Club member for more than a half-century.

Sally's last beat was for The Sunday Patriot-News before she hung it up at 80. She didn't die until she was 93. She was the last of the true society writers who also was a socialite.

Irish Walker, the "Roundabout" columnist, became the jolly Methuselah of Harrisburg journalism, from 1921 when he headed the Carlisle bureau of The Telegraph through to the 1980s when he was writing for The Patriot-News. For 19 years The Telegraph featured his column, which in style and arcane wisdom was as eclectic as its originator—that child of the century, white hair flowing, bow tie, pipe sticking out of the right side of his mouth, a mildly nonconforming, haphazardly garbed peripatetic enthusiast of mirth.

Actually the son of an immigrant London bobby and a graduate of Johnstown High and Dickinson College, Walker quickly became the quintessential Harrisburger. His columns started March 1, 1928. He devised a format so he could begin any subject where he wished, insert diverting items that came to mind, and then close off with whatever seemed to fit—such as, "Enjoy pollution, live dangerously, breathe deeply, A-aaahh!" His fictional irregulars also contributed: Bill Blithers, Oneeda Keys, Habeas Corpus, Rosie Rumer, Polly Esther, Spearhead Jones, The Old Timer, Stime Lairds, Sally Forth, and a host of others. "The names 'dood it,'" Walker liked to explain of his popularity.

Ron Drake was the airwaves' Sally Harris and Paul Walker from 1946 until his retirement in 1982. "You don't have to be good, just corny," he said, "and I'm good and corny." With the corn, he had a touch of comic artistry, gentle sarcasm, near-perfect phrasing and timing, and marvelous characters like "Professor Schnitzle" and "The Bird Lady." No other radio talk jockey in town was ever threatening competition to Drake.

53.

THE NEWHOUSE NEWSPAPER

WITH THE DEATH OF VANCE MCCORMICK in 1946, his Patriot-News' 44-year duel with the Stackpoles' Telegraph ended. No other Harrisburger had ever owned, managed and dominated a newspaper longer than McCormick.

McCormick was McCormick, a singular phenomenon. The Stackpoles, father and sons, were press lords for 46 years. The Newhouse family should eclipse that, because Samuel I. Newhouse himself was the Patriot-News proprietor through his private corporation for 32 years until his death at 84 in 1979.

Though an ardent free enterpriser, McCormick neglected to provide for the future of his newspapers, for either their management or their capitalization. So his heirs, his widow and his stepdaughter waited a bereaved 14 months and then in August of 1947 sold the papers, with a combined circulation of 86,529, to Mr. Newhouse Sr. of New York through his emissary, Edwin F. Russell.

With papers in Staten Island, Newark, Syracuse and Jersey City at the time, Newhouse ventured west and added the Patriot-News, and then in five months he had the Stackpoles' Telegraph.

On Market Square the Patriot and Evening News broadcast, and displayed, the first game of the 1940 World Series between Detroit and Cincinnati.

Never before in Harrisburg history did a newspaper grow faster. In the first year under new management, Patriot-News circulation shot up by 14,900, followed by another 14,326 the next year. Meanwhile, the Newhouse group began emerging as the nation's third largest, and in 1983 has 27 papers with an average daily circulation of 3.2 million.

On Good Friday of March 26, 1948, The Telegraph announced to a shocked Harrisburg that its Saturday edition would be its finale after 117 years. That closed 155 years of locally owned, locally folded, and locally sold-out newspapers, at least 25 of them. The community required outside leadership because it failed to invest and reinvest in its daily press. Nobody even wanted the Telegraph Building. Finally in 1978 it was added to the National Register of Historic Places, only to be razed five months later for a parking lot.

McCormick and the Stackpoles once had been all too visible—what modern ethic-conscious journalists call "walking conflicts of interest." They didn't just manage the news, but sometimes City Hall, the National Guard, the banks, some churches, the private schools, select industries, horse shows, automobile clubs, toll bridges, and even political parties and candidates. Earlier local press czars—like John Wyeth, Simon Cameron, George Bergner, Theophilus Fenn, Oramel Barrett and Benjamin Meyers—had operated in that fashion, too, but McCormick and the Stackpoles were more pervasive and persuasive about it. Nostalgia blurs what an oligarchial and elitist old-boys network they enjoyed.

As Front Street changed, so did the management of banks, hospitals, brokerages and, for that matter, other media like radio and television. Stalwart Harrisburgers faded away, and outsiders took their places.

Sam Newhouse, lawyer and capitalist deluxe, probably needed a road map to tell him whether Union Deposit was on the East or West Shore, but he required little instruction on how to prepare a newspaper for the most economically competitive era in history. He feared not that Harrisburg was a graveyard for the press. This inconspicuous, 5-foot-2 gentleman was like a ubiquitous minor character in a John O'Hara novel. He left the daily newspapering to his publishers and editors, but he stayed committed to his business for 57 years.

The first major task in the post-McCormick era was to build an adequate newspaper plant, and in 1953 Newhouse invested $3 million to give the Patriot-News its first new home in its long history. In 1949 he launched a Sunday newspaper, something McCormick and the Stackpoles had overlooked. By 1959 starting reporter pay was more than $100 weekly. A modern colormatic press was installed in 1969, just in time to be waterlogged in the 1972 Flood. An expensive computer system for typesetting began in the spring of 1975, replacing "hot type' with "cold type." A new third floor was added to the Patriot-News Building in 1980, guaranteeing the paper would remain in center city.

Harrisburg had almost 16 decades of proprietary newspapering, with its colorful characters, politicking in print and fortissimo editorializing. Never was that style so right for its time as at the turn of the century when Vance McCormick and Ed Stackpole could scream and wake up the entire town.

54.

WALLOWER'S PENN HARRIS

AS THE NEW CAPITOL IN 1906 symbolized the advent of Renaissance I in Harrisburg, the opening of the $2.5 million Penn Harris Hotel in 1919 was the epiphany of the reborn city.

"If anybody ever tells me Fort Penn's a hick town—they won't be able to tell me that again. This is practically the Waldorf-Astoria," a character in John O'Hara's *A Rage to Live* exclaims. The hotel project sparked such civic excitement in the real Harrisburg that O'Hara fictionalized it in his novel.

The grand opening was a gala, black-tie New Year's Eve party to greet 1919. That in itself was a change, as Harrisburgers traditionally ignore New Year's Eve, usually sleep through it.

Gov. Martin G. Brumbaugh and Mayor Daniel L. Keister led 500 honored guests in a rousing, "Hail, Hail, the Gang's All here." The toast was: "This handsome hotel will be a key to open the doors to the future hospitality and prosperity of Harrisburg." Then the celebrators dipped into their snapper soup—called turtle soup in Harrisburg.

Elias Z. Wallower, the prime investor, joked: "People prefer to visit a city where living conditions are just slightly above par."

The 10-story hotel—expanded to 12 stories and 400 rooms in 1924—was class for a town that long had spurned luxury.

When Charles Dickens visited the city in 1842, he was appalled seeing legislators spit tobacco juice on a hotel carpet. As a legislator, 6-foot-4 Boies Penrose had his own enlarged bed built so he could get a good-night's rest for his 300-pound frame in a local hotel.

The Penn Harris was different. It was so modern it had telephones and bathtubs in each room. And so good was business that in its second year it paid its stockholders a 30 percent dividend, and raised that to 35 percent in the third year. Once President Judge Homer L. Kreider had a jury for a murder trial sequestered in the hotel. He was astounded when the court was presented a $3,000 bill. The jury foreman from upper Dauphin County had seen shrimp cocktail on the menu and ordered it for his fellow jurors for breakfast, lunch and dinner.

The Penn Harris faced the Capitol on the windy corner of Walnut and Third, the site of the Grand Opera House that burned down in 1907. After the hotel was in business 54 years and was demolished the Harrisburg Redevelopment Authority paid $2.8 million for the location of Harristown's Strawberry Square.

"The Penn Harris Hotel was created in response to a civic need," stated the hotel in its 25th-anniversary pamphlet. "The enterprise was distinctly a community affair. Almost all of its stockholders then were, and now are, citizens of Harrisburg." In fact, as early as 1916 the Chamber of Commerce and the Harrisburg Rotary Club joined to raise the financing.

The hero was Wallower (1854-1941), a white-haired, grandfatherly moustached gentleman who resembled his contemporaries Milton S. Hershey and J. Horace McFarland in looks and enterprise.

The Penn Harris Hotel, built by E.Z. Wallower, is the "Nesquehela Hotel" in John O'Hara's novel A Rage to Live. *It was "once a part of the soul of Harrisburg," writes Beers, and a "temple of Renaissance I."*

Wallower was the son of a city councilman who politicked for Simon Cameron. He started out as a printer, was a stenographer for the Molly Maguire trials in the coal region, and after that he became a go-getting capitalist. At 22 he was the publisher of the first penny newspaper in town, The Daily Independent, spending $19,000 for the building where Pomeroy's is today. Space he didn't use he rented for $1,800 a year to Dives, Pomeroy and Stewart, the original department store that moved from its old quarters at the Opera House.

Wallower headed the group that built the People's Bridge, or the Walnut Street Bridge. He also helped put together the Harrisburg Electric light Co., Harrisburg Steam Heat Co., and with lawyer-landowner Ehrman B. Mitchell Sr.—whose son would be an architect for Strawberry Square—he helped save the distressed Harrisburg Steel Co.

He resided at Front and Maclay streets, was a respectable cigar-smoking Republican, was active in the Harrisburg Country Club and the Central YMCA, and with perfectly attuned noblesse oblige regarded the city as his domain and something that he must care about.

In his final years he still had the spirit to write 226 pages of *Reminiscences*, and, accurate as always, he jotted down that building the Penn Harris was "the crowning achievement of my career."

55.

PENN HARRIS PEOPLE

ATTRACTING INVESTORS and supported by the Chamber of Commerce and Harrisburg Rotary, E. Z. Wallower paid $230,000 for the empty hole that had been the Grand Opera House. Then in the middle of World War I when most private construction was halted, he built the Penn Harris Hotel.

The Penn Harris had one of the first public investing subscriptions for a hotel in the United States, and was among the first to be built of reinforced concrete.

The hotel was jointly owned, with a single board of directors, by the Harrisburg Hotel Co. and the United Hotels Co. of America, established by Frank A. Dudley of Niagara Falls, N.Y., with the Ten Eyck Hotel of Albany, N.Y., as its flagship.

Like the white Christmas tree with red balls the hotel always had in its lobby for the holidays, the town's most visible personages were its directors. Among them were Henderson Gilbert, George W. Bailey, Harper W. Spong and Edward J. Stackpole Sr., who was succeeded by his older son, General Ed Jr. After 1926, the famed Franklin Moore was managing director. Moore, a dynamic figure became potentate of Zembo Temple and president of Harrisburg Rotary. For years Ben Keil was resident manager, in charge of 425 employees.

The
PLANTATION
"Place of Plenty"
In the hustle and bustle of our modern life, a touch of the leisure and charm of the Deep South offers welcome restfulness.
AIR-CONDITIONED
PENN HARRIS
HOTEL
HARRISBURG
PENNA.

The Penn Harris Plantation Room was famed as the state legislators' rendezvous and featured southern cuisine.

For 52 of the hotel's 54 years, bell captains Nimrod Johnson and German Jackson escorted the most humble and the most illustrious to their rooms, including John F. Kennedy and Babe Ruth, the latter of whom had purple pajamas in his satchel in case he didn't carouse all night.

Glamorous actresses checked in, but none had the panache of "The Old Gray Mare," Emma Guffey Miller. For decades it was the custom of the Federation of Democratic Women to place a courtesy bottle of bourbon at the room door of their founder, and until she was in her 50s one bottle often wasn't enough. Emma was an outspoken advocate of women's rights and what she called "sensible liquor laws."

Even minor figures, like lieutenant governors, used the hotel as their Harrisburg residence. The Pennsylvania National Horse Show, the YMCA,

YWCA, Zembo Mosque, Community Chest and War Bond drives made the hotel their campaign headquarters. Rotary, Lions, Kiwanis, Soroptimists, and Quota clubs had their civic luncheons there.

The Pennsylvania Railroad stationed its lobbyist at the hotel, not far from the Tuesday Club on the mezzanine overlooking Third Street. Harve Taylor spent hundreds of tea times enjoying his bourbon straight at both inner sanctums.

The hotel had 14 private suites and four restaurants, and was a pioneer in the luxury of having all of its major rooms air-conditioned.

The food, though hardly nouvelle haute cuisine, satisfied Harrisburg's modest tastes. Welsh rarebit, onion soup and pecan pie were popular at the Harris Ferry Tavern, and chicken pot pie at the English Grill. In its first quarter century, the hotel itemized it served the ribs from 6,000 steers, the loins from 5,500 beef, a half-million pounds of ham, 165,625 pounds of lobster, shrimp and crab meat, and 6,150 barrels of oysters. Many also recall the Penn Harris dishing out tons of boiled-dry chicken, but the hard rolls were always tasty.

On its marquees, put up in 1937, the hotel advertized "Famous for Southern Dishes." As Harrisburg is a northern city, that was a strange boast, but the Penn Harris also called its main dining room for many years the "Plantation Room." A Harrisburg black politician in 1967 in that same room charged the town with "Plantation Politics" to describe the age-old, low-keyed, plutocratic type of control over patronage and votes in the black wards.

John O'Hara in *A Rage to Live* featured a fictional "Nesquehela Hotel," and called its dining room the "Commonwealth Room." In latter years, though oblivious of O'Hara, the Penn Harris supplanted Plantation Room with Commonwealth Room.

It was in that lustrous setting Grace Caldwell Tate, the provocative protagonist of the O'Hara novel, would have the corner table, bathed by the noontime sunlight, for her Friday $1.25 luncheon. On a formal occasion, Grace entered the room "wearing a sealskin cloak over a simple black taffeta gown, and her only jewelry was a thin diamond necklace, but she was the one. She was what the younger women could hope to be, and what the older women, who knew her age, could take pride in." Grace was all of 37.

56.

EVERYBODY'S GATHERING PLACE

THE PENN HARRIS HOTEL was a golden success for more than four decades because it defied two Harrisburg social principles. It refused to be dull, and it reinvested its profits rather than squirrel them away.

The hotel made its $1.5 million enlargement in 1924. After ghastly Prohibition lifted, it opened its Harris Ferry Tavern in January of 1935 and its Esquire Bar in September of 1936.

For the Susquehanna Room of its downstairs English Grill and Coffee Shop, the hotel in 1940 hired George Gray and Helen D. Manahan to do a mural series of 29 Pennsylvania scenes that included William Penn under the elm, Old Camelback Bridge, the early Steelton rolling mill, and Cornwall Furnace. Gray, the bachelor son of an engineer of the Broadway Limited, went to Harrisburg Tech and later studied under N.C. Wyeth before he became a nationally known World War II Navy illustrator. Miss Manahan was a Central High graduate, a student of the Capitol's muralist Violet Oakley, a founder of the Harrisburg Art Association, and for many years admissions officer at Polyclinic Medical Center.

After the Penn Harris was detonated, Commonwealth Bank rescued the paintings for its Market Square headquarters.

Off its spacious lobby, the hotel developed the "Rue de la Ville," a cozy luncheon spot favored by the local judges for their weekly imbibing when they didn't want to mix with the crasser crowd at the Esquire.

Upstairs, the hotel had the "Governor's Suite" for small banquets and its ballroom for gatherings of 500 or more. In 1938 a stage was built to accommodate the press' Gridiron Dinners and the Art Association's Bal Masques. The town's earliest pigeon-hole parking was set up next door, but proved to be a money-loser.

Unlike so many other local enterprises, the Penn Harris neither rested on its assets nor let profits be drained by hometown wastrels and out-of-town relatives. As this city's modest version of Philadelphia's Bellevue-Strafford, it was almost everybody's gathering place.

Arch's Drugstore was in the downstairs corner from 1928 through 1965. Samuel E. Arch was a pharmacist for 52 years and the brother-in-law of Harry Buch, whose famous apothecary at Second and State streets lasted from 1922 to 1972.

Sam's store became a political hangout. Boss Ed Beidleman stopped by every morning and conferred with his protégé, Harve Taylor. Gov. Arthur E. James played the pinball machine. Gov. James H. Duff tied his dogs outside before he came in for a nickel Coke. Gov. Gifford Pinchot bought ice cream, and Gov. George H. Earle in the midst of the Depression purchased his aspirin there. Across the street the ever-alert reporters hung out at the bar of the Columbus Hotel, whose highballs were 10 cents cheaper than the Penn Harris'.

Arch's best seller was a 50-cent bromide mixture with peppermint water—a bottle a week to calm stress in the days before Valium. Sam Arch, another Tech grad, worked the shop 55 hours weekly and performed public service by ministering to many of Harrisburg's always numerous hypochondriacs. Closing up was usually a problem. One night Sam leaned across the counter, "Harve, we close at 10 p.m." And the senator replied, "Sam, I've been thrown out of a lot of places, but this is the first time I've been bounced from a drugstore."

The Bal Masque moved into the ballroom in 1955, and for 18 years it was the town's wildest affair. Stodgy Harrisburg let go of its inhibitions for this annual February gala. The 1963 circus-theme Bal Masque honored Mary Barnum Bush Hauck, and its showstopper was the Seven Lively Artists' six pastel elephants prancing before zany ringmaster Shim Lehrman.

With a Bal Masque theme of classic movies, a Bowman's sales woman was carried in as Cleopatra on her barge, more suggestive than the Egyptian queen would have dared to be. A pregnant hausfrau was a prize winner with a banner, "The Birth of a Nation," draped across her belly. And the year Broadway musicals were featured, a Harrisburg policeman stopped two hillbillies entering the hotel with shotguns. "L'il Abner," they explained. "Go right in then," the cop said understandingly.

After the Penn Harris closed, the Bal Masque lost its magic. It made nine more attempts to recapture the glamour and fun, but finally was discontinued.

57.

JIMMY DELIBERTY

AT THE

ESQUIRE BAR

"HE WAS HERE BUT HE JUST LEFT," Barman Jimmy DeLiberty explained to dozens of telephone callers daily at the "Esquire, the Restaurant for Men."

Generations of creditors, bosses, girlfriends and mostly wives heard that line from DeLiberty, the noble guardian of his all-male patrons' privacy. DeLiberty, a railroader's son, was the barman, except for its first week, the entire 37-year history of the Esquire.

"It seemed appropriate to provide one restaurant which the fair sex could not invade," the Penn Harris Hotel stated, "where men might meet with men and loiter at the bar or sit at tables in comfortable booths and discuss with due profundity the problems presented to the masculine mind."

Once DeLiberty inadvertently left the switch up on the amplification system. The telephoning hausfrau loudly suggested that since her husband had "just left," he might still be found on Walnut Street and should be informed that if he weren't home within 15 minutes his supper would be cooling in the dog's bowl. Patrons' faces blanched as the sharp soprano voice broadcast threats of domestic disturbance throughout the saloon. The intended victim was bought another scotch in sympathy.

The Esquire opened in September of 1936. With its décor of George Petty girls from the Esquire magazine of that month, it had art-deco style. And with a street entrance, it was an accessible sanctuary.

Successful as the Esquire was, the Holiday Inn Town never duplicated having a tavern with street-entrance convenience. Worse yet, Strawberry Square, built on the site of the Esquire, ignored designing a similar first-floor bastion.

The Esquire provided the "Five Harrisburg H's": Hangovers, headaches, heartburn, hoarseness, and horse manure. Few could bum there even two hours and not be surfeited with the Five H's. Yet a gentleman's code prevailed.

Former Gov. John Sidney Fine, victim of Pennsylvania's first sales tax, hadn't been back to the Esquire in years, and then one day in his broad-brimmed hat he strolled in. "This is one place I can go where I won't hear, 'A penny for John,'" he sardonically mentioned about that hated slogan that followed him to his grave and beyond. He was right. Old Esquire hands extended cordial greetings, and none murmured the distasteful wisecrack.

The late Jimmy DeLiberty is still regarded as Harrisburg's nonpareil bartender. He estimated that at the Esquire he walked 52,000 miles, or the equivalent of twice around the world, and that he poured at least a million drinks.

Among his customers were Clark Gable, Jimmy Stewart, Frank Buck, Jack Dempsey, Jim Thorpe, Billy Conn and Eleanor Roosevelt, who ordered by phone an orangeade sent to her room. Among the local illuminati were Hobert Hopkins, Freeman MacBeth, Norman Law, Don

Stabler, Buzz Rosenberg and Hain Wolf. The Esquire's "Senator" was 6-foot-3, 212-pound John Maxwell Moore, who came from DuBois in 1928 and worked briefly for the state in one of at least 50 jobs he held in his lifetime. Splendidly garbed, with pomp and garrulity, Moore played the role of statesman better than the expense-account ones.

DeLiberty, only 5-foot-7, was an ex-athlete who could vault over the bar, using one hand as a lever and the other as a hook to spin a disturber of the peace through the swinging doors. Once he did that, only to learn he had tossed out the hotel's entertainer paid $500 nightly. Another guy he chucked out got to his feet and threw DeLiberty back into the bar. Unknowingly, DeLiberty had picked on the bodyguard of Gov. George H. Earle. Ending service one night, DeLiberty refused to pour a final drink. "Hey, that's the vice president of the United states," a patron shouted. So Jimmy poured one for Alben Barkley.

The Esquire closed forever Dec. 29, 1972, but two years before it besmirched its noble escutcheon by succumbing to women's liberation. As skirts swirled, the tone of the Esquire fell. Upstairs, the august Tuesday Club held fast, though when it moved to Third and Market streets even its restriction against women "not beyond the bar" soon was disregarded.

The Esquire's feminine conquest was complete when two patrons, one a gentleman and the other a curly blonde invader, were married, the exact kind of entrapment avoided in the good old days.

58.

A CITY'S HEART

THE $1.3 MILLION HOTEL HARRISBURGER opened Aug. 1, 1930, to be a partner of the Penn Harris Hotel astride the entrance to Capitol Park. In tandem they provided 700 rooms and seven restaurants.

"Harrisburg's Tower of Hospitality," as the 17-floor, 300-room newer hotel called itself, had the Tack Room, Pickwick Tavern and Appian Room. Its Caucus Room competed for 33 years with the Esquire as the watering hole for politicians.

Ray S. Shoemaker built the hotel, as well as Zembo Mosque, Grayco Apartments, Mary Sachs and Payne-Shoemaker Building, and was its president until his death at 56 in 1940.

James A. Johnston, out of Altoona, was its astute manager, and a quarter-century ago the assistant for four years was Edward R. Book, now chairman of Herco and under his domain is the "Queen of the Hill," the Hotel Hershey.

The Harrisburger unfortunately was modeled after New York's Commodore Hotel, so its doors opened into a grand staircase taking up too much of its costly ground-level space. Many preferred the Harrisburger, especially its food, but it was always second in status to the Penn Harris. Though newer, it was the first to feel the drastic economic plight. It closed in October of 1969, at sheriff's sale for $253,500 and $750,000 assumed debts.

The Penn Harris began to falter as early as 1950, when the Pennsylvania Turnpike was opened from Middlesex to Philadelphia. Travelers by the droves stopped coming to Harrisburg. The Penn Harris' occupancy was once a predictable 95 percent, and it dropped by 17 percent. One-way Harrisburg streets in 1961 cut access to the hotel, so by 1963 the Penn Harris Motor Inn was in operation on the West Shore.

Once a part of the soul of Harrisburg and an establishment with visible and civic-minded management, the Penn Harris retrenched and its sterling reputation plummeted. The place became shabby. When the Holiday Inn Town with 260 rooms opened in 1964, the once-great Penn Harris was no longer the crème de la crème.

After the 1972 Flood when the Penn Harris required overdue major renovations, its ownership decided to bail out. Heedless of tradition and perhaps too obtuse to care, the management canceled a farewell New Year's Eve party and bolted the doors two days before 1973 arrived. It was poor taste—something the original Penn Harris never was accused of. Worse yet—the mortal sin—was the lack of grace the shipwreckers displayed by not vowing they would return to the town that had enriched their enterprise for 54 years.

Pete Wambach dashed off a verse that had more sentiment in it than ever expressed by the last of the Penn Harris proprietors:

"There in the Ballroom, wedding parties danced, And Bal Masque costumes busted out the walls. There Gridiron Shows in secret raised their hell, And college cheer re-echoed in the halls.

"The two-fisted drinkers in the Esquire drank, The manhood of a half-a-century, While wives within the Tavern filled the space, With chatter, gossip and a cup of tea.

"Wherever shall we find a city's heart, So perfectly attuned in one such place?"

Grand hotel that it was, the Penn Harris at its demise proved vividly that it was of better stuff than the meretriciousness doing it in. The hotel had market value of $1,565,410 and was worth $40,000 annually in local taxes, but it was treated as if it were a beggar. Imported salvagers in the once-splendid lobby huckstered the hotel's flatware and even telephone book covers. It was as if modern Visigoths by legal means were looting Harrisburg's temple of Renaissance I.

PAYNE-SHOEMAKER BUILDING AND HARRISBURGER HOTEL, HARRISBURG, PA.
2093-30

The Harrisburger Hotel and Payne-Shoemaker buildings were first-class spaces. The Harrisburger also groomed and watered politicians.

So when the demolitionists came early Sept. 3, 1973, the old hotel stiffened up in pride. The hired blasters in 33 years had leveled 307 structures, but none gave them the trouble the Penn Harris did.

As Mayor Harold Swenson finished a count-down, he saw chunks of the hotel's steel beams, like Sampson's arms, swing out and crash down upon Rogal's Travel Service and David's Clothier. The Penn Harris was reaching out to the community one last time, taking down into the dust with it a bit of the town. The film coverage was so dramatic Madison Avenue used it for commercial advertising spots.

The wreckers stealthily returned Oct. 21 to finish the job. The last blasts were safe and sure, but the great Penn Harris didn't go to its death quietly.

59.

FROM PATRIARCH TO ORPHAN

By 1920 Harrisburg was a prosperous contemporary city, far beyond the wildest hallucinations of its most visionary citizens just 30 years before.

There was a splendid new Capitol, a landmark St. Patrick Cathedral, the redoubtable Penn Harris Hotel, one of the nation's leading park systems, busy railroad service on the New York-to-Chicago Main Line, and inner-city trolley network never again surpassed, an expanding job market in government and at the mills, a growing quality educational program, and all the pleasant conveniences of neighborhood living.

Harrisburg the City Beautiful in 1920 had a population of 75,917, or a record 36 percent of the entire citizenry of Dauphin and Cumberland counties. Prestige went with a city address.

The Chamber of Commerce glowingly predicted that soon Harrisburg's population would soar past 125,000—that this Baghdad by the Susquehanna was on its way toward becoming another Rochester, Hartford or Richmond.

"Our citizens are forward-looking and progressive and I believe in the years to come will cheerfully bear their share of taxation for all the improvements necessary to make our city all it should be," former Mayor Vance McCormick told the Chamber of Commerce in 1915. "Our best men and our best brains are needed to place our city in the forefront of

RIVER FRONT DRIVE ALONG SUSQUEHANNA RIVER, HARRISBURG, PA.

Front Street modernized, beautified, and utilized around the 1920s, exactly as the planners intended. It was once the city's main dirt road.

American cities, where she rightfully belongs—men of great breadth and foresight who can see the future needs of a great city. Isn't this old city of ours worth some sacrifice and some personal effort, and isn't she worthy of the very best within us rather than indifference and exploitation at the expense of others?"

The "great breadth and foresight" required were not to be realized. Though Harrisburg grew to a peak population of 89,544 in 1950, its role as the hub of Dauphin and Cumberland counties slipped to 31 percent. None knew it, but that ratio was on a greased chute, down to a weak 13 percent by 1980.

As Harrisburgers in 1920 enjoyed their contentedness and conformity, they forgot the Teutonic imperative of "Lebenseraum"—more living space. A fortress mentality took hold, and the old pioneering spirit ebbed.

Until the restrictive state annexation law of 1937, Pennsylvania cities had almost unlimited expansion privileges. During Renaissance I, for example, Pennsylvania offered its cities the contiguous-city annexation provision, and all that was necessary was to obtain a petition from a majority of property owners who wanted to be absorbed into the city.

Harrisburg reached its outer boundary on Allison Hill in 1910 and in the Uptown with Riverside in 1917. In 1926 Harrisburg opened its two new campus high schools on virtually its city lines, and through the 1940s it enrolled students from the lesser provinces of Susquehanna Twp., Penbrook and Paxtang.

Boss Ed Beidleman, once lieutenant governor and the mentor of Harve Taylor, engineered the dual high school system to satisfy his political constituency, but this able lawyer lacked the insight to foresee a future that, as Philadelphia's later Mayor Richardson Dilworth so vividly stated it, would put the "white noose" of suburbia around urban-troubled cities.

The "white noose," like a hangman's knot, got tighter as the decades went by. The life blood seeped not just from Harrisburg but also from the other 47 third-class Pennsylvania cities, which in the 1960s and 1970s lost 19 percent of their population, or almost 300,000 persons.

With this change went political and social power. After 1964, Harrisburg usually didn't have a resident state senator. For 16 years it didn't have a resident congressman. By the 1980s all the county judges but one were suburbanites. Steelton, which had a court seat for 43 of 49 years, also was no longer considered when its population declined from 14,000 to 5,000. And the political impotency often was annoyingly tangible, such as in 1977 when a Susquehanna Twp. Republican legislator voted against the state appropriation of $100,000 for Harrisburg fire protection because he was perturbed by Democratic Gov. Milton J. Shapp.

The 1902 City Beautiful reformers never envisioned the day when Harrisburg wouldn't be foremost. But in 1982 only one of 17 board members of the Harrisburg Symphony lived in the city and only nine of 23 on the Community Theater. Just four presidents of 27 of Harrisburg Rotary and two of eight of the Wednesday Club after 1960 were city residents.

Once the patriarch of the community, Harrisburg became its orphan.

60.

"THE NARROW IRON SHELL OF LIFE"

Of the Harrisburg of 1920, John O'Hara in his 1960 novel *Ourselves to Know* observed:

"Fort Penn was ruled by conservative thought, but as the capital its social life was more active than that of cities of comparable size, and this produced a social manner that would have been usually encountered in much larger cities. It was a worldly manner."

His heroine, Hedda Steele Millhouser of Lykens, thought Harrisburg "a miniature Paris...with its substantial Capitol and other commonwealth buildings, the wide, tree-lined residential streets, the shops where she was called madam, the hotels, busy and ornate, and with music always in the background, the bridle path along the river front, the quite numerous automobiles..."

Yet fancy as the city was and worthy of two O'Hara novels, the Pottsville master was more sardonic than complimentary about the local character. "Genius was occasionally stifled," O'Hara noted, and the community had a way of settling for too little, because "the source of its pride was in its approximation of compact, continuous conventionality, never in its eccentrics or their caprices."

George P. Donehoo, the local churchman and historian, had prophesied that the striving Harrisburg soul would forge a man that "someday will be what he seeks to be." Dr. Donehoo neglected to consider that the values achieved might be so shoddy as to be nugatory, or worse, dangerously psychopathic as a street criminal's.

Native-born James Boyd called it Midian in his 1935 Front Street novel, *Roll River,* and he criticized "the narrow iron shell of life in this and other little places."

Indeed, the Harrisburg of 60 years ago was a marvelous blend of city conveniences and amenities: 23 neighborhood elementary schools, 90 churches, 42 auto dealers and garages, 14 banks, 16 coal dealers, 14 architect firms, 38 bakers including Steelton, two Turkish baths, 21 pool halls, 17 boarding houses, 46 cigar stores, 68 dressmakers, 37 druggists, six fishmongers, 14 florists, 12 hardware stores, 11 ice dealers, four income-tax experts, 14 laundries, three manicurists, 16 paperhangers, 49 registered plumbers, 29 printers that included 12 proclaimed publishers, five shoeshine shops, 61 tailors, and an amazing 269 neighborhood groceries plus the 15 American Stores and the 13 A & Ps.

The town, at the same time, had bolted-down segregation, with few black professionals and no black entrepreneurs. It had no college, and little incentive for average students to pursue higher education anywhere. It had no broad social goals, certainly no organized planning.

Harrisburg obliviously rode the wave of its prosperity and advantages, and it did so, as the characters in O'Hara's and Boyd's novels, by basking on incessant busyness, exaggerated family and neighborhood togetherness, mindless familiarities, and daily portions of easy contentment. Its biases weren't seriously challenged.

Civic awareness became blurred and underdeveloped. Dissent was dismissed as ill manners. Patronage—as much in business as in government—replaced enterprise. Beyond professionals seeking credentials, ambition waned.

With the tightening of the "narrow iron shell of life," social, business and political problem-solving stopped. The community's key industries—such as AMP, Harsco, Rite Aid and Terryphone—were either developed by outsiders or those not in the Harrisburg mainstream. Newcomers, often on a transient basis, soon were managing the religious, banking, utility, educational, transportation, publishing and sometimes even the political interests. Harrisburg sat back as a proprietary vacuum occurred. By the 1950s Harrisburgers weren't even drinking hometown beer.

Through civic epigenesis, Harrisburg lost better than 90 percent of its leadership. Suburban Levites in their locked, air-conditioned arks entered and departed the City Beautiful, passing by on the other side, for their 40-hour weeks. There was little need for most to have any personal allegiance or affection for Harrisburg.

Had the State Arsenal on Herr Street fired a 17-gun salute to Harrisburg, as it did to celebrate Old Home Week in 1905, many suburbanites would have thought the blast just another round of street crime back in the city.

City DISCONTENTED

61.

THE FIRST MODERN RIOT, 1969

ON FEB. 18, 1969, for the first time in 142 years, Harrisburg closed its public schools for a "cooling-off period." State troopers and city officers patrolled the corridors, as the community defended itself from its youth.

It was the anniversary to the day—three score and seven years—of the birth of Renaissance I, when Harrisburg the City Beautiful passed its $1.1 million municipal improvement bond issue and elected Vance McCormick mayor. But instead of these reformers' prophecy coming true, it was Jeremiah's "young lions" roaring, yelling and laying the land to waste.

The once City Contented had become the City Discontented.

The disturbances began Valentine's Day, not with an apple for the teacher, but with a boycott of a John Harris High afternoon assembly by students who regarded it as inadequate recognition of the recent Black History Week. In the aftermath, fights broke out, a sit-in occurred at William Penn High and a local electrical store was set afire.

School resumed the next day, only to have classes terminated at noon because of "open rebellion," as Superintendent Glenn Parker called it. "It is impossible to teach under these conditions," a teacher said. Ten days of tension followed, with 23 arrests, including three adults, and 27 students suspended.

Four months later, Harrisburg had its first modern riot. A week-long curfew was clamped down after an 18-year-old was slain, at least 15 people were injured, and eight known cases of arson occurred. After 103 people were arrested, seven were convicted of inciting to riot and other offenses.

The trouble started that Monday of June 23, two minutes before 9 a.m., at what Renaissance I knew as Mount Pleasant. A black woman entered a pharmacy at 13th and Market Streets to buy cigarettes and was told the store was closed. In the scuffle that ensued, her shoe was caught in the drugstore door.

Such were the banalities of inchoate conflict that befell the new Harrisburg. In many of its residents' lifetimes, the Pleasant City had become the Afraid City.

The populace registered its disapproval with its feet. The city's population dropped by 9,847 in the 1950s, by 11,636 in the 1960s and by 14,797 in the 1970s. A racial switch resulted. There were 87 more white children than blacks in the Harrisburg schools at the time of the 1969 emergency. That autumn the blacks became the majority by 949.

For the first time, fear and outright racial hostility prevailed in the capital city, a town that for generations managed to maintain a surface tranquility among the races. Genuine harmony had never existed, and not much tokenism, among Harrisburg's professions, politics, churches, schools, financial, business and cultural interests.

So when black assertiveness came, there was no structure throughout the Harrisburg area for devising new social accommodations. Mutual contempt flared so rapidly that the old repressed pattern of separatism was now taken literally—for whites and blacks to live as far apart as possible. Before the riot there had been all-white enclaves on the East and West Shores. After the riot, real estate in these Caucasian centers boomed.

As American riots of the 1960s went, Harrisburg's was minor league, but it has taken 15 years—and suburbia offered no Marshall Plan—for Harrisburg to begin re-interesting whites and blacks in the city.

On March 9, 1976, Mayor Harold A. Swenson reviewed data before a State Senate committee that showed the city losing almost 1,000 residents a year since World War II. Even blacks were leaving, said Swenson:

"If that rate of decline were projected for future years, the city should be totally depopulated by 2036. The demographics of the situation clearly show that the outward movement concentrates on the well-to-do, younger, more productive segments of the population, leaving to the cities a high proportion of the old, the poor, and the minorities, who cannot afford or are not allowed similar freedom of movement."

In the first third of the century, Harrisburg was "the most prosperous and hustling city of its size in the country." Now it had become, to many of its own inhabitants and to many disdainful suburbanites, nothing more than an unwelcomed $10 annual occupational privilege tax.

62.

WILLIAM LYNCH MURRAY

AND THE

GREATER HARRISBURG MOVEMENT

If there were to be a Harrisburg Renaissance II—a supposition still unproved—it was appropriate to begin where the last grand moment of Renaissance I died. On Dec. 12, 1972, a crowd of 400 gathered in the Ballroom of the Penn Harris Hotel for the unveiling of the Harristown Project by the Greater Harrisburg Movement.

In 15 days the Penn Harris, symbol of the once-modern Harrisburg, would bolt its doors forever. The hotel proprietors sold their city spoils to public redevelopment and defected to the West Shore. They expressed no interest in ever reinvesting and re-establishing themselves in what was once their home city. The taproots of this oak of 54 years of hotelling hadn't really gone deep.

"When people cross the Susquehanna, they're in a different world," William Lynch Murray complained only two months before. "It just won't work. If you have a rotten core, you're going to have a rotten periphery, no matter what you've got on the periphery. It's an idiotic notion that never the twain shall meet," he said in the Harrisburg YWCA.

Murray, Shipoke-born, a successful architect and dapper civic leader, was president of GHM, the innovator of Harristown.

Charm and exquisite manners belied the Scotch-Irish doggedness in Bill Murray. He and Dr. Roy Stetler in 1946 had been the last vice presidents of the Harrisburg League for Municipal Improvement, the Vance McCormick organization that launched Renaissance I in 1901.

When the United Way in 1962 was reclining from six successive losing years—in 1961 it actually collected less than 1960—Murray took over as president and Robert M. Mumma Sr. as campaign chairman. The two backslapped and bullied the town, so that giving increased by $93,715, more was raised than ever before in 42 years, and the United Way was saved.

"There wasn't a single person I talked to in this campaign who can take any type of failure lying down," Murray said as he turned the United Way over to Heath L. Allen and Fred B. Dewey, and in 1983 they started it on a series of goal-breaking triumphs unduplicated in Pennsylvania.

It was Murray, Mayor Albert H. Straub, HACC chairman Bruce E. Cooper and others who put GHM together, busting out in style with a flashy dinner in Hotel Hershey. William Keisling, fresh from managing Straub's mayoralty campaign after having been a Scranton administration whiz kid, was hired as GHM executive director, "I gotta ride that boy" President Murray snorted once, "but I'm not staying up to 4 a.m. until he finishes work for an 8 a.m. meeting."

A month before the unveiling of Harristown, Murray and Jack Hanckle of PP&L brought American City Corp. to town to explain its planning for the Greater Hartford Process. Leo Molinaro, a Philadelphian who was president of American City, told how 24 Hartford leaders, starting in 1969, raised $3.35 million, floated $30 million of bonds and were rebuilding the Connecticut capital to be worth $3 billion in 10 years.

"The American despair about the city is almost at the point of pervasive disbelief," said Molinaro. "The toughest part of our job in Hartford was to come up with a believable image of what life could be like if all systems—jobs, traffic, safety, etc.—could work. The disbelief is so great that both the people in the ghetto and those in suburbia don't expect anything to work. They equally enjoy the same disadvantages of malfunctioning community life, though the suburbanites aren't as candid in admitting their discomfort."

Knowing his fellow Pennsylvanians' frailties, Molinaro added prophetically, "No group can do the job alone, although any group can stop it."

The all-day session was remarkably free of double-talk and old-fashioned Harrisburg palaver, but it needed a show-stopper to pique the dormant sensibilities of the local enervated business executives. Just before everyone adjourned to the bar, an unidentified Harrisburger interrupted one of the planners:

"If you're equating the progressive business and community leadership of Hartford with Harrisburg, then you don't know this town. I mean, we just don't think in terms of a $30 million front-end mortgage to promote $3 billion in community growth. What can we do for a dime?"

After the laughter faded, there were Harrisburgers who didn't think the observation was so funny.

63.

HARRISTOWN PROCLAIMED

The day Harristown was announced in the Penn Harris Hotel, Dec.12, 1972, William Lynch Murray observed that in the 39-block center of the once City Beautiful there were only nine buildings worth saving. The Penn Harris itself, to be closed in 15 days, wasn't one of them.

Architect Murray, president of the sponsoring Greater Harrisburg Movement, could have added that in a quarter-century of the post-World War II era, only one new retail establishment had been built in the Downtown—Kresge's at the site of the old courthouse.

Harrisburg, quipped Murray, had the dubious reputation for being the "city of committees." He said he had stacks of reports on what to do with Harrisburg as high as he could reach, "all gathering dust, just gathering dust." For whatever Harristown would be worth, he laughed, it at least would put an end to futile committees and dusty reports for a decade.

GHM as the designated consultant to Harrisburg had reviewed $250,000 worth of plans of the last 20 years, and only the Gladstone Report indicated a desirable direction. Issued a month before the 1969 Riot, it called for "Strawberry Square," named for Strawberry Alley. The Victor Gruen Associates Report, five months after Gladstone, reaffirmed the need for a covered retail center joined to the adjacent Capitol Complex. Tied into this entrepot would be various new projects already up or going up such as City Towers, ground for which was broken only three days before Harristown's going public.

The name Harristown came from "hometown," said the development corporation's first president, James W. Evans. It would create a "profit situation" for the dying Downtown, which was so flaccid the average property was selling at 60 percent of market value and tax yields were a 20th of potential.

Asked the chances for failure, Evans dismissed the question—a jaw-jutting tactic of his that won him success as an old quarterback, Marine, and trial lawyer. A scrappy Welsh coal-cracker, Evans had never been fully assimilated into the Dutch lethargy of his adopted city. He was co-founder of the Harrisburg Area Community College and chairman of the City Charter Commission, and he stimulated his adrenalin by taking on Harrisburg's traditional doubts and procrastinations. "Jim wants to put himself on the credit side of society's ledger," his law partner, Arthur Goldberg, later explained.

Harristown would be the developer for "the melding of the private and public sectors of interest for the only show in town," said Evans, rattling off mixed metaphors. The city, the commonwealth and perhaps the county would form the public sector, with the Harrisburg Redevelopment Authority—beholder of $41.7 million of grants between 1957 and 1983—as the land merchant with the power of eminent domain. Private investment and tax-free bonds would raise much of the money, and the state and Bell Telephone would be the prime leasers in the pioneering years.

Other towns, such as Detroit, Denver, Oklahoma City, Cincinnati, Indianapolis and Hartford, were into this sort of thing, but they weren't Harrisburg.

A different sort of concept was the "Empire State Plaza Plan" that Gov. Nelson A. Rockefeller in 1962 decreed for Albany. "Rocky's edifice complex" was a $2 billion, 10-building state job, narrower in scope than

Harristown but more architecturally ambitious. Rocky used big government to clear out 98 acres of Albany blight.

The safeguard for Harristown would be that it would be watched over by "two 800-pound gorillas," the mayor and the Harristown Corp. itself. No one in 1972, with the wary Harold Swenson as mayor, expected that someday these two gorillas might put banana peels under each other.

The grand adventure was launched with a $150,000 kitty, a "bold concept…more than just a plan, but a proposal of action," as The Patriot-News called it. A third of that stake was put up by Gov. Milton J. Shapp who called it "one of the most ambitious inner-city rebuilding projects to be undertaken anywhere in the United States."

Skeptics watched to see what the bankers would do, the guys who "look at the fingernails of their left hands" when they speak, in the words of novelist John Cheever. Within 45 days all the major financial institutions in Harrisburg made their commitment to Harristown.

"They used to say they could never get anything done in Harrisburg. That's changing now," commented Bill Murray.

64.

RENAISSANCE II?

A month after he became mayor in 1968, Albert H. Straub told Harrisburg Rotary "the town was allowed to drift and to drift badly" for 30 years.

The threatened ruination, in Straub's opinion, began during the Great Depression. He didn't have to itemize what hadn't been done—industrial development, municipal and school annexation, the establishment of a college, more enlightened politics, more competitive business investing and, of course, the public's simple recognition that racial brotherhood was overdue.

Eight years after Straub's speech, James W. Evans retired as Harristown's first president. It was 1976 and he still had to warn: "To do nothing is to guarantee disaster. To push the Harristown concept as hard and as fast as we can is the only chance, though not a guarantee, we have at survival."

Harristown was based on the theories of Elenezer Howard, an English urbanologist of 1904 when Harrisburg's Renaissance I was launched. What his contemporaries Albert Einstein was to relativity and Sigmund Freud to the unconscious, Howard was to visionary urban planning. "The growth of a city must be in the hands of a representative public authority, and the best results could be achieved only if this authority had power to assemble and hold the land, plan the city, time the order of the building, and provide the necessary services," Lewis Mumford interpreted the Howard principles.

Adopting modern economic enterprise, not textbook civics, is what Howard espoused in his planning and management schemes. Harristown should be the welcomed alternative from the negligent local politics that had let the Downtown core disintegrate.

Whatever its shortcomings—including its illusions—Harristown when it was proposed in 1972 was a comprehensive concept.

Ironically, the fresh idea came out of a community almost oblivious to most of the national crazes of the 1960s and 1970s—assassinations, bombings, confrontations, marches, Vietnam politics, and civil rights and feminist agitations. "The people here are difficult to arouse and even when they're aroused, they're not very aroused," former mayoral candidate Jack Lynch said in 1972.

Harrisburg proved its Dutch culture's notorious reputation for stand-fastness. The anti-war and environmental movements had limited followings here, and no effective black or female power structure developed.

The headlines out of Harrisburg were vivid enough—The U.S. Supreme Court case about possible discrimination at the Harrisburg Moose Club, the 1969 riot, the Berrigan Trial and the 1972 Flood. Yet these engendered minimal local social consequences.

Harrisburg drifted, as Al Straub could see, not just physically but mentally.

If there were to be a Harrisburg Renaissance II, as the Harristown founders prophesied, it must work against cynical pessimism of gigantic proportions.

Renaissance I was lucky. At the turn of the century, the city fell into step with the new Capitol and the enthusiasm of the Teddy Roosevelt generation. Racism then was immense, but it didn't have to be faced. Personal greed wasn't uncommon, but people also shared a bully faith in "The American Dream," undefined as that may be. Few were indifferent, and a counter-culture was unheard of.

Harrisburg in 1902 had the wealth to recapitalize itself. By 1972, in contrast, the city and school district were $25 million in debt, outmigration and poverty were extensive, and the tax load, as Ed Endress in 1971 reported in The Patriot, made the capital city non-competitive with the choicer suburbs.

Headlining all the problems was crime.

In 1969, the year of the Harrisburg school closing and riot, the area offered a quantum leap in crime—property loss to $1.3 million with stolen goods doubled, crime complaints up by 48 percent, arrests up by 16 percent and the FBI per capita crime rate doubled. The Harrisburg area romped ahead of Philadelphia and Pittsburgh in its increased crime rate. York was under curfew because of "hit-and-run guerilla warfare" the night Neil Armstrong peacefully stepped on the moon.

The stout-hearted could endure a deteriorating city, such as Harrisburg obviously was, but no one was content with an unsafe city, as Harrisburgers perceived theirs to be.

65.

THE STATE IN THE CITY

"Patience, O God, and how we have needed it," prayed the late Rev. Dr. Sheridan Watson Bell on April 5, 1975, in his invocation for the groundbreaking of Harristown's first major project, the $51.4 million Strawberry Square. "May the future of Harristown be as bright as the sun shining today," added Gov. Milton J. Shapp.

At the very time Mayor Harold Swenson, the governor and Harristown President Jim Evans were turning over a spadeful of earth on the south side of Walnut Street, Bryn Mawr's Sen. Richard A. Tilghman on the north side of Walnut had a lawsuit against Harristown headed for Commonwealth Court.

Tilghman, ranking Republican on the Senate Appropriations Committee and the suburban advocate with little fondness for any of Pennsylvania's cities, was adamant against Democrat Shapp's committing the commonwealth to an obligation of $480 million—starting at $11,230 a day on Aug. 1, 1978—for leasing Harristown properties the state would never own.

The court 16 months later set down Tilghman's suit, as it did one against the Department of Community Affairs for approving a $34.4 million city bond obligation. A third suit was instigated by Anna M. German, the aging spinster daughter of a prominent landlord of the Renaissance I era. Miss German until her death in 1980 lived next door to Strawberry Square and wanted to block the Harristown $105 million bond issue.

Renaissance I proceeded 15 years without court troubles. Renaissance II had expensive lawyers filing briefs before the mortar was poured.

Ironically for old Republican, home-bound Harrisburg, the men first on the political firing line for Harristown were Democrats and the natives of other states.

Shapp was born in Cleveland. "Brilliant businessman, knew leverage and dollars and cents," Mayor Swenson commented about Shapp's role. Swenson himself came from Brooklyn. And the state Secretary of General Services who facilitated the leasing was Ronald Lench, a native of Bridgeport, Conn., who had been a legislator from Beaver Falls before he moved to Susquehanna Twp.

The fortuitous line-up came about because after 90 years there was a Democratic governor and mayor, Shapp and Swenson, from 1971 to 1977. The last time that had happened was 1891–92 with Gov. Robert E. Pattison and Mayor John A. Fritchey.

It was Harristown's position that the state and the city, like a town-and-gown community, must not exist in isolation. It illustrated that theme in a full-page newspaper ad, showing the old red-brick Capitol in 1829–89 when it was surrounded by an iron fence keeping out Harrisburg.

Swenson told Tilghman's Appropriations Committee that the state was using $195 million worth of tax-free real estate, or 27 percent of Harrisburg's property. If it paid city, county and school taxes, the bill in 1970 would have been $6.1 million. To make his point, Swenson drew up a huge bogus tax notice to the commonwealth for its unpaid municipal tax of $1.98 million.

Statehouse politicians argued Harrisburg would be a wasteland without the Capitol. As of 1972, one in every five state jobs was in Dauphin County and one out of every 25 living Dauphin Countians was a state employee. Furthermore, by 1973 the state had $2.5 million worth of leased rentals in the county, including $1.36 million in Downtown Harrisburg.

West shore politicians, for their part, forever condemned state expenditures as they tried to get state rentals in their districts.

The Greater Harrisburg Movement in 1971 called the commonwealth "the biggest freeloader." But there were editorials and anguish when Gov. David L. Lawrence in 1960 almost sent the Bureau of Motor Vehicles to Scranton, and in 1965 when Gov. William W. Scranton did transfer the State Workmen's Insurance Office's 135 jobs to his hometown. Yet two years later, in the 1967 mayor election, Jack Lynch urged Gov. Raymond P. Shafer not to acquire Verbeke Street property and wipe out 1,000 residents and 100 small businesses. That plan was discarded when Harristown offered office space to the commonwealth. Shapp talked up Harrisburg, but he did move the Bureau of Vital Statistics to New Castle and a minor office to Lewistown.

In the computer age, government was as portable as the terminal circuitry. Even Harristown critics acknowledged that the project was the most sensible way to keep the government they fed on, if not loved, in the capital city.

66.

STRAWBERRY SQUARE

The game plan for Harristown if it were to anchor itself as Renaissance II in a city that had had a riot, a catastrophic flood and the worst emigration in its history—all in less than a decade—was to make haste before pernicious lethargy set in.

With the exception of enticing a hotel to replace the old Penn Harris—and that's a big exception—Harristown's Phase I was fast afoot.

It took a mere 42 months from the 1969 Riot to launch the Harristown project. Then it was but another 39 months before the old YWCA was leveled and the 12-story Strawberry Square got underway.

The new building—the first new retail structure in the center city in 30 years—covers 2.2 acres and has a three-story atrium. One of its designers was a Harrisburg native, Ehrman B. Mitchell Jr., whose father founded Beaufort Farms and whose mother started the Harrisburg Symphony. The week of April of 1976 when ground was broken for Strawberry Square, Harristown also announced plans for a 334-foot-tall building at 333 Market St. for the Department of Education. It would be the tallest building between Philadelphia and Pittsburgh.

It took only 23 months to build Strawberry Square and on March 6, 1978, Bell Telephone began occupying nine floors with 1,000 employees on a

The excavation for Strawberry Square, circa 1976, was an impressive event in itself. Construction was the first phase of the Harristown project.

38-year lease at an annual rental of $1.4 million. The area codes of 717 and 814 would be managed from this Bell center, covering telephone users from Stroudsburg to Warren. To prevent a recurrence of the 1907 Opera House fire at the same site, the nation's most modern alarm system was installed.

Hervey W. Froehlich, a native of Camp Hill, was behind Bell's commitment. He was Bell's vice president and general manager for its Central Area. While Hervey moved the latest technology into the new skyscraper, his dapper Uncle Jack at Cameron and Market streets was pumping gas as he did for 60 years. Jack Froehlich perhaps was Pennsylvania's senior gas station proprietor and undoubtedly its most natty attired. Ole Jack sported a snappy Ivy League cap and a tweed jacket, just as he had when he filled the Duesenbergs of the Beidlemans and Haldemans. While Nephew Hervey often worked late, Uncle Jack would close shop early to go to the YMCA, where he was acclaimed "the greatest volleyball player ever to perform in our gym."

After Bell's occupancy, it took Strawberry Square only nine months for its first retailer, I. Mishkin in January of 1979. Isaac L. Mishkin's parents, Moe and Pauline, had a woman's apparel business in downtown Harrisburg for 40 years. Arguing "the market is as good as you want to make it," son Ike and partner Kay Cooper moved quickly to recapture the smart woman's couture trade abandoned by Mary Sachs and Junior Dress of yesteryear.

A year from Mishkin's opening, the Education Department moved into the 333 building.

Then to celebrate $147.6 million of investment—by far the greatest economic venture in Harrisburg history—Strawberry Square on Nov. 13, 1980, threw a gala "Grand Opening." Lights glowed in its 41 shops as 3,000 guests at Harrisburg's biggest party ever toasted the triumph of a city that had begun to believe it might have pride in itself again.

This hurried-up timetable fit the hyperactive, fretting personality of the Harristown generalissimo, William Keisling. An Eagle Scout from Scranton, briefly a newspaperman and in politics since he was 23, Keisling took the helm of Harristown at 36 and put the stamp of his own character into the project. Keisling proved to be both a public jovial figure and, alternately, a low-profiled, furtive type, resigned to his role of no praises for wonders accomplished and always a target for those with urban grievances.

Speed was absolutely necessary for Harristown, for there were thousands of inveterate naysayers ready to exclaim, "I told you so," if another Fifth and Walnut resulted. That was the 1967 debacle when an apartment across from Old City Hall was razed for a promised $40 million sports center and motor inn. The site is a parking lot yet.

Since 1950 Harrisburg had expended millions in redevelopment—of which at least $563,922 couldn't be verified by auditors because of faulty records. Much had gone up—Taylor Bridge, Town House Apartments, Jackson-Lick, Ben Franklin and the School Administration buildings, B'nai B'rith Apartments, City Towers and Morrison Towers. But all was piecemeal, uncoordinated "slum clearance."

The unified rebuilding of the city's core had never been tried until Harristown.

67.

EVERYBODY'S OUT OF TOWN

"Next to drinking brandy before breakfast, the most fatal mistake a man can commit is to isolate himself in the country," humorist S. J. Perelman penned in the 1970s while he sniffed brandy at his bucolic estate in Bucks County.

Post-war America opted out of cities, and it just wasn't Harrisburg that was left behind. In the 1960s and 1970s, the 48 third-class cities in Pennsylvania lost 297,723 of their populations, or 19 percent—the equivalent of Allentown, Lancaster, Reading and Wilkes-Barre all shutting down.

"There seems to be a growing alienation between the city and what most people conceive of as the American way of life," William H. Whyte Jr., the urbanologist from West Chester, predicted as early as the 1950s. Penn State alumnus Vance Packard entitled his 1972 book, *A Nation of Strangers.*

Jane Jacobs, originally from Scranton, in 1961 published her memorable *The Death and Life of Great American Cities,* and argued that population density is a vital component of civilization. "We cannot have it both ways: our 20th century metropolitan economy combined with 19th century isolated-town or little-city life," she said.

Tim Doutrich, as ex-mayor in 1982, recalled an exciting Harrisburg of the 1930s and 1940s with "congeries" of people "elbow to elbow" in center city. It was a town where the lines from a Raymond Chandler mystery of the time applied, the gal saying to her guy: "Get dressed, sweetheart, and don't fuss with your necktie. Places want us to go to them."

Then the "galloping gangrene," in Miss Jacob's words, set in. "Everybody's Out of Town," said B.J. Thomas in 1970, a song particularly applicable to Harrisburg: "Where have the peo-ple gone? Seems like there's no one hang-in' on. Look through the win-dows, the hous-es are emp-ty—Hey—Everybod-y's out of town. Seems like—I'm the on-ly one a-roun'."

Two decades of urban renewal, 1950-1970, failed to stem the tide. Worthwhile projects—Town House and Presbyterian Apartments, to cite just two—joined the Harrisburg skyline, but they weren't enough. Cultural advantages were increased with the State Museum and Art Association Center, but they weren't enough, either.

Even leadership wasn't lacking. Mayor Nolan F. Ziegler was alert and active from 1956 until his untimely death of cancer in 1963. He launched urban renewal and began implementing a plan for steady modernization, but all seemed to be little more than prolonging the pulse of a comatose patient in intensive care.

There was "a pervasive sense of defeatism," Francis B. Haas recalled. He was city solicitor for Mayor Harold Swenson and then attorney for Harristown. The Chamber of Commerce noted 700 businesses leaving the city between 1969 and 1975, with retail dipping to 11 percent of the community's total as compared to 70 percent in 1950 and with hotel space down to 16 percent from 61 percent.

What was so disheartening about Harrisburg's case was the attitude seemed to be anti-city rather than pro-suburbia. People fled out, like refugees, but weren't seeking to build new communities as their pioneering American ancestors had. John O'Hara had said, "Harrisburg isn't Paris." But the new suburban settlers didn't desire a new Paris but "an all-American flavor reminiscent of the Midwest," as Bill Costopoulos and John Baer put it in *The Price of Acquittal,* their book about a 1976 West Shore slaying. The suburbanites "shovel snow in the winter, mow lawns in the summer, and follow Penn State football in the fall," said Atty. Costopoulos and Baer.

68.

SHUTTING UP SHOPS IN THE 70'S

When the last spigot was shut off at Graupner's Brewery on May 14, 1951, the old Germanic burg along the Susquehanna had made its final draught of hometown beer. Fink's and Doehne's previously had closed, and beer no longer was brewed in Steelton either.

Now all the beer was trucked in. Some distributors even moved beyond the city limits, such as Wilsbach, a name famous in Old Harrisburg Tech football and a keg merchant since Prohibition was lifted.

The Graupner closing was at the time no more than "a chronicle of small beer," as Shakespeare would have put it, but it foretold the desolation ahead.

During the 1970s too much too quickly was closing down in Harrisburg. Shutting up shop became contagious.

Mary Sachs, Bowman's for more than a century, J.H. Troup the music house since 1881, Junior Dress, E.G. Hoover jeweler, Doutrich's, Allan Stuart clothier, Davids, Stark Brothers, Shenk and Tittle sporting goods, Jeannette Shop, Cantor's Shoes, Greenberg's, Sam Levin's Penn Book Store after 40 years, and Letts as the nation's oldest photography shop since 1860 and whose supplies probably were used to make pictures of the carnage at the Battle of Gettysburg—all closed in Harrisburg during the 1970s.

The Linden Tea Room shut, as did the 210 Club for jazz. Eugene W. Zimmerman's Holiday Inn Town after 15 years was bankrupt by 1979, but new ownership kept it open. The Harrisburger, Governor and Plaza hotels joined the Penn Harris in closing. Auto dealers row on Cameron Street almost disappeared. The city's first skyscraper, the U.S.F& G Building, was vacated. The Telegraph and Donaldson buildings, other landmarks from Renaissance I, were razed.

The magnificent State Theater was reduced to rubble and a lock was put on the Colonial Theater with its huge balcony. The only movie place left in town showed X-rated movies exclusively.

Education took to its feet. The city's two fine nursing schools faded into history, the Harrisburg Hospital's in 1974 after 69 years and 2.525 registered nurse graduates, and the Polyclinic's in 1976 after 65 years and 2,303 RNs. The Central Pennsylvania Business School, downtown for 48 years, was bought by Bart A. Milano, and after its enrollment dipped to 15 students he built a handsome campus at Summerdale. Thompson Institute, successor to Beckley College of 1918-1934, had only 125 students by 1972, so it departed to Lawnford Acres.

The ultimate crash was the bankruptcy of the Penn Central on June 21, 1970. The original Pennsylvania Railroad was chartered in this city in 1846, its tracks went through the middle of town, and for generations it was the largest employer. Even by the 1950s the Pennsy was the nation's fifth largest enterprise with $3 billion in assets, 10,100 miles of track and as many employees as the commonwealth. During early Renaissance I, the old PRR had more workers than the Army had soldiers. Going broke for the Penn Central was the equivalent of three Bethlehem Steels, plus PP&L, AMP, Harsco, Hershey Foods, Rite Aid and Quaker Oats, all crashing at once.

Just as bad as the failures—in some sense more humiliating—were the successes that moved out of Harrisburg.

Three firms listed on the New York Stock Exchange that began in Harrisburg are Rite Aid, Harsco and AMP, yet by the 1970s their corporate headquarters were in the suburbs. The biggest engineering firm, Gannett, Fleming, Corddry and Carpenter, headed there, and Modjeski and Master followed. Iceland Products departed from Steelton. Book-of-the-Month and Berg Electronics settled first in suburbia.

The ITT Terryphone, named for Kent J. Terry, in 1954 was designed in the basement of trucker John N. Hall's building on Second Street and staked to a $6 million loan by a city bank. It ended up on 12 acres off Eisenhower Boulevard, while Hall, once an aspirant for mayor, took his fleet of tractor-trailers to the Carlisle Pike.

The old capitalists had their shops and factories right in town, and they often walked to work. The new capitalists wanted expressways outside their office door.

69.

THE RESTAURANT BOOM

Harrisburg never had more than three good restaurants, John O'Hara asserts in *A Rage To Live,* but he discreetly never mentions which three.

A paradox of the tumultuous 1960s and 1970s was that as people left town and businesses shut down, a restaurant renaissance took hold. At last Harrisburgers had a choice for dining out, even in style.

The locals still would gripe, but for a town whose specialty dish is chicken corn soup much of the commissary complaining shouldn't be considered informed. This was the place, The New York Sun reported in 1887, where folks put sugar on macaroni, mixed cucumbers with stewed onions, fried their asparagus, devoured pretzels, and ate sauerkraut every Wednesday night. Besides, Harrisburgers crave quantitative eating, not the qualitative culinary arts.

The restaurant boom, beginning with Sam Weinstein's Maverick in 1961, was part of the "reverse economics" Harrisburg went through. As the city lost high-profit and high-employment enterprises, it gained in the less-profitable amenities. Ironically, it often was improving the quality of life usually for those who no longer lived in town.

Harrisburg never had an art gallery. Suddenly it acquired three non-taxable ones: the Art Association's own building at the Governor Findlay Mansion on Front Street in 1964, the William Penn Memorial Museum in 1965, and the Doshi established by the late artist Maya Schock in 1972.

Long an orphan in higher education, the city in 1961 got its first daytime classes at what became the University Center, and then the Harrisburg Area Community College, the commonwealth's first, opened in 1964.

To save lives, River Rescue was founded in 1960 by Gus Spagnolo, Bill Stimeling, Buz Klinger and others, with volunteer lawyering by the late Earl J. Melman and George W. Gekas. It was the first citizens' river-safety patrol in Pennsylvania, and in 1971 it added ambulance service. Meanwhile the Central YMCA Health Club, a magnet for businessmen, opened in 1975.

Culture, learning, candlelight dining, water safety and improved body tone, while praiseworthy, lack the economic impact that a single, high-tech industry could have provided. The one taxable influence these diversions did have was to make parts of the old burg more attractive to gentrification, or the refurbishing of old properties for upper-middle-income living. The Historic Harrisburg Association was founded in 1972 by Marianne D. Faust, later two-term councilwoman.

In its darkest decades, Harrisburg took itself to the dining table, often by expense account, to forget its troubles.

Weinstein, once the proprietor of the Be-Bop jazz joint off Seventh Street, created such a class place at the Maverick that John F. Kennedy tried its fare. In 1974 George Giannaris bought the place and stepped up business even more. Soon following were such eateries as Au Jour Le Jour, The Brown Bag, The Gazebo, Caruso's, Harris House, The Colonade, Zorba's and, on the west bank, Catalano's, popular with politicos.

The genius of this chow revival was Joe Lombardo, who in 1965 opened his Gaslight Restaurant on Seventh Street in what had been a slum.

Lombardo had gone through 10 previous restaurants, was a so-so waiter at the Esquire Bar and had been broke twice, but he made it big at the Gaslight and later before his death in 1978 at new quarters where the State Theater had been. Joe stole the winning idea of a blackboard menu special from the Giannaris family, who first used it at its Belmont Restaurant on Chestnut Street in 1954.

Part of the renaissance, too, was not surrendering heritage. Jimmy Kaldes' The Spot opened on Market Square in the 1930s, was replaced by the new City Hall and only increased business when it moved its grill a block away.

The landmark is Harry's Tavern at 13th and Vernon streets, owned by Harry and Mary Touloumes and bartended by Jerry Muth. Ex-GI Touloumes bought the bar in 1949. Four years later he repainted its pinkish ceiling that dated to 1939, and in the last 30 years patrons have watched it bedim into a mellow nicotine yellow. As the surrounding city went through a metamorphosis and menopause, Harry's steadfast inertia carried on—the lone remaining sanctuary where suburbanites and blue-jeaned socialites can browse with pluralistic inner-city settlers in crowded evenings of old-time Harrisburg garrulity.

70.

THE FOURTH LARGEST CITY IN PENNSYLVANIA

By 1980, the 12 West Shore municipalities had a population of 98,416, the equivalent of being the fourth largest city in Pennsylvania. They had more people than 36 Pennsylvania counties.

But the West Shore was not a city, and didn't aim to be. There are no cities in Cumberland County, though it has been settled for 260 years.

On the East Shore, the six neighbors of Harrisburg, exclusive of Steelton, had a population of 83, 087. Lower Paxton Twp. with 34, 830 was bigger than Williamsport, almost twice as big as Pottsville and, in all, had more people than 37 Pennsylvania cities, but it, too, had no intention of becoming a city.

Had American suburbia, in its quaint ways, rejected the social, evolutionary, civilized impulse of humankind going back to the City of Ur in Mesopotamia 4,000 years ago?

Had the cities become so identified with the Four Bs—blacks, boodle, booze and bums—that the pristine "residential nurseries" of suburbia wanted nothing to do with them?

More directly, was the cold-shoulder and sometimes the repugnance shown Harrisburg by Pleasant Hills, Pennsboro Manor, Point Ridge Farms or Paxton Crossing an attitude not so much anti-Harrisburg but anti-city anywhere? Had suburbia become so self-sustaining that its residents would be bored in Paris, uncomfortable in London, disenchanted in San Francisco, morose in Boston, and trembling in New York?

Anguished Harrisburg in the 1960s and 1970s exposed its impuissance, but perhaps the real fault for its heartbreaking decline wasn't so much its own doings as the fact that marketable alternatives to a supposed safe and clean new world were just a short commute away.

The $6.4 million M. Harvey Taylor Bridge opened June 24, 1952, to relieve the traffic jam at Market Square—but it also relieved the traffic jam at the Lemoyne Bottleneck, that age-old gateway to the West Shore.

Marking the 15th anniversary of the Taylor Bridge, Fran Fanucci, then the Patriot-News' West Shore bureau chief, devised a sure-fire headliner: "West Shore, Pa.—Someday?" The Patriot-News in 1887 certified the independence of suburbia by inaugurating its West and East Shore weekly tabloid sections.

Fanucci's question was hardly an original one. Back on Dec. 18, 1925, Robert Lee Myers I, a former legislator and president of Lemoyne Trust, addressed the Chamber of Commerce and urged such a Cumberland County city. "The time is fast coming" were Myers' immortal words.

William B. Whittock in 1967 gave Fanucci the modern answer. He was the engineer for Camp Hill, Shiremanstown, and Fairview and Silver Spring townships:

"It will come, but only to a point. There will never be a megalopolis on the West Shore. I don't think they will ever again build a city. By that I mean, cities as we have known them, with grid street layouts and the jammed traffic, with buses, subways and confusion. It would be a shame if that were ever allowed to happen on the West Shore, but I think too many people are too wise to allow it. The townships and boroughs are so different. The way I see it, they will never lose their identity as separate places. There will always be a Lemoyne, a Camp Hill and a New Cumberland."

Like there'll always be an England. And such reassurance was just what the returning G.I.s in 1945 sought. Displaced from their old city neighborhood and farms and weary of crowded Army barracks, they took their government loans, got married, had 2.3 children and became first-generation suburbanites with the same enthusiasm their immigrant grandparents were first-generation Americans. Other than being obsessed by crabgrass, charcoal grills, golf and keeping up in their new consumer culture, this new white-collar elite was happy.

Pennsylvania had invented suburbia in 1881 with Wayne, outside Bryn Mawr, according to Penn sociologist E. Digby Baltzell. The next year, appropriately, America's first country club opened. Baltzell profiled what he called "the suburban nomads," the executive families who relocated ad infinitum from suburb to suburb, their houses as conventional as their wardrobes.

"Mortgaged up to their rain gutters," snorted novelist John Cheever, these West and East Shore patio pioneers didn't so much detest Harrisburg as they were oblivious to it. They told their old Army and college chums and their in-laws in Wichita that they "are living in Harrisburg" and sometimes indeed they had a Harrisburg mailing address. But they not only never saw Muench Street, they couldn't pronounce it correctly either.

71.

GILDED PROVINCES

As Harrisburg depopulated, the East and West shores blossomed. A new America dawned, not in Goattown, the Bloody Eighth Ward or the Lower End of Steelton, but in Devon Manor, Twin Lakes Park, Green Lane Farms and Allendale.

There was a style of sorts to this suburban spectacular, even in garbage. Camp Hill purchased a bright orange Mercedes-Benz garbage truck for the 1970s. Lemoyne valiantly provided the last municipal free trash collections through 1981. And the great interstate highway system on the West Shore became a thoroughfare for trucking refuse away from contented consuming communities.

Prosperous, pampered, snug, well schooled and professionally credentialed, Harrisburg suburbanites were the new bourgeoisie, not rednecks or liberals but moderate conservatives. As each generation must have its revolution, theirs was to create one of the most comfortable living conditions ever known on earth. Temple Beth El Rabbi Gerald Wolpe once said it was easy to warn against the Holocaust, but how does one cope with the country club?

"In many ways, Cumberland County is a microcosm of white, middle class, suburban-rural Americans," the 1981 county library study reported. "Its people would not feel out of place if the county were to be somehow transported en masse to Vermont or Kansas or Southern Virginia. On the other hand, they probably would feel uncomfortable in Pasadena, Brooklyn or Miami." The study noted Cumberland County was 98 percent racially homogenized—a higher white percentage than at the time of the Battle of Gettysburg—and it had seven golf courses and 14 movie theaters but not one showing X-rated films.

While haranguing against "big government," these cunning suburbanites fashioned two of the biggest taxpayer social programs in the nation's history to their advantage—superhighways and school construction. With billions spent on these two staples—far more than it would take to rebuild Harrisburg top to bottom—the suburbanites then went about devising viable alternatives and attractive communities to the Harrisburgs they left behind.

For the first time in history, it became convenient for those in the Harrisburg hub not to live in Harrisburg.

The schools accompanied the post-war baby boom.

After the Central Dauphin District of 120 square miles was formed in 1950 to cover seven municipalities, Eisenhower Boulevard opened to give the East Shore north-south access. After the Taylor Bridge opened, the West Shore School District was formed in 1953. The new Cedar Cliff High School opened in 1958, or less than two years before the South Bridge Expressway.

The ribbon to the expressway was cut Jan. 22, 1960, and the politicians adjourned to lunch on the West Shore. In 1982 the South Bride—never called the John Harris Bridge—was widened. In a ceremony the politicians drove an antique auto across—to the West Shore again.

In the mid-1960s Trinity High School came, giving the West Shore an alternative to Bishop McDevitt. The East Shore's I-81 opened too, and so did new high schools for Susquehanna, Lower Dauphin and Central Dauphin East. Eventually the school construction spree faded, but not the roadway building—the River Relief Road to upper Dauphin County in 1968; the George N. Wade Bridge in 1973, and the Cameron Street Cloverleaf in the late 1970s.

Lifestyle amenities, like white and lavender crownvetch, clustered by the highway exits.

Harrisburg's gilded provinces at last count had 19 golf courses, plus health clubs, cocktail lounges, weight-reducing salons, swimming pools and racquetball courts, as well as houses of worship, mortuaries, the largest supermarkets, fast-food joints, saloons for take-out six packs, and the resplendent lodgings of physicians, attorneys, accountants, stockbrokers, pharmacists and analysts.

Real estate was king. In the 1960s Upper Allen's population increased by 178 percent: in the 1970s, by 45 percent. Lower Paxton in the 1960s went up to 30 percent and then 50 percent in the 1970s. Harrisburg Schools' property valuation between 1967 and 1977 increased by 26 percent, but Cumberland Valley's by 231 percent, Central Dauphin by 136 percent and the West Shore District by 94 percent. In their taxable worth, CD at $551 million, the West Shore at $401 million and Cumberland Valley at $351 million had more to pluck than Harrisburg's $323 million. The median Cumberland County house during the 1970s boom increased in value by almost threefold, to $48,200.

The 11 school districts on the West Shore saw their enrollment peak in 1971, the same time hundreds of households wished their driveways were twice the size to fit the family's three cars.

72.

EAST SHORE, WEST SHORE

The Blue Danube is merely the boundary of Czechoslovakia, Hungary, Yugoslavia, Romania and Russia, as the Rhine separates Germany, France and the Netherlands.

But the Susquehanna slits the East and West shores, creating an unarmed but formidable barrier between political jurisdictions, school systems, chambers of commerce, schoolboy sports and, some say, even the quality of pizza.

Poor Harrisburg extends to the last slapping molecule of the Susquehanna, within a centimeter of the pavilion of Catalano's Restaurant where lanterns at dusk glow like a scene out of *The Great Gatsby*.

It is a different world outside the city, or even beyond Dauphin County.

The average income in Cumberland County was $10,821, or more than $1,000 higher than in Dauphin, reporter Carmen Brutto discovered when he compiled data from the 1973 Pennsylvania personal income tax returns. Dauphin County had almost 7,000 more poor, or persons claiming less than $4,000 annual income.

Dr. James W. Selgas, research chief for HACC, at that time assembled demographics showing, among other curiosities, that while Cumberland County had a lower percentage of its adult women in the job market—only

38 percent—it had a higher percentage of its married women working—63 percent. One conclusion might be that female professionalism is higher on the West Shore. Another inference could be that keeping up with the West Shore standard of gracious living required more family income.

The Greater Harrisburg Movement in 1978 produced a housing survey that counted 28 apartment complexes with "a phenomenal vacancy rate of only 2.3 percent," but virtually all the new units were outside the city. More than a third of the respondents told GHM that residential and commercial development in suburbia was "too fast," and the survey itself found "virtually no enthusiasm for faster growth."

The city at that time was struggling to attain any growth at all. During one year in the late 1970s, there was but one single new residence built in Harrisburg.

The West Shore, by both intention and plain good fortune, came up with an enviable public economic situation by 1983.

While Cumberland County has only 54,000 fewer persons than Dauphin, its county budget is $15 million, or a third, lower. Its county property tax per capita is three times less, too. In nine public services on a per capita basis, Dauphin outspends Cumberland. Harrisburg's 1983 municipal budget of $16 million could meet the combined needs of Camp Hill, Hampden, Lower and Upper Allen, South Middleton, New Cumberland, East Pennsboro, Mechanicsburg, Fairview Twp., Silver Spring and Lemoyne.

The West Shore thinks itself so non-urban that it is able to get by without an incinerator, a juvenile detention home, a full-time district attorney, a unified police force, and fewer other comprehensive social services.

Despite some of the most rapid growth in Pennsylvania, Cumberland County remains a contented confederacy of 12 boroughs and 22 townships.

"We are no longer scattered communities with farm areas between the built-up sections," wrote former Camp Hill councilman Ivan L. Craig in 1970. "Municipal boundaries go through living rooms, wander along and across streets. Only informed local citizens—and tax collectors—know where boundary lines are. Clearly the West Shore has become one community."

Craig, a Bell Telephone engineer from Maine, settled in Camp Hill in 1926, was a public official for 37 years and learned a lot of civics. In 1971 he became one of the founding fathers of the West Shore Council of Governments.

The Susquehanna, not quite a mile wide and usually not more than a few feet deep, is the great divide. Businessmen, not generals, build the best Maginot Lines.

The West Shore Businessmen's Association was founded in 1947, and then, to the shock of Harrisburgers, it evolved in 1955 into the West Shore Chamber of Commerce.

A conciliatory Harrisburg Area Chamber in 1976 as a bicentennial unity gesture voted unanimously for a "Harrisburg Metro Chamber." The West Shore leadership voted it down, 10 for, 10 against and one abstention. Economic considerations weren't the issue, the West Shore president reported. "Maintaining our own identity" was what "called the marriage off."

73.

THE MALLING OF HARRISBURG

The shopping mall is the most recognized artifact of modern American middle-class suburban life.

Once the courthouse, the railroad station or even a gothic church symbolized local identity. Now the low-storied, pastel-colored rows of box structures assembled like retail cases encircled by parking lots, denote the next settlement of Americans out beyond the city limits.

Theodore H. White in his *Making of the President, 1972,* discovered shopping malls as handshaking stands for political candidates. He was a bit late. William B. Lentz began his 1964 campaign upset of Sen. Harvey Taylor by passing out balloons at the Colonial Park Plaza.

"Impermanent temples of commerce," White misnamed the malls. The first opened in Kansas City in 1922. As White was writing a half-century later, there were 13,000 in America—and the last of 26 in the Harrisburg area, the Capital City Mall, was going up. The new secular temples have the practicality and non-aesthetic appeal of styrofoam cups. Anonymity reigns. Who owns, manages and promotes these malls? Once, there had been a Mary Sachs, an Ed Schleisner, a Harriet Hommer, a Clarence Shank and a Charley Tittle, a tribe of Goldsmiths, a Charley Feller, a Bowman clan and even a George Pomeroy. But the malls usually are blandly named and unadorned landmarks with faceless proprietors who have no discernible community allegiance.

Downtown America used to have a tangible spirit, and each city center was different. The malls, for all their varied artificiality, have the suburban uniformity of a checkout counter.

Two country-boy capitalists started the malling of the Harrisburg area.

Josiah W. Kline (1882-1961) was a Cumberland County Dutchman and son of a village storekeeper. Short and stocky, he was a pageboy in the 1899 Legislature and then in Congress. He also was a butcher boy selling newspapers on the Reading Railroad, a gas meter reader, and eventually state law librarian from 1914 to 1929, though he had no college education.

Kline began in real estate in 1911. Within 20 years he built Harrisburg's first high-rise, the 117-unit Parkview Apts. Then came the Thornwood Apts. He sold houses for Wilson Park, the land for Bishop McDevitt and John Harris high schools, and at last he put up his shopping center. Kline Village, at the end of Market Street, opened Nov. 15, 1951.

Luther B. Smith (1898-1968) received a grammar-school education in Maytown and went into trucking, autos, aircraft, construction, heavy equipment and land developing. Unlike Kline who was childless, Smith had a daughter, the noted civic leader Ferne Smith Hetrick. Like Kline, he left a foundation.

Kline set the style. He properly located his shopping center between Harrisburg and Susquehanna Twp., and next to a cemetery so he would have no competition. He paced off the acreage, and no shopper needed to walk more than six car lengths to a store.

Smith was just as smart with his West Shore Plaza, opening in 1955. Ironically, after both farm boys passed on, their malls made it big with a new idea—the urban farmers market.

Downtown Harrisburg retailers remember Christmas of 1955—it was the first they ever had serious rivalry for shoppers. Once they did 70 percent of the community's business. By 1974 before Strawberry Square opened, center city was down to 11 percent.

Once the mall craze hit, it became a flurry: Camp Hill Shopping Center, 1959; Colonial Park, 1960 and enclosed in 1970 and expanded with Pomeroy's East in 1974; Pomeroy's West, 1968; the 80-store East Mall 1969; Union Deposit mall, 1973, and Capital City Mall, 1974.

As Pennsy Supply poured interstates, the malls followed. The Harrisburg Expressway was described jokingly in the early '60s as the "Korvette's Expressway." Roadside strips also went up so that the Susquehanna Valley began to rival New Jersey in urban blight.

Motor Inns, as first cousins to malls, filled in available real estate. Actually, the Penn Harris Motor Inn, Harrisburg Host, Hershey Motor Lodge and Sheraton West, to cite four competitors, were in business before the Penn Harris Hotel closed. Hershey added its convention center in 1974 and in 1980 in Harrisburg the Marriott opened.

The President's Task Force on Suburban Problems warned in 1968 of "the contrived homogeneity" that could come. Within a decade Harrisburgers couldn't remember where they had seen a movie, because all the mall theaters look alike.

74.

COLONIZING

AND

CARPETBAGGING

By 1983 the 30-year, cozy colonialization of Harrisburg is so arrantly effective it takes a blatant insult to stir city pride.

Surrounded by a suburbia four times as large, and at least four times as wealthy, Harrisburg is easy pickings for a modern-day subjugation Rudyard Kipling a century ago called "White Man's Burden."

Intruding outsiders don't consider themselves that, as they regard the East and West Shores as "Harrisburg," but not when they explicitly select out-of-city residencies and school districts. Defensively they argue, and often with justification, that the city dwellers are too lethargic to provide civic, cultural and business leadership.

Sixty years ago Harrisburg lorded over suburbia. Today suburbia either ignores or cashes in on Harrisburg however it pleases. As there are no bumptious exploiters, the isolated city often can't tell friend from foe when its advantages are shared but its disadvantages are rejected.

This past July [1983], City Hall's feud with Harristown reached the embarrassing point where a mediating 11-member committee from business and labor was required. When the all-male participants were named, nine didn't live in Harrisburg.

"I recommend that we ask that the names listed in the agreement be withdrawn," said council woman A. Jane Perkins, her voice marinated in sarcasm. "We should then ask them to list appointments which will better reflect our total community: city residents, minorities and females, as well as the important interest and support of non-residents and our 'city fathers.'"

Carpetbagging is an ongoing comedy, as happens after loyalty and esprit de corps break down.

When Harristown charged that Economic Development Director Horace L. Morancie actually lives in Brooklyn, N.Y., where his family lives, Morancie countercharged that Harristown's executive William Keisling lives over the city line in Susquehanna Twp. Meanwhile, Business Administrator David C. Latshaw in a go-around with firefighters noted the union chief didn't live in town. "I wonder if he has looked around and seen how many $10-a-year carpetbaggers he has who are not living here but are drawing very nice salaries," retorted Penbrook's Barry Buskey.

The Buskey rejoinder alluded to the $10 occupational privilege tax, the limit exacted from outsiders with a city livelihood and which the suburban-dominated Legislature doesn't intend to increase.

Morancie, Keisling, Latshaw and Buskey no sooner were done brawling than City Treasurer George E. Kauffman Jr. resigned because he was "harassed" for building a home in Swatara Twp.

Residential realty—or genuine hometown loyalty—began slipping when Harrisburg started slipping. In the early 1960s Councilman Eugene "Shorty" Miller, once the great Penn State quarterback and then Edison

Junior High principal, moved to Susquehanna Twp. and forgot that made him ineligible for Harrisburg elective office.

When Harrisburg teachers in 1976 went on strike, letting pupils roam the streets for 27 days, The Patriot-News discovered that only 180 of the 702 teachers lived in the district and another 180 had their own offspring in other schools not closed. That same year council fought over a City Hall residency requirement, because 475 of the city's 891 employees didn't live in town, including 16 of the 24 bureau chiefs, 80 of the 107 firemen, and 127 of the 168 policemen.

Angry Councilman LeRoy Robinson said of the residency ordinance that lasted only until 1979: "Cities live by the fact that people live in them. By this residency bill, we are telling people who live in the city and who pay taxes that we are concerned about them."

Capital cities are often absentee cities. In business, the Harrisburg Academy, Advertising Associates, Anesthesia Associates, Barber School, Bridge Club, Delivery Services, Dental Services, Display Service, Education Association, Explosives, Gastroenterology Ltd., Hunters and Anglers, Mini Maid, Paper, Truck Body and X-Ray Associates aren't in Harrisburg.

None of the 38 governors and 25 lieutenant governors ever sent children to Harrisburg schools. Milt Shapp vacated the flooded Governor's mansion for six years for a West Shore rental, and at least three-fourths of the top officials in the Thornburgh administration don't live in town. Dick and Ginny Thornburgh broke precedent by registering to vote in Harrisburg and becoming active local citizens.

"It's not how many people live in a city. It's how many people who use it," said James Rouse, developer of Baltimore's Harbor Place. Certainly Harrisburg is "used," pun intended.

75.

ONE OF THE WORLD'S BETTER-KNOWN CHUNKS OF REAL ESTATE

Within a mere 10 years, Harrisburg took three stiff punches on the nose—a civic disaster in the 1969 Riot, a natural disaster in the 1972 Flood, and a technological disaster in the 1979 Three Mile Island incident.

Already caught in competitive attrition with popular suburbia, Harrisburg was most vulnerable to the dire consequences of these emergencies.

"No More Harrisburgs," placards proclaimed in Sydney, Australia, and suddenly this quiet Central Pennsylvania city was more than just a dot on the world map. Harrisburg became the recognized dateline for the nuclear industry after the Unit 2 accident of March 28, 1979. CBS, NBC and ABC still rerun their film clips of the four cooling towers as nuclear symbols and the name "Har-ris-boorg" is intoned across the airwaves, though the city is 13 miles north of TMI.

Comedians playing Harrisburg or Hershey continue to pop off, "This place makes you glow."

Only as a tourist attraction has TMI in Londonderry Twp. been of any genuine value, and even in this regard there is an obvious hesitation to ballyhoo "the festering sore," as it has been called. Wasn't it nice when the area was known only for the Capitol, Hersheypark, the Eisenhower farmhouse and the Dutch hex signs on red barns?

Photogenically and videogenically would that TMI were undistinguishable, but alas, it is marvelously identifiable. Like modern pyramids, the hyperbolid-shaped towers, grayishly foreboding in the mist off the Susquehanna, at 372 feet are not only 100 feet higher than the Capitol, but are the most massive structures on the horizon viewed by visitors arriving at the Harrisburg International Airport. To vivid imaginations, they are the incarnation of the popular 1979 movie, "The China Syndrome."

More words and film about Harrisburg have been distributed because of TMI than the accumulation of all the previous publicity in the city's history.

President Kennedy neglected the 100th anniversary of Lincoln's Gettysburg Address to make his fatal visit to Dallas, but President Carter was compelled to appear at TMI on April Fool's Day of 1969 to reassure a world that the globe's first major nuclear mishap was under control.

TMI is "one of the world's better-known chunks of real estate," as described by the Pennsylvania Historical and Museum Commission, a phrase it has never used about the Capitol in any press dispatch. Of course, TMI is a $2 billion problem, or is it $3 billion?

Oddly, the name dates to only 1963 and a geological survey. The island is only 2.5 miles long but lies about 3 miles from Middletown. Previously it was known as Musser's, Conewago, Elliot's and Duffy's island, and then was of use only to tenant farmers and off-shore bass fishermen.

TMI captured its horror image by a strange misplacement of history. The Susquehanna flowing by its banks during a week in June 1970, as TMI was in the planning stage, almost earned that notoriety. An abandoned coal mine in Cambria County began spilling 17,000 pounds of untreated acid daily into a stream feeding into the river.

"Except for an 11-hour mobilization of the state's resources, unprecedented in scope, the Susquehanna would have been polluted over its entire 500-mile length to the Chesapeake Bay. The bay itself could have been affected," reported The Pittsburg Press. It called the threat of a dead river "an ecological disaster that could make the Santa Barbara oil spill seem mild by comparison."

The commonwealth hurriedly committed more than $1 million to treat 200 miles of the West Branch to Milton, saving the great river and probably the Chesapeake's shellfish industry. Gov. Raymond P. Shafer and Attorney General Fred Speaker were the unheralded heroes.

The media unfortunately almost missed the rescue story, busy as it was in an election year documenting another state budget mess in which the commonwealth was losing $1 million a day as angry politicians put off adopting a personal income tax.

76.

"WE SURVIVED TMI"

The Harrisburg area was given its costliest mishap in history when a pilot-operated relief valve was left open for 140 minutes at Three Mile Island. An immediate 11-day crisis in 1979 ensued when 133 tons of uranium fuel threatened possible nuclear meltdown.

The full tab for TMI should be astronomical, though at first the power plant was promoted as an economic asset, not a liability.

In the last five years alone, the TMI cleanup bill amounts to $435 million, or the equivalent of educating all the public school pupils in Dauphin and Cumberland counties for that period.

When the General Public Utilities Corp. in 1966 began planning for TMI and 2,200 jobs, most Harrisburgers welcomed the project. The community had been hard hit by the record 116-day steel strike in the late 1950s. In late 1964 the Defense Department began phasing out Olmsted Air Force Base, stripping away 15,000 jobs.

TMI's Unit I was licensed April 19, 1974, and that Sept. 2 commercial operations began. Down river in York County, Peach Bottom already was generating 25 million kilowatt hours of nuclear electricity a day. Plans were under way for more plants upstream at Berwick and Meshoppen.

Protests against Three Mile Island continued long after the accident in 1979. Nearly 40% of the residents within fifteen miles of the reactor had evacuated during the crisis.

"The Susquehanna Valley is fast becoming the nation's most concentrated region of nuclear energy generation," editorialized The Patriot-News in 1976. "Just as Thomas Edison himself in the early 1880s came to Sunbury to establish the world's first central generating station and the earliest electric companies were started in Harrisburg and along the Susquehanna, so the nuclear energy developers have spotted the great river as an invaluable resource."

Six years later, the paper saw it differently: "In a sense we have become hostage to TMI…Nuclear power has become such an intrusion into the day-to-day life of people, with the potential to create monumental havoc, it is time to consider whether all of this is not too much a price to pay."

The great expectations were dashed March 28, 1979, or 89 days after TMI's Unit 2 went on line while Unit 1 was being refueled.

When a hydrogen bubble was reported developing in the TMI reactor vessel, 144,000 of 370,000 persons living within 15 miles of TMI evacuated—a rush that outdid the 1863 panic before the Battle of Gettysburg. Pandemonium almost occurred as the bubble hovered over 36,816 nuclear fuel rods and that "Black Friday" at 10 a.m. City Hall's civil defense alarm accidentally was sounded.

For two centuries the Harrisburg area had an old-world Dutch hypersensitivity to fear and rumor anyway, with a past that included witchcraft, medicine shows and fakirs, end-of-the-worlders, flying saucers and assorted superstitions. There were critics of Jonas Salk's anti-polio vaccine, and it took Harrisburg 30 years of brawling before it fluoridated its drinking water in 1972.

But with the TMI's live dramatization of "The China Syndrome," for once the local credulous and sophisticates were united in their apprehension.

Three years later, the uneasiness continued. Voters in Dauphin, Cumberland and Lebanon counties were 36,688 to 19,130, or 67 percent, against restarting Unit 1 until Unit 2 was decontaminated.

Once such a promise, TMI became the community's leading headache, as well as an economic liability. In his 1982 thwarted bid for the legislature, Joe O'Connor observed of TMI, "Its district would like New Jersey to annex it or have the dump trucks build a hill around it so people could protect their psychology."

Yet there is something to be said for Harrisburg's stubbornness and serene sensibilities. Quick as the community could panic, it also had the resiliency to relax. It may loath that world-famous nuclear mega-bete noire, but it also ignores it. The citizenry seems to have assimilated the monster, defanged it and de-frightened itself.

TMI might always be there, but only curious outsiders gape at it these days. The locals when traveling often will say, "I'm from Harrisburg, that's near Three Mile Island," in a stiff-upper-lip tone to indicate they're making the best of such a hazardous-duty existence.

77.

32.8 FEET, 650 BILLION GALLONS

The patrons of the Silver Lake Inn, near Pinchot Park, were celebrating the arrival of spring on Wednesday night, June 21, 1972, when heavy rains began outside. One fellow peered out the barroom door to see what was happening. A fish flapped in and landed on the dance floor. Or so that fish story goes.

A 90-year-old widow on Harrisburg's Catherine Street, where she had lived since 1904 through three major floods in her lifetime, said, "I was busy writing letters to some friends and preparing some bills when I realized the water had reached my ankles on the first floor.

The late M. Louise Aughinbaugh, daughter of the leading local jeweler of the turn of the century, had been a beloved school teacher, a patroness of the arts, and the town's only self-declared "socialite." When firemen carried her from her home, the protesting, frail grande dame warned them not to be "bold" and "pinch" her. In the rescue boat, Miss Aughinbaugh jollily informed a British television reporter that her Second Street now looked like Venice.

Mayor Harold A. Swenson and his wife Elsie, surprised by the flood like everybody else, set up command headquarters at a dry City Hall, but went four days without a solid meal. "After you have everybody out, all you can do is stand at the water's edge and wait," said a frustrated Swenson.

Future Mayor Stephen R. Reed, then 22 and the county head of assistance and vital statistics, lost 12 pounds evacuating himself and his mother from Second Street. That accomplished, he became one of the genuine heroes of the volunteer River Rescue effort.

The 1972 Hurricane Agnes Flood was catastrophic, probably twice as damaging as its 1936 predecessor which was regarded as "The 100-year flood." Swenson said the 1972 Flood hit Harrisburg with an impact that "3,000 to 5,000 fires would have."

Water swirled into almost 6,000 area houses, but not one in the city was covered by the federal-guaranteed flood insurance plan, including the new Governor's Mansion. The Red Cross counted 83 houses destroyed, at least a $5 million loss. All of Steelton's West Side was wiped out forever, while some of Harrisburg's Cameron Street apparently was permanently destroyed.

The Red Cross spent $1.28 million in the community and had 339 shelters. Harris Haven North, the temporary mobile-home settlement by the Farm Show, still had 212 families six months later at Christmas. The major complaint in the government-issued trailers was that many leaked when it rained.

At least 616 small businesses were either destroyed or heavily wrecked, and 12,000 industrial and commercial establishments suffered according to Dun and Bradstreet. Business damages were at least $200 million, with a $36 million inventory loss.

The flood was the last thing Harrisburg needed, only three years after the 1969 Riot. City government suffered $3 million in damage; Dauphin County schools, $1.2 million, with the city schools half of that; HACC $500,000, and Lykens, $5 million, including the loss of all seven bridges over the Wiconisco Creek to the borough.

Governor Milton Shapp was not prematurely evacuated from the executive mansion during the 1972 flood. The mansion was not covered by flood insurance, nor were 6,000 other houses.

The Enola Yards, Bethlehem Steel, Harrisburg Steel and many businesses in Highspire, West Fairview and elsewhere were covered. The Patriot-News' press was 28 feet underwater. There were 132 abandoned autos in Harrisburg alone, 45 million Pennsylvania lottery tickets in storage at the airport were destroyed, $3 million worth of warehouse liquor was spoiled, and mail delivery was put back a week.

Harrisburg seldom gets hurricanes and nationally it had been the quietest hurricane season in 42 years. The winter's snowfall was below normal.

Agnes came gently. She passed over, reversed her field and hovered about, carrying 28 trillion gallons of water. On June 21 she unloaded 5.39 inches; on June 22, 7.16 inches, and as she left on June 23, a parting fifth of an inch. The river at first was at 4.82 feet, or well below its 17-foot flood stage, but by Saturday, June 24, the Susquehanna was a small ocean, cresting at 32.8 feet, or 3.6 feet higher than the 1936 Flood.

As the Paxton Creek rose at a record 6 feet an hour, the Susquehanna swirled 650 billion gallons of water past Harrisburg on June 24, in comparison to her normal daily flow of 23 billion.

78.

OUT OF THE MUCK AND THE MIRE

Five months after the 1972 Flood, Mayor Harold A. Swenson, in presenting his 1973 budget to City Council, gave his usual 12-minute speech, but it was the best in his career.

The city, he said, "suffered its greatest disaster in history and it survived. A weak, wobbly, dying city could not have done that, but Harrisburg was able to withstand a near-fatal punch and has made a recovery which has been impressive in scope and pace. Individuals and businesses have pulled themselves out of the muck and the mire with a confidence and determination which tells much about this community's stamina and the character of its people."

There was Old Testament grit to that effort, but the difference was that the children of Harrisburg weren't the chosen people in the Nixon, Ford, Carter and Reagan America.

Swenson let fly a marvelous wisecrack when half of Downtown was under water and Cameron and Second streets were navigable streams, yet there were hordes of curiosity seekers. "It takes 400 National Guardsmen, 60 state police and the entire Harrisburg police force to keep people out of Downtown Harrisburg who a week ago said it wasn't safe to go Downtown anymore," quipped the Mayor.

A disaster does bring publicity and to its victims it often temporarily stimulates their untapped energies and their latent sense of brotherhood. "When the community suffers tragedy, its people seem to unite, almost without call, and display courage, as they have done in 1972, that honors them," The Patriot-News editorialized.

All that unity and courage did play a role in Harrisburg's unofficial acceptance of the Harristown Plan six months after the flood. Actually the 1969 Riot touched off the first thinking about a possible organized Renaissance II, and the flood three years later only convinced more persons that the rebuilding scheme was by now a dire necessity.

Beyond the Harristown Plan, the city didn't gain a thing from Hurricane Agnes. Being in the floodplain didn't make much of Harrisburg any more favored a spot for relocation by a single suburbanite or businessman. The additional impoverishment created by the flood unfortunately also coincided with federal and state cutbacks in aid to the poor, the dependent and the urban-dispossessed, as well as to urban redevelopment altogether.

It would have been better, the locals joked, if during World War II the Eighth Air Force, under Pennsylvania's Gen. Tooey Spaatz, had bombed Harrisburg to smithereens. That sort of calamity, not indigenous flooding nor riots nor even the latter-day Three Mile Island episode, could touch the souls and pocketbooks of Congress.

When Agnes swept out to sea, she also took city businesses and residents who never returned.

The graffiti-like stains of floodwaters remain a decade more. More insidiously damaging—perhaps more destructive than the immediate havoc Agnes caused—was the emigration she sparked.

Much of the Jewish community, established for a century and by now the core of Harrisburg's leadership and professionalism, hurried to the safer hills of the affluent developments along the Linglestown Road. Harrisburg school enrollment dropped by 818 students that fall, its second greatest loss exceeded only by the exit after the 1969 Riot.

Harrisburg always lacked flood protection. The year after the flood, Washington had a plan—similar to the one advanced 36 years earlier after the 1936 Flood. The project would cost $28 million and be completed by 1982. Nothing was done. By 1978 the proposals were up to $80 million, and by 1983 there was a scaled-down version costing $123 million. This would the completed 20 years after the 1972 Flood and a broke Harrisburg's share would be an impossible $43 million.

Besieged by flooding military and social deficits of their own, the White House and Congress didn't want to hear about torrents in Harrisburg.

The results of the 1972 Flood plague Harrisburg yet and contribute to hard times. But pundits and politicians don't deign to make the connections, preferring to think of the recent past as long gone and the flood as one of those episodes triumphed over by the valorous American spirit. So little is done, and the next flood will swirl down the same paths the 1889, 1902, 1936 and 1972 floods did.

79.

THE FANCIEST TRASH COLLECTION

Three months before Tropical Storm Agnes hit in 1972, Harrisburg got embroiled in one of its favorite old commotions: "pull-out trash" vs. "push-out trash." It was political garbage, literally.

A dismayed Mayor Harold A. Swenson, though facing re-election the following year, refused to sign an opulent ordinance reinstating "pull-out trash." Since 1968, the city had limited its black trashmen to collecting garbage no farther than 40 feet from the curb. That was "push-out trash," meaning occupants exercised by lugging their trash cans from the backs and sides of their homes weekly to help the trashmen and also save tax dollars.

Swenson maintained Harrisburg couldn't afford to return to valet trash collection. The city already was paying $1 million a year in mortgage payments for its "Rolls-Royce incinerator," not yet operating. Like 10-cent millionaires, Harrisburgers were going broke but weren't about to give up maid service.

The "push-out trash" rule also might have encouraged citizen responsibility for municipal cleanliness, as the once "City Beautiful" was becoming the "City Ugly."

There seemed no way, however, to remove the blinders from the eyes of Harrisburg and suburbia. Beyond the myopia of civic indifference, almost everywhere was clutter, litter, blight and monotonous uniformity smeared across what landscape planner Warren Manning 70 years before called one of the handsomest natural settings in the world for an urban community. The Carlisle Pike and Route 22 weren't far behind Seventh Street in their hideousness. As Front Street was being ravaged so were the major arteries to the most exclusive residential suburbs.

The City Beautiful reformers in 1910 argued convincingly that conservation and cleanliness meant profits.

By the 1970s, especially after the 1972 flood, Harrisburg needed all the profits it could get. Moody's Investors Service wasn't impressed by the sputtering incinerator nor "pull-out trash," and it lowered the city's bond rating from AAA to Baa.

While City Council opted for luxury trash collection, one councilman and a public works official were behind $11,000 in their city water, sewer and trash bills, and 8,400 other property owners were in the hole for $2 million over the years. Accounts receivable for real estate taxes hit the $700,000 mark, with the Republican Club, among others, in arrears.

After 1965, Harrisburg joined all America in rushing into debt—the federal and state governments, corporations, mortgaged homeowners and credit-card consumers. In the land of the once-cautious Puritans and the once-timid Quakers, all government by 1982 was $2 trillion in the red and the private sector, not including corporate debt, owed $1.6 trillion. Even conservative Hershey Foods Corp. between 1974 and 1982 had its long-term debt expand almost fourfold, but its $140 million was moderate compared to many businesses' IOUs.

Harrisburg was on a spree, at the inopportune time it was losing business and citizenry.

Tax-supported municipal debt by 1979 amounted to $25.18 million, up from $8.8 million in 1965. City Hall's unfunded pension liabilities sped to $29.8 million by 1982. The school district required $12 million for repairs while it already owed another minimal $12 million for its 1975 Middle School and $1.6 million in 1977 to cover under-estimated expenditures and bond costs. Harristown was into at least $150 million, but that was backed up, like collateral, by long-term leases of nearly $500 million in rentals by the commonwealth and Bell Telephone.

When The Evening News' Don Sarvey in 1977 figured the Harrisburg debt per resident, he came up with a surprising $3,185—as compared to the commonwealth's statewide per capita debt of $330.

Although most of Harrisburg's debt bore interest rates under 8 percent, when the prime rate was twice as high, staggering obligations like these weren't advisable. To attract potential business and residents, Harrisburg should be competitive with suburbia, even have a tax edge. What smart money would buy into long-term indebtedness like that?

Offsetting the dire economics, Harrisburg boasted it had the fanciest trash collection.

80.

DEBT CRUNCH

A corporation without debt probably is poorly managed, for it can't be doing much investing in its future. But a community with too much debt and built-in obligations severely curtails its daily operations.

By 1983, Harrisburg's City Hall and schools owed $1.50 for every $1 taken in, while Hershey Food's net sales were 10 times its long-term debt.

As Harrisburg began Renaissance I in 1900, it could afford to increase its borrowing and expenditures one hundred-fold because it was one of the nation's lowest-taxed and indebted cities. By the 1970s, in contrast, the city was hard-pressed to survive financially day by day.

The Swenson administration at its outset in 1970 estimated $75 million was needed to redo public works. By 1980, water improvement alone had a price tag of $30 million, or two years' worth of the entire city budget. The 1972 Flood knocked out the City Island filtration plant, one of the prizes of Renaissance I, and left the city with a single 42-inch main from Dehart Dam in Clark's Valley to provide the necessary 15 million gallons of water daily.

The DeHart system, named for the late Councilman William DeHart, opened July 1, 1940, but since then received no major modernizations nor little upkeep. Surplus water rents were put in the city budget to keep it solvent. When Gov. Milton J. Shapp made acreage available next to the state hospital for an auxiliary reservoir, the city lacked the credit to build it and repair the water system.

Flood protection seems out of the question. At least $43 million in city money is needed to match anything the Army Corps of Engineers could get from Congress.

Unfunded city pensions for employees, the police and firemen climbed to being a $26 million liability by 1973, and a decade later to almost $30 million. That Harrisburg had 911 full-time employees in 1981, as compared to Lancaster's 595 and Altona's 556, partly was due to its being a capital city and also to the stalwart tradition of patronage politics Simon Cameron began in 1824.

The School District couldn't afford anything more after getting the Middle School in 1976. The city, meanwhile, went without a stadium, a convention center, a library of its own or a tourist bureau. As early as 1973, the Dauphin County commissioners backed out of sharing the new City Hall—that $12.3 million Market Square edifice occupied on the 10th anniversary of Hurricane Agnes, no less.

In most cases Harrisburg was not extravagant, though the definition of that term in a Dutch community depends upon whether a deep conservative or just a plain conservative is speaking.

In 14 years, 1969 through 1983, city property taxes went up 7.8 percent annually and Dauphin County taxes by 3.4 percent. The national consumer price index, in contrast, was up 10.04 percent annually in the 1970s. The 1 percent wage tax, shared with the schools, came in 1966, the year after the city budget hit $5 million. As the budget leaped across $10 million, the split property tax on land and improvements took effect in 1974. By 1981, the budget was over $15 million.

The School District kept a faster pace in taxes at 8.3 percent annually, and its budgets were $10 million in 1968, $20 million in 1975, and $30 million in 1983. But between 1965 and 1979, the commonwealth's general fund zipped at an annual average of 26 percent.

Though Harrisburg had extraordinary costs, like incinerator and parking garage deficits, riot expenditures and school busing, it didn't drown in red ink. In the pre-Reaganomics era, help was available: $24 million, mostly federal dollars, for 1972 Flood renewal; $1.4 million in 1973 federal school grant and a $1.2 million City Hall revenue-sharing: a $1.2 million public-works grant, and in 1981 a $900,000 federal oil-entitlement check, etc. But by 1981, President Reagan and Governor Thornburgh were cutting back on such outside assistance.

The new self-reliance hurt. The town by 1978 had 20 percent of its residents below the poverty level and 60 percent of its pupils from poverty families. The property tax landed on modest homes, three out of four built before 1940.

The crunch was vividly illustrated during a 1981 legislature inquiry to switch school taxes from a property base to family income. A Harrisburg educator testified it would be to the city's disadvantage, as the aging housing was worth more to tax collectors than the meager household incomes.

81.

THE INFERNAL FURNACE

It was Mayor Al Straub in a mellifluous moment in 1969 who called it "the Rolls-Royce of incinerators." But even Straub never suspected the solid-waste flambeau eventually would cost more than a new city hall or even the HACC campus.

Only the gilded West Shore province could really afford such a luxury, and it didn't want to be partners. "There's plenty of room for garbage for at least 30 to 40 years," a West Shore township manager explained. One answer was to truck West Shore waste by interstate highway to distant landfills. As a classic Evening News headline put it, Mayor Reed pleaded: "City Invites West Shore To Send Trash."

Nothing could symbolize the financial futility and constant malfunctioning of the modern American city like Harrisburg's incinerator. It's the champ, the stumblebum cousin of TMI.

When council OK'd the project on Sept. 20, 1966, the cost was to be $4.5 million. When the city began paying, Dec. 15, 1969—though the first test burnings weren't until 34 months later—the bond issue was $12.5 million, or $20 million when amortized. After repeated breakdowns, the incinerator's cost became $30 million. That figure might not include 1983's estimated needed repairs of $3 million, plus a projected $1.7 million deficit.

Straub should have said the incinerator was 400 Rolls-Royces.

Mayor Swenson called it "a facility that far exceeds our needs and our ability to pay." Built to handle 720 tons daily, it could torch all the junk between Millersburg, Carlisle and Palmyra. No landfills should be necessary, but within the shadows of the incinerator there were many—such as Lower Paxton's giving off methane gas. To pay for itself, Harrisburg's furnace should run at 85 percent capacity, but usually it has been at 60 percent.

The Lower Dauphin Solid Waste Authority, supposedly in business in 1964 but to this day still studying the "garbage explosion," as early as 1975 called the incinerator a "white elephant." By then the incinerator was notorious for its poor design, faulty equipment, inefficient operation and malfunctioning salvage. At one point, 90 specific deficiencies were cited. There weren't enough pressure gauges and some didn't work properly—a prophecy to come of TMI downstream.

As technology was taking Americans to the moon, the Harrisburg incinerator couldn't effectively dispose of an old washing machine. In 1978 it even had a $593,000 explosion and fire, which insurance covered at $549,000.

Harrisburg has had a long history of smoldering Gehennas. An early dump faced today's Polyclinic Medical Center. After World War II, Wildwood Park became the dump. In 1963 there was a rubber-tire fire and the black smoke screened Beaufort Farms from the Blue Mountains. When the stench threatened the executive suites of the state Health Department, the city was ordered to close the dump, just as the HACC campus and the new Lucknow Industrial Yard opened.

Susquehanna Twp. held its nose and voted as early as May 12, 1966 not to join Harrisburg in the incinerator project. Other suburbanites remained uninterested, so in the midst of the 1967 mayoralty election the city committed itself.

"Nothing could symbolize the financial futility and constant malfunctioning of the modern American city like Harrisburg's incinerator," wrote Beers in 1983. It caught fire itself in 1978.

The 60-acre Cameron Farm was purchased and the court rejected citizen objections by Rep. George Gekas, Jim Rowland Jr., Sebastian Natale and Joseph Klein. Meanwhile, Cumberland County "generally approved" building its own $7.2 million incinerator, but Mechanicsburg said not near its beautiful borough so the West Shorers let Harrisburg be the goat.

An episode at the incinerator's 1979 cave-in epitomized all the comedy and tragedy of this diabolically spendthrift infernal furnace. As the earth parted, former Councilman Jack R. Karper, managing the incinerator, hurriedly rescued the garbage reserve so there would be trash to feed the flames and make steam for PP&L. Explained a jubilant Karper, "Thank God we saved the garbage. It represents dollars."

82.

RACIAL SEPARATISM

It is one of the most depressed and deteriorated communities I have ever seen—houses in disrepair, crowded, dirty streets," wrote an unidentified board member of the Methodist Mission. "A survey taken a year or so before I came showed 108 children in one block."

The town was Harrisburg, and the year was 1954.

Until almost 1960, Washington and Harrisburg had two things in common: Grandiose Capitols and rickety, wooden-shack black slums within a block of them.

Time and progress stood still for the Harrisburg black community. The inner-city neighborhoods were only more congested in 1900 than what Charles Dickens saw here in 1842. Facsimiles of such Harrisburg poverty lasted a century after Dickens. So-called suburban Edgemont, beyond the state hospital in Susquehanna Twp., didn't get water and sewer lines until 1970, replacing outdoor plumbing and a private well system 66 percent polluted.

There was no real organized Harrisburg black community during Renaissance I. There were just 4,500 blacks in 1910, fewer than 5,000 by 1920, and it was only in 1960 that the black head count exceeded 15,000.

A subservient class embedded in poverty, the early-day black minority was as contained as it was neglected. What ethnologist John Bodnar found true of Steelton applied to Harrisburg: "Neither blacks nor immigrants ever escaped blue-collar work in any large numbers." Eight out of 10 spent their lifetimes in it. Until World War II, many did odd jobs and lacked steady employment. Career blacks scarcely existed. It was the rare black who graduated from high school. Bodnar noted that Steelton High was ahead of its time in having almost 40 blacks graduate between 1880 and 1910.

As late as 1954, only 98 blacks were employed in state government. Black professionals in Harrisburg were limited to a handful of physicians, lawyers, dentists and pharmacists, and there was maybe a dozen black businessmen. Before 1949 no hospital had a black staff doctor.

With its paucity of self-employed and middle-class families, the Harrisburg black community was as restricted as if apartheid were law. For example: Pennsylvania desegregated its schools in 1881 and adopted modern compulsory education in 1893, but these laws were meaningless without a black literate class to insist upon their implementations.

Early Harrisburg ostracized—rather than overtly discriminated against—the unequal blacks. Ostracism was a cunning form of Jim Crowism, or a process of rude dismissal and indifference. Whites didn't want outright control over blacks, because it was more effective to retain for themselves the perquisites of social acceptance and upward mobility.

Harrisburg's racial separatism was patterned after Philadelphia's, not after Baltimore's more congenial southern brand of selectivity.

So entrenched was the racial stratification that Harrisburg before World War II had few duly recognized blacks.

The list is almost complete with William Howard Day, the state clerk with a master's degree on the school board; Turner Cooper, the freed slave who built homes on Allison Hill; Peter S. Blackwell, the Steelton editor and councilman; W. Justin Carter Sr., the lawyer from Richmond who became boss Ed Beidleman's political secretary; Dr. Charles H. Crampton, the William Penn High trainer and Republican leader; Professor Charles F. Howard, principal of Steelton's Hygienic School for decades; Professor John Paul Scott, the leading city black educator for 47 years; and H. Edwin Parson, the first black druggist whose daughter, Sara Alyce Parson Wright, in 1974 became the national YWCA's executive director. Among the few black women of eminence, but not affluence, was the black YW's Ella Frazier.

The strongest bond the black community had was in its closely knit churches, some of which went back to the early 1800s, and had been stations on the Underground Railroad. But without a substantial middle and professional class, the local blacks couldn't make a dent in Harrisburg's virtually impregnable racial barriers.

Earlier than most states, Pennsylvania in 1935 adopted an open-accommodations law. The impetus for that admittedly much-disregarded legislation was that the splendid Penn Harris Hotel, facing the Capitol no less, wouldn't rent rooms to black school principals attending a conference here. A quarter century later, national tennis champion Althea Gibson came to town and couldn't get lodging either.

83.

LIFE FOR HARRISBURG BLACKS

Life for Harrisburg blacks went on for decades much the same. The 1930s differed from the 1880s only in that the hard menial labor was a little less physical and sweaty.

A majority of Harrisburg blacks dropped out of school to become laborers, cooks, chambermaids, stewards or chauffeurs for Front Streeters, or the beaded-browed steelworkers who did the messy job of brick-lining the open hearths. In earlier days, blacks were barbers, livery-stable keepers, blacksmiths, cobblers and hired hands.

Many blacks came into the community as imported strikebreakers at the Steelton mill in 1891 and again in 1919. Their reward was to stand on the curb in 1925 and watch the Ku Klux Klan parade up Harrisburg's Market Street.

The blacks forged their own culture. They had their all-star baseball Black Giants and the semi-pro football Harrisburg Trojans. They had their churches and cemeteries, their social clubs and saloons. The "white-only" ban at many membership swimming pools and golf clubs persisted until the 1970s.

When big-name entertainers came to town—such as Earl "Fatha" Hines, the Pittsburgh pianist playing the Chestnut Street Auditorium for a black gathering in 1935—they didn't book rooms at white hotels or eat in the better restaurants.

Progress didn't happen. Head-nodding, not heading up, was the lot for the Harrisburg blacks. As an underclass, they were expected to remain stable, stagnant and servile. A true black middle class didn't emerge, and as a result there was limited Harrisburg-bred black family leadership. By the 1970s and 1980s when the blacks began to gain local professional and political acceptance—such as president of HACC, city school superintendent, and president of the medical society—probably fewer than half these respected black leaders were native Harrisburgers.

For too many generations the Harrisburg blacks had been demoralized and stifled, especially in educational advancement and business.

A vibrant Harrisburg Harlem never developed. Black artistic talent was lost. Status symbols such as a black country club weren't developed, though such a club was briefly discussed in the late 1950s—after the noted success of the Jewish community's Blue Ridge Country Club, an enterprise established in the early 1930s by Dr. Ben Gainsburg, Ed Schleisner and Jake Miller.

That true liberation hadn't occurred was reflected in the marketplace, where the jobs available to blacks usually were subservient in nature, subsisting in pay and dead-end in career opportunity.

The ghettoes told the story of how confining racial ostracism was. Many of these black neighborhoods outlasted the white railroaders' and the Front Streeters' domains. "Integration is simply the time between the arrival of the first black and the departure of the last white," social organizer Saul Alinsky once quipped, but the Harrisburg area didn't share much of this modern American racial "block-busting" tradition. The dark-town sections remained dark for generations.

It was rare that a black would be found outside of Harrisburg, Steelton, Carlisle or rural-like Edgemont. Perry County in 1970 had 100 fewer blacks than it had in the Civil War era, and during the 1970s its non-white population declined again, from 35 to 28. Cumberland County lost 50 blacks in the 1960s and gained only 655 in the 1970s.

No one ever preached deliberate segregation in the Harrisburg area. The flirtations of the Klan amounted to nothing. Overt bigotry was neither condoned nor widely practiced.

Earlier this year internationally known, white jazz singer Susannah McCorkle remembered Harrisburg as an alienated town when she was a student at John Harris High School in 1960-63. Her father was an anthropologist for the state Health Department, and the family found Harrisburg "unpleasant." Blacks and whites didn't mix. "There was nothing we could do together outside of school," she said.

84.

PLANTATION POLITICS

AND

NIBS FRANKLIN

Harrisburg specialized for decades in "Plantation Politics"—named for the politicos' hangout, the Plantation Room of the Penn Harris Hotel, and an applicable term for a community only 36 miles from the Mason-Dixon Line.

By the late 1960s, "Plantation Politics" meant "$2 and a swig of booze," as scornful black leaders said, for a promised vote and menial patronage.

"Plantation Politics" also gave Harrisburg well-deserved notoriety for fraudulent voting, a reputation that went back to the 15th Amendment in 1870 guaranteeing black franchise. Democrats then opposed civil rights, knowing Simon Cameron's Republicans would sweep the inner-city wards for every available vote but would do little to earn black support.

When Cameron's henchmen said Democrats had enticed a few of the city's new eligible black voters, the old Patriot and Union, then a virulently Democratic sheet, fired a blunderbuss: "Not a single Negro vote was offered in the City of Harrisburg and none ever will be as long as the white men in this community have any say in the matter."

The blacks and the "Party of Lincoln" conspired in setting up zero wards, phantom voters, ghosts and dead souls. A favorite trick was "400 votes and six pages of the calendar." The first six voters would stuff calendar pages into the ballot box, so their real marked ballots could be rotated for the 400 voters. The precinct would tally a 400-0 Republican victory, plus six calendar pages.

All this action, well into Harve Taylor's day, produced GOP triumphs, kept insurgents from capturing primaries, and strengthened Dauphin County in the statewide Republican circles.

A showcase figure like the Hon. William Howard Day became the North's first black city school board president in 1891—courtesy of the GOP machine.

Former Democratic Mayor Vance McCormick was popular with blacks but when he sought the governorship in 1914 he was a threat to Republicans. So he lost his own Harrisburg by 2,259 votes, and 663 of that margin came from the black 7th and 8th wards.

Boss Ed Beidleman going for the state Senate seat told a black leader it wouldn't look proper if he received 100 percent of the vote in a Cameron Street precinct. He got it anyway. "Boss, they love you too much to listen to reason," the ward heeler explained.

As a sidelight, this controlled politics didn't bother the flourishing prostitution trade.

"Plantation Politics" were so powerful that the system didn't buckle under Roosevelt's New Deal in the 1930s nor in the 1950s when Democratic Gov. George M. Leader gave blacks their first top state jobs.

City sanitation inspector Charles Franklin, as supreme field boss, earned mention in the Rev. Franklin L. Henley's charge that an "immoral environment" existed in the bought ghetto wards. Called "Nibs" by the whites and "Nip" by his fellow blacks, the burly Franklin became a legend. He departed this life in 1965 while under indictment for tampering with and "injuring" a voting machine in his 7th Ward.

Nip followed in the tradition of Charlie Osborne, who in 1929 produced a 609-0 vote. Under protest, Osborne re-fixed the fix to be 607-2.

In 1947 Franklin engineered a 400-0 vote in the 2nd Precinct of the 7th Ward and in the 5th Precinct he produced 976 votes from a 953-voter registration list. The next year, Nip served 30 days for assault and battery at the polls. In 1963 he had 12 winners for nine offices receive an identical 627 votes while the losers got between 52 and 54 votes. Best yet, he even had four referendum questions fixed.

Franklin's last election in 1964 was his masterpiece. For Taylor's losing primary, he gave his old pal a 640-4 vote. Of the four wayward voters, he told reporters in his husky voice, "I'm going to find out who they were." Then in November, he recorded a 378-303 count for Sen. Barry Goldwater in Sibletown, the nation's only pro-Goldwater vote in a black neighborhood. What Harrisburg white financiers would die for, Nip Franklin received gratis—front-page mention in The Wall Street Journal.

85.

DISMANTLING TOKENISM

When Harrisburg's long-standing racial ostracism finally began to dissolve in the 1960s, it was outside pressure that set the gradual change in motion.

The national civil rights movement made the major impact, opening Harrisburg's eyes to how far behind the times it was. For once the white hegemony in the city and the suburbs was criticized and put on the defensive.

The all-white Harrisburg Fire Department fell first, in June of 1963—a century after the Battle of Gettysburg. White firefighters enjoyed a strange local distinction. Though Isaiah Parson had become the first black policeman 60 years before, Harrisburgers felt it improper to integrate the fire stations. Actually, hiring a few black firemen took place without incident—Harrisburg's usual aplomb in not letting historic changes disturb the serenity.

After there were 2,000 civil rights demonstrations in more than 300 American cities in the spring of 1963, Harrisburg recognized the trend. The Mayor's Human Relations Committee was established that July of 1963, and on Aug. 3 the city had its first Freedom March. The parade up Walnut Street was conspicuously impassive. It was more important that it happened than that anything interesting didn't happen. Harrisburg blacks proved to be as laid-back as Harrisburg whites. The most outspoken remark to the 600 marchers came from the Rev. Franklin Henley: "It certainly would be a real novelty in Harrisburg to see a Negro reading an electric meter or a gas meter."

Dismantling tokenism had a long way to go. In public housing, de facto segregation existed since 1938 when the William Howard Day Homes were built and named for that distinguished black man.

But it wasn't until the Jackson-Lick Apartments in 1962 that a second black was honored. C. Sylvester Jackson, another Republican, had worked for the Boyd family estate and also was executive secretary of the nearby all-black Forster Street YMCA, which in the mid-1960s was razed for the new Camp Curtin YMCA Branch. Jackson was active when the black Y started in 1919 and then in 1928, with leaders like Dr. Charles H. Crampton, Dr. Morris H. Layton, W. Justin Carter and Walter J. Hooper, raised $125,000 for its building, $5000 of that a gift from Rep. I. H. Doutrich.

Public-housing integration, both in name and fact, wasn't realized until 1971 when the $2.5 million Morrison Tower was dedicated on Chestnut Street. Clarence E. Morrison, a young black lawyer from Charleston, S.C., had been the first black assistant district attorney and then president of the Harrisburg Housing Authority. Morrison moved to Susquehanna Twp., and in June of 1981 was appointed by Gov. Dick Thornburgh to be the first black Dauphin County judge, and that November he was elected by an overwhelming vote.

Steelton, meanwhile, opened the county housing project, Cole Crest Apartments, named for Samuel Cole, one of the authority's officers from 1958 to 1976. Cole, a 1919 Steelton High graduate and once a mill worker, was principal of the Hygienic School for 23 years and also served two terms on the school board.

The Martin Luther King Jr. assassination in April of 1968 goaded Harrisburg blacks to assert the day of second-class citizenship was over.

Only a year before, City Hall got its first black official, Glenn E. Williams Jr., 40, an accountant, as city controller. His father had been doorman at the Penn Harris Hotel. Young Glenn, with a world of potential, became Harrisburg's first black to try for statewide public office in 1972, but lost the state treasurer post in a Democratic sweep. At 52 in 1979, he died of cancer.

The year after the Dr. King assassination, Stanley R. Lawson became the first black councilman, at the same time Mrs. Miriam Menaker became the first Jewish and the first woman council person. The following month, James H. Rowland Sr. became president of the school board. Rowland had been president of the West Virginia State Board of Education and subsequently would be president of the Pennsylvania board, the only American ever to head two such top state educational agencies. He also was a founding father of HACC.

As a respected voice in the white and black communities, Rowland in 1971 made a bid to be the first elected black judge, but he was eliminated in a crowded field of primary candidates. In retrospect, Jim Rowland proved to be a decade ahead of the community's acceptance of a black in a black robe.

86.

THE WORLD

OF THE

MOOSE LODGE

The fervor of civil rights in the 1960s and 1970s was vivid at the state Capitol, made acceptable modifications in the City of Harrisburg, and had virtually no observable impact upon suburbia. So go the three worlds of the Harrisburg community.

Because so many Harrisburgers are cautious, dutiful civil servants, they don't take to the ramparts—usually they don't even know there the ramparts are.

When the welfare righters in 1970s, with partial justification, became incensed at the state government, it was a Philadelphian, not a Harrisburger, leading the picketing, though the city riot had happened less than a year before. Roxanne Jones made headlines by throwing her slipper through the transom of Gov. Raymond P. Shafer's office door, and she ended up serving five days in the Dauphin County Jail for disturbing the peace.

Raging Roxanne was a charismatic figure, and so was Commonwealth Secretary C. DeLores Tucker, who became the first black woman primary candidate for governor in 1978 after Gov. Milton J. Shapp fired her in a fracas for accepting high fees for her oratory. Roxanne and Cynthia De-Lores no more dented Harrisburgers' consciousness than if they had been visiting vaudevillians from Erie.

The most celebrated case was when K. Leroy Irvis took on the Harrisburg Moose Lodge 107 on State Street, just down from the Capitol where Irvis was employed as Democratic majority leader in the House of Representatives. It was Dec. 29, 1969, that Irvis, a legislator for 10 years and holding the post Thaddeus Stevens once had, took a few colleagues to the Moose for a late dinner. He was denied service, and before he was finished, Attorney Irvis had the Moose before the U.S. Supreme Court.

After the court by a 6–3 vote upheld the Moose to restrict its private accommodations to members, Irvis in his prophet-like demeanor predicted America if it went on this way would have black massacres within a decade. Discouraged, he threatened to retire from politics, but he stayed on and in 1977 became the nation's first black speaker of a state House of Representatives.

The Patriot-News commented on the Irvis case: "The truth is that today the President of the United States can dine at the Grand Hall in Peking and at the Kremlin, but, because of the controversy, would hesitate to walk into the Harrisburg Moose." Yet it wasn't astonishing that it took a Pittsburgher like Irvis to challenge this unnecessary form of insulting discrimination Harrisburgers had shut their eyes to for generations.

Harrisburg, as always, had its own peculiar agenda that sometimes passeth all understanding but can be successful in its way.

In the dozen years after the 1969 Riot and Irvis case, 10 blacks went on the school board and eight to City Council, including LeRoy Robinson Jr. who in 1982 would be national president of the Family Service Association. By 1981 council's four blacks, with the first black woman, Mrs. Judith Hill, outnumbered the three whites.

With few headlines, blacks made their way up: Dr. James A. Odom, president of HACC for seven years; Benjamin R. Turner, first black school superintendent for six years; All-American basketball player Julius McCoy, first serious black contender for mayor; Middletown Mayor Robert G. Reid, Pennsylvania's first black mayor; Mrs. Le Gree Daniels of Edgemont, Republican State Committee member and first black Pennsylvania woman on the Electoral College in 1980.

Nathan H. Waters, first black to seek a legislative seat in 1972; Barton A. Fields, first black Secretary of Commonwealth; Dr. Claude E. Nichols, first black president of the Dauphin County Medical Society; Mrs. Juliet Rowland, first black president of the Junior League in 1979; and the indefatigable Mrs. Sarah Jones, once a charwoman who cleaned the Governor's Office at night and in her 70s as a mother of eight, foster mother of three, grandmother of 18 and great-grandmother of nine was the spokesperson for the Uptown Civic Association and Neighborhood Center.

87.

A NEW SEPARATISM

If the good news of the last 20 years is the Harrisburg black community's march out of obscurity, the bad news is fewer whites are watching the parade. The novel experiment of desegregation received almost universal—and hypocritical—approval, but it wasn't backed up with the necessary demographics.

A new separatism of economics, plus racial preference, replaced Ole Jim Crow.

Dauphin County's black population in the 1970s increased by 5,004 to 31,275, but half that increase was concentrated among the city's 23,215 blacks.

The Susquehanna River remained a racial Checkpoint Charley. Cumberland County in 1980 had only 2,457 blacks, or 1.4 percent, and almost half lived in Carlisle. Harrisburg had almost as many Spanish-speaking citizens, 2,296, as all of Cumberland County had blacks. Little Steelton had more blacks, 1,742, than the combined 14 West Shore municipalities 10 times its size.

Whites literally gave ground. About 18,960 of them departed Harrisburg in the 1970s. By 1980, the city whites retained a slim numerical majority, their 28,190 amounting to 53 percent.

In the fall of 1969, after the February school emergency and the June riot, Harrisburg schools for the first time became "a black district," as some sharply put it, with 54 percent black. The next year as desegregated schooling and busing began, the black percentage went to 56.7. The 1972 Flood sent more whites fleeing, and the schools increased to 62.8 percent. By 1982, it was 71 percent black, 20 percent white and 9 percent Hispanic and other minorities.

As the Harrisburg black community came of age, the white social and corporate influentials disappeared. Only a few with convictions, or a genuine love of urban living or an appreciation of spacious old housing, didn't abscond. Ethnologist John Bodnar noted in his Steelton study how after 1941 when the mill hands got involved politically, the elite quit borough council and the school board and the mill superintendent transferred his residency to the leafy suburbs. "The old stock departed. Steelton now belonged to the newcomers. No one else wanted it," concluded Bodnar.

Some white suburbanites used a ludicrous argument: "The blacks own Harrisburg." That not only was false economically, but the case more likely was that nobody "owned" Harrisburg any longer and the city suffered from not being the concern of proprietors.

Certainly no "new order" emerged. Like the departed whites, some blacks could be indifferent about their community and project selfishness, ignorance and racial misconceptions. After 200 years of all-white rule, the new blacks were just as capable of playing shoddy politics in City Hall and the school district and selling out for patronage. The whites never produced a Harrisburg Thomas Jefferson. The blacks have yet to bring forth a Harrisburg Martin Luther King.

A "Black Pride" did evolve, but not the macho-type black supremacists boast about and white supremacists scorn.

It is a sign of community maturity that since the 1969 Riot there hasn't been another one. Nearly 15 years later, there still isn't a black mayor or legislator and once in 1973 five blacks were defeated for City Council, yet the black community hasn't panicked. For 12 years after the Cedar Cliff football game, Harrisburg High was subjected to unwarranted humiliation, but city blacks kept their dignity. Harrisburg blacks, furthermore, could see a black school superintendent and a black board president replaced by whites and accept that as equal opportunity, too.

By every measurement, racial tension has eased, even during the 1981-83 recession when far more blacks per capita are jobless than whites.

Never known as a "model-community"—in fact, once called the "Mississippi of the North"—the Harrisburg area endured and made some racial progress that is extraordinary. That the achievement goes unrecognized is, as blacks with long memories know, an old and sad American story.

88.

THE URBAN SCHOOL PROBLEM

In 1919, there were Harrisburg students who staged a strike to gain admittance to the new Edison Junior High School. Fifty years later, classes were dismissed at William Penn and John Harris high schools because of sit-ins and disturbances.

The "urban school problem," as one Harrisburg school director called it, was the new reality.

The Prophet Isaiah foretold that a "little child shall lead them," but he also envisioned wolves, lambs, leopards, kids, calves and young lions lying down together. Contemporary America, instead, misled its city children by concentrating its social, racial and economic antagonisms at the schoolhouse door.

Once the schools were sanctuaries from the hassles of public life. The schools were structured to be independent community citadels—not just architecturally as brownstone fortresses, but in separate districts with governing and taxing boards having the power of debt, self-management and tenure, their own codes and even policing privileges.

Pecksniffian though many of the old-time educators could be, most were clad in the armor of a righteous cause. As the ultra bourgeois of the bourgeoisie, they enjoyed the esteem of their community. They were neighborhood, church and civic leaders, though until the 1940s most didn't earn more than $100 a month.

For more than a century, or since the founding of the Harrisburg School District in 1827, the classrooms were ruled by martinets and school-marms. Few had more than s two-year normal school education, but often they were called "professor" as they imperiously preached American middle-class morality to youngsters whose parents were fresh from the farm or just off the boat.

How shocking it was when one of these teachers, with a prominent local name and acting as if he were from a John O'Hara novel, in 1960 murdered a lover in a sordid incident at Riverfront Park. And how disillusioning it was to learn during the 27-day school strike in 1976 that many teachers were regarded as "outsiders," because indeed more than five of every seven of them did live outside the city's neighborhoods. Harrisburg Tech didn't have a parking lot. Harrisburg Middle School needed a parking lot larger than an athletic field.

By the 1960s, Harrisburg schools were in the midst of what its first black superintendent, Benjamin F. Turner, called "the throes of social upheaval."

Cheap politics were part of the problem. A stronger political hand, as the old days had, might have brought some composure to the school situation. But the worst cause was the warring outside community, which often seemed to be a diverse mob with contradictory demands wanting to dump chaos where once calm learning had prevailed.

During the 1960s and 1970s, there was more screaming in Harrisburg schools—and at school board meetings—than anywhere else in the city. Director John Hope conceded that the district "operated in a climate of partisan political chicanery and backroom maneuvering." When Turner resigned in 1980 after a six-year stint, he said, "As an educator, I decided I could no longer give 100 percent to the kids."

Inner-city children in this era of Vietnam and civil rights weren't docile or innocent either. Caught up in the maelstrom of a society that accentuated adolescent assertiveness and loosely defined "identity"—their T-shirts bore the slogans—city youth all too often became purposeless cogs in a routine where disorder, disrespect and disinterested academics reigned.

Little of the "War on Poverty" affected the youngsters. Many were left in poverty, which didn't have the acceptable status of "being poor" in 1910.

It was a good school day when Harrisburg absenteeism was under 20 percent. It was a rare child, especially white but also black, who expected to take all his elementary and secondary education in the city. Like having loving parents, children also need the stability of place, and too few received that.

In 1978 Superintendent Turner, explaining a 30 percent withdrawal rate, observed that 24 students of the group really shouldn't be considered drop-outs. They had been transferred by the court to state correctional institutions.

89.

THE CITY'S LARGEST TAX COLLECTOR

That Harrisburg schools even made it through the 1960s and 1970s was a heroic achievement.

Amidst the daily vicissitudes, the school district endured as it mirror-imaged the community's chaos. The misfortunate demographics were disheartening enough to wither the optimism of the town's most stout-hearted, adding to a vicious losing cycle.

In the quarter-century after 1957, the city school enrollment fell from 15,000 to under 9,000. The city birthrate declined by 24 percent in the 1970s alone.

Every loss of a student was the loss of parental support. Harrisburg schools ended up the city's largest tax collector but a minority operation, directly serving fewer than half the population in students and parents combined. This attenuation of clients was doubly dismaying in a town where by 1983 the district had 49 percent of its property tax exempted, or $103 million worth.

Marketing such a shrinking enterprise was almost impossible when within a few miles was a comparatively new and gleaming district like Cumberland Valley—even its swimming pool a Taj Mahal—or a resplendent giant such as Central Dauphin. In 1969 CD replaced Harrisburg as Dauphin County's largest district. Its two high schools serve 120 square miles—a wide expanse for cross-township busing of these students whose parents fled Harrisburg because they said they didn't like cross-town busing.

Had cost-conscious taxpayers found Harrisburg schools a bargain, that might have made a difference. But by the 1970s Harrisburg's equivalent school taxes were matching Camp Hill's. In fact, in 1982 when Harrisburg raised its school millage by 7, Camp Hill dropped its by 2. The year before, Harrisburg schools doubled its occupation tax to $75, and that might have put the lid on any economic incentives for families willing to become urban pioneers.

Harrisburg's school budget, like many third-class city districts, soared as enrollments swan-dived. From 1968 to 1983 the district budget tripled to $30 million. The rub was that after 1980 the commonwealth began reneging on its 1945 commitment to meet half the local educational costs. This shortfall added more mills to Harrisburg taxes and then in 1982, the year of the record 7-mill jump, Harrisburg lost another $170,000 in a subsidy formula modification, or the equivalent of still another mill of local taxation.

The district was a partner with the city is suffering from municipal overburden. Inner-city schools require more management and evaluation, and also more special classes and programs. Truancy is costly. Desegregated busing began in September of 1970 and by 1973 was a $773,546 item, or eight times the transportation costs of 1969. Schoolboy football could not longer pay for itself.

Patronage is expensive, and in the late 1970s Harrisburg's flourished. City Hall had elected school directors on its payroll, while the district had some old City Hall faces on its payroll.

The school's business management won no prizes, either. In 1973 the district understated expenditures by $44,000, maintained poor attendance records, and was subjected to an investigation by the state Auditor

General. Five years later the district, at its debt limitation, required court approval to borrow $1.6 million because it needed quick money to cover underestimated expenditures. The $10.7 million bond issue in 1973 for the Middle School pushed the annual debt service to almost $1 million and had the district perennially broke.

Like TMI and the incinerator, the Middle School stumbled onward. After only eight years it required a $580,000 new roof—in contrast to the nearby Capitol that went 66 years with its original roof. Worse than that, the Middle School was designed to have "classrooms without walls," an "open space" concept of questionable utility for 13-year-old street kids. By 1982 the new superintendent, Robert F. Kelly, agreed that district repairs would require $12 million over four years, some of which would go for interior walls for the Middle School.

90.

"BLACK" AND "CITY"

"The city, above all, has been victimized by the national unwillingness to accept the social consequences of the melting-pot tradition insofar as it implies a multiracial society," wrote Arnold A. Rogow in his 1975 urban study, *The Dying of the Light.*

Dr. Rogow, a political scientist at Stanford and CCNY, was an Eagle Scout and in the 1940s one of John Harris High School's brightest students. The famous Rabbi Philip David Bookstaber became his legal guardian after Rogow was orphaned at 13.

Harrisburg by the 1960s had a public image of "black" and "city"—two of the most defeating epithets in modern American society.

Harrisburg schools sometimes had to cope with epic intolerance, such as occurred after the 1971 Cedar Cliff football game. They were the first mentioned when it came to such "bad news" as drugs, vandalism, pregnancy, rowdiness at athletic contests, drop-outs and even arson, as if these weren't troublesome also at the more favored suburban schools. Illogically, only black Harrisburg was said to have the "racial problem."

The situation was invidious, a regression to the community's repugnant attitudes that created racial ostracism in the beginning. Pluralistic education, like a multiracial society, was feared—and only Harrisburg, Steelton-Highspire, Susquehanna, Central Dauphin, Middletown and Carlisle really had it.

There were brave whites and blacks who wanted integrated education and regarded a 100 percent white suburban school as unacceptable as a 60, 70, 80 or 90 percent black Harrisburg school. But many true melting-pot integrationists didn't stand a chance in the racial polarization.

Harrisburg schools were 12 percent black in 1930, up to 45 percent in 1966, to 54 percent in 1969, and in 1981 were 71 percent black and 9 percent Hispanic plus other minorities. After 1970, there couldn't have been many white racists sending their children to Harrisburg schools. By 1980 when there were only 2,300 white children in the schools, for a white public-school family to remain the city was either an act of social conviction or a result of poverty.

The 1970 desegregation plan was one of Harrisburg's noble gestures—perhaps its noblest, because it required sacrifice by its middle and upper classes. The Pennsylvania Human Relations Commission "got our attention by hitting us over the head with a mandate for racial balance," as Superintendent David H. Porter later wrote. All but two of Harrisburg's 18 grammar schools in 1969 were racially imbalanced, with 99 percent black at Downey and Hamilton, 97 percent at Ben Franklin, 95 percent at Woodward and 88 percent at Lincoln.

Integration brought the early childhood center, a single high school and busing. Harrisburg High opened Sept. 8, 1971, giving the city its first unified high school since 1893. Within three weeks, 60 students were suspended as trouble-makers. It took years to achieve a one high-school spirit, split as Harrisburg allegiances had long been between Allison Hill and Uptown.

By the second year of busing in 1971, Harrisburg was transporting 53 percent of its enrollment. The national average was 42 percent, exceeded in many Harrisburg suburbs where busing took 60 to 98 percent of the students.

The U.S. Supreme Court in 1974 decreed black city students could be bused to white suburbs, but that option was almost unheard of in Pennsylvania. The Pennsylvania Supreme Court upheld Harrisburg's desegregation, but the district immediately lost 100 white students.

Despite all the hollering, a citizen poll by Bell Telephone in 1972 revealed Harrisburgers' biggest grievances remained crime and high taxes, while only 18 percent mentioned busing. Tom Wicker in his New York Times column in 1976 lauded Harrisburg for achieving an orderly integration without the racial bitterness seen in Boston and Louisville.

91.

THE WEST SHORE COSMETOLOGICAL CRISIS OF 1970

The "Hirsute Hassle," or the West Shore's "Cosmetological Crisis" of 1970, was comic slapstick, though to many serious suburbanites it was Armageddon between destructive libertines and respected authority.

The length of boys' hair was an issue that troubled the West Shore School District, and within two years spread to the Middletown and Bishop McDevitt high schools and then on up to the Pennsylvania attorney general and a U.S. federal court, as the Constitution itself was cited.

All the to-do was over "what grows only a half-inch a month, or more slowly than crabgrass in Green Lane Farms," as this columnist observed at the time.

Chasing urchins with long hair was a diversion when much of the rest of America was inflamed by the Vietnam crisis or when across the river the future of urban multi-racial education was at stake in the Harrisburg schools.

Long hair didn't set a suspicious fire at Camp Hill High in April of 1971 nor cause vandalism at Hershey and Mechanicsburg schools, but a backlash against unshorn male locks was an approved, collective subconscious way to retaliate against the anxieties created everywhere by galloping cultural pluralism. And what is more pluralist than hair—"curly, fuzzy, snaggy, ratty, knotty, shining, gleaming, straining, knotted, twisted, beaded, braided, powdered, flowered, bangled, tangled and spangled… Hair," as the hit musical of 1970 put it?

The local apocalypse started at sedate Cedar Cliff High when more than 100 teenage males violated the school dress code with hair flowing over their eyebrows, ears and collars. Then 75 brazen kids at Red Land staged a brief sit-in under the banner, "Lincoln had a beard."

Trim-clipped principals, solicitors and school directors mobilized. The West Shore's chief administrator, Dr. Harold F. Hench, threatened to call the gendarmes if "disorder" continued. Cedar Cliff principal Louis S. Edwards attempted a dialog. Asked one youngster, "Why do you contend that parents who you say are best able to teach sex education are not capable of telling us how to groom ourselves?" Edwards forthrightly conceded he couldn't be too specific in replying to that apt analogy.

After at least 25 "males with manes" were suspended, Cumberland County Judge Clinton R. Weidner upheld that classroom "distractions and diversions" would occur if sideburns when below the earlobes. "If and when the time arrives when the extremists are willing to serve, and able to be elected by majority vote, they should then serve, change the rules and others will abide with their rules. But until then, the community has declared its approval of those now dedicated to an educational system free of extremes and proven efficient by the test of time."

Without endangering property rights or shedding blood, teen-age boys now had the accolade of being "extremists"—something they could boast to their grandchildren in years to come.

The "Reporter at Large" column of April 24, 1970, jumped into the fray: "All the noise floating across the river shouldn't be overrated. The youths are a lot more straight, even in hair style, than they'd care to admit."

Who really are the hair freaks, asked the intrepid columnist: "What age bracket is crowding into beauty shops on Thursdays and Fridays and spending the green to thwart nature's mousey shades?"

The column also noted that suburban living obviously hadn't enervated all the spunk out of the kids. And what had happened to the "generation gap" when the court berated a father for standing behind his son? And how smart were suburban educators and especially the hired guns, the lawyers, because "the case put forth was intellectually shabby...The elders went into the crisis unprepared, and then when they were caught short became arrogant."

The column concluded: "Conformity isn't rampant on the West Shore, and the crisis reaffirmed that happy fact."

With a time advantage Harrisburgers never has for its difficulties, the West Shore District diligently restudied its dress code and by September of 1974, or a high school generation later, had a revised code to promote cleanliness, safety and placidity. Two months later a former York County school superintendent, the popular William P. Goodling, was elected to Congress. He proceeded to sport a lush masculine mane that remains the envy of all the balding Republicans in his West Shore district.

92.

FRIENDLESS HARRISBURG

The West Shore squabble over long hair was a farce, but the Cedar Cliff football game of Sept. 17, 1971, and its aftermath were shameful.

Fans created a ruckus, but only one side—Harrisburg—was blamed and excommunicated for 10 years. Worse, a struthious suburban silence enveloped the ugly episode. In a year rife with protest, this modern Dred Scott case was not denounced.

Harrisburg blacks as a community were humiliated yet they stood tall with extraordinary maturity, too proud to stoop to retaliation.

The new Harrisburg High had just opened for a district 58 percent black. The once Harris Pioneers' crimson and silver and the Penn Tigers' orange and black were amalgamated into the Harrisburg Cougars' black and silver, the colors of the Oakland Raiders.

Eight days later the Cougars opened their first season in West Shore Stadium losing in the final minutes, 17—14. It was their only loss in a 9-1-1 year.

There were never any complaints about the action on the playing field. Harrisburg School Board President James E. Rowland Sr., once a star athlete, saw the game and confirmed that. In fact, within four months

Cedar Cliff played basketball at Harrisburg, lost a 55-54 thriller, and there were no disturbances.

Spectators that season at the Cedar Cliff games at York and Williamsport were rowdy. The very day of the Cougars' game, Bishop McDevitt played at Steelton-Highspire for the first time since 1945 when it was Catholic High, and there was a brief fracas. The game between Central Dauphin East and Reading had trouble, too.

There was at least one Confederate flag down in the Colts' stands for the Harrisburg game. According to a committee official of the Pennsylvania Interscholastic Athletic Association, "verbal abuse and agitation," including racial taunts from cars, also took place. What mattered was that six injured fans were hospitalized briefly. Cedar Cliff never filed a formal complaint—that would have been awkward, as it was its responsibility to police its own home games—but the PIAA took reports and concluded the "unacceptable conduct" was all by Harrisburg.

The District Three Committee of the PIAA, though neither publicly elected nor a recognized judiciary, exacted quick punishment. Harrisburg High was put on a two-year minimum probation, with no practices nor contests to start later than 4 p.m. The PIAA, with all its directors white and 1,200 of its 1,206 accredited officials white, didn't reprimand Cedar Cliff, though that school on its own switched its remaining season's night games to daylight hours.

"I'm a little disturbed that only Negroes were arrested. I don't think we got the whole story," the district justice nearest Cedar Cliff said, as jurisdiction was given to a Mechanicsburg justice. Four of seven young blacks were indicted, and three were given prison terms of six to ten months and the fourth was fined.

"It's plain foolish for a group of men to sit around and punish a whole school," exclaimed Harrisburg's first black councilman, Stanley R. Lawson. Mayor Harold Swenson and Council President Tim Doutrich also were critical. Harrisburg sought an injunction against the PIAA, but the Dauphin County Court denied it. Two years after, the Pennsylvania Supreme Court, citing "judicial noninterference," rejected a Harrisburg appeal, but 24 hours later, on Sept. 20, 1973, the PIAA lifted the Cougars' probation.

The law's heavy hand should have been enough, but two months after the game Cedar Cliff announced its withdrawal from the Central Penn League to form the South Central League, without Harrisburg, of course. The Central Penn went back to 1947, and Cedar Cliff, a member since 1962, was walking out with its first and only championship. Valiant Steel-High stuck by Harrisburg until the Central Penn at last collapsed in 1978.

Without the league, friendless Harrisburg had to arrange schedules with as many as 55 different schools, traveling at times to Washington when it couldn't cross the Susquehanna for a game. "We would hope that we can join together in continuing cooperation and respect," the Harrisburg School District said to its neighbors after the 1971 game, but the cold shoulder got icier.

It wasn't until February of 1981 that Harrisburg received an invitation to start talks with the West Shore District. A new league, the Mid-Penn Conference, was formed. Competition resumed when about 500 intrepid Colt fans journeyed to Severance Field on Sept. 25, 1982, a balmy and peaceful day. "Cougars Welcome Cedar Cliff, 30—6," as The Sunday Patriot-News reported the outcome.

93.

RACIAL EDUCATION

In the best of times, achieving pluralistic racial education would be a demanding exertion for any school district. For Harrisburg, that challenge was just one of many.

The District would retain a semblance of continuity only in its administration and faculty. Amazingly it had only four superintendents from the mid-1960s through 1983.

Dr. Glenn C. Parker bowed out after the 1969 school closings, "a casualty of the urban school problem," as one school director put it.

Dr. David H. Porter, the one veteran Harrisburger and true community leader, was assistant superintendent for 17 years and then from 1969-1973 guided the desegregation plan with an expert hand and calm voice. He retired in June of 1974, respected after 36 diligent years as the dean of Harrisburg's public officials.

Benjamin F. Turner was hired as a school planner in 1971, after 14 years in Philadelphia education. As an innovator he established the Riverside Center for the Arts and student evaluation and was ready to assume the role as perhaps Pennsylvania's leading black superintendent. He lasted six years, battling a teacher's strike, a quarreling school board, and conflicting support from community banks, the public, the press, and even his own staff.

Once the passionate expounder of urban education, he announced his resignation six months in advance and then quietly departed for Cleveland.

Replacing the first black chief in a district at least 60 percent black with another white could have meant a split community, but Harrisburg rose above the temptation. Dr. Robert F. Kelly, a New Yorker with previous superintendencies in Virginia and the San Francisco area, settled in and proved to be as fair and colorblind in the front office as his predecessors were.

Overlapping superintendents, from 1963 to 1976, street-smarts Samuel A. Evans was a power behind the throne. Evans began in 1951 as a clerk and rose to business manager and board secretary and eventually to deputy superintendent, coupling his final five years with an interest in the Capital Area Tax Collection Bureau. Evans, almost indispensable, knew first names and middle initials, as well as budgets and patronage. By 1978 he was a Republican city chairman, and his son was a school director.

Part of rebuilding Harrisburg education meant paying for it, and six times in the dozen years between 1971 and 1982 the district raised property taxes. On a seventh occasion, because of county reassessment, it got a revenue increase without higher millage.

Turner said Harrisburg schools "must devote all available time, money and creativity to increasing learning achievement of every student." That goal, however, didn't receive everyone's undivided attention.

Instead there were headaches over truancy. Another major task was making the new middle School function properly after it opened in 1975. It didn't help, either, when a 15-year-old set a fire in the high school and caused $75,000 in damage.

A tug-of-war at the Middle School on June 13, 1978, gave Harrisburg national headlines it didn't need. About 2,200 youngsters participated in an attempt to set a Guinness world record. The braided nylon rope burned

200 of them, sending 80 to the hospital and four required partial amputations and another five received fractures.

Though East Pennsboro and Cumberland Valley had limited warfare teacher strikes, Harrisburg's 27-day disruption in the fall of 1976 was as harmful as it was emotional. Right after it began, 288 students transferred to other districts—some to where the teachers came from, because 522 Harrisburg teachers didn't live in the city. In fact, during the next few years when Harrisburg was cited for having improperly certified staff members, some of them didn't live in the city either.

Fired years after the Harrisburg strike, the Pennsylvania State Education Association, then friendly with Gov. Dick Thornburgh, successfully lobbied a statewide law banning optional teacher residency restrictions. But school strikes weren't outlawed. If history repeats, it is possible once again for commuting public employees to keep city kids out of school while their own offspring attend classes elsewhere. The pontificated principle of home rule for besieged cities never was absolute.

94.

GUERILLA THEATER

Of all its exasperations in the 1970s, Harrisburg should have tolerated the least the brigand-type politicking in its school system, bombarded as it was by constant emergencies. Yet the school board became the most raucous back-alley of angry politics in the community.

Before the Seventies, the Harrisburg School Board was a coterie of nine mutually admiring members. There was one 12-month period under President Carl B. Stoner Sr. that the board, showing "no polarities" as one member said, voted unanimously on 350 issues. Stoner, a lawyer and local historian out of Central High, went from being part of the anti-Taylor Fighting Five of 1951 to the school board for 18 years. He diligently devoted 20 hours weekly to this volunteer job, intelligently pursuing harmony and quiet progress.

In the fall of 1969, after the school disruptions, Stoner bowed off the board. But decorum still prevailed. That May 8, 1970, the board voted 6–2 to adopt the racial and economic plan for desegregation. It was afterward that the school management, reflecting the city, became highly politicized.

By 1980 when school directors themselves staged walkouts and spectators screamed insults at board meetings, the situation had degenerated into "guerilla theater at its best," as former board member John Hope wrote in his newsletter "Schoolwatch."

Democrats secured control in December of 1975 for the first time in modern Harrisburg history, but that lasted only two years for President Tom Connolly. When Harold Swenson was defeated for a third term as mayor, the Republicans regained the school board and selected Gordon B. Hicks president.

Hicks was the third black to be president, but one of his first actions was to demote the second black, Jim Rowlands Sr., from school solicitor to assistant solicitor. "Big Daddy"—Hicks was 6 foot and weighed as much as 356 pounds—was born in Steelton but grew up in Harrisburg. He was one of the last of the old "Plantation Politics" crowd, a GOP fieldhand since 1936 for such masters as Harve Taylor and U.S. Sen. Hugh Scott.

Big Daddy could be smart, charming and persuasive. As treasurer of the old Forster Street YMCA and a founder of the new Camp Curtin Y, he knew the neighborhoods and the white power structure. Yet with such advantages, Hicks wasn't a Jim Rowland when it came to statesmanship. Rather than conciliation, Big Daddy didn't' hesitate to make the school board as partisan as it could be.

Hicks seemed to relish chaotic confrontations and public commotion. Taxes got passed at his meetings. Political friends were hired. Superintendent Ben Turner survived a motion to be fired. Somehow above the din of too many loudly voice demands and too many rude accusations, the school system kept afloat—or seemed to, as when a 1977 deficit of $305,000 was made to appear to be a $206,500 surplus.

A carnival atmosphere ensued. Elected board members switched parties. One jumped twice, brazenly explaining his second sell-out as "a change intended to help end excessive partisanship." Some got relatives and friends jobs, while having no visible means of a livelihood themselves. A few were suspect as to their city residency. Of course, it was the aberrant board member or administrator who had his or her own children in the school system everyone was battling about.

Hicks was more of a ringmaster in this circus than a savant. He was forthright enough not to duck responsibility, and it was probably no single individual's fault that anarchy reigned. Hicks' successor, John C. Staley, quit in mid-term, and Staley was followed by Miles D. Thomas who needed a record 24 ballots to be reappointed board president.

Harrisburg schools once had been a sanctuary from tumult and a citadel of rectitude. When City Hall and the courthouse were the sinecures of ward-heelers, the school district had been proud, progressive and professional. Now in the 1970s, the school system's management was in disarray.

Yet as citizens howled like wolves, as security was summoned to maintain order at board meetings, and as harangues and impoliteness dominated almost all proceedings, back in the classrooms of Harrisburg some purpose seemed to be taking hold. Compared to the disputing adults, the students were behaving themselves.

95.

REPUBLICAN HEGEMONY

When John F. Kennedy stopped by Harrisburg in 1960, he had no delusions he could win the hearts and minds of Republican Harrisburgers. He made the pilgrimage here only to convince Gov. David L. Lawrence, an Adlai Stevenson supporter, that a fellow Irish Catholic could be a viable presidential candidate.

Though Kennedy almost doubled Vice President Nixon's crowd in his Market Square rally, he fared worse locally at election time than even liberals like Abraham Lincoln and Franklin D. Roosevelt. Kennedy in 1960 didn't carry a single precinct of Cumberland County's 76, and he managed majorities in just 18 of Dauphin County's 145.

Sweeping 92 percent of the precincts was the way Harrisburg area Republicans liked to straight-ticket an election.

From the Battle of Gettysburg to Watergate, local Republicanism reigned with Simon Cameron's winning formula—the Protestant Ethic, Social Darwinism, economic laissez-faire, neighborhood stability, and generous patronage for the faithful. For 108 consecutive years, four bosses held power—Old Simon, his son U.S. Sen. J. Donald Cameron, Lt. Gov. Edward E. Beidleman, and Sen. M. Harvey Taylor.

Not only were all the schools named for Republicans, but so were the streets—except for Verbeke, which the locals called Broad Street, anyway.

The few Democrats who survived could be more conservative than their rival Republicans. William K. Verbeke, Dr. John A. Fritchey, Vance McCormick and John K. Royal won the mayorship. On FDR's coattails in 1936, the popular Dutchman Guy Swope made it to Congress for one term and George Kunkel, an ersatz Democrat, to the state Senate, but otherwise Harve Taylor masterfully kept his Dauphin County immune from the enticing coalitions of the New Deal.

The Kennedy and Johnson presidencies had no appreciable effect on local Democrats, except that perhaps they feuded more among themselves. In 1961 Guy Swope's younger son Lee did become the first elected Democratic county judge, but this victory belonged to his efforts and not his party's.

Ironically it was the West Shore that retained coteries of stubborn Jeffersonian and Wilsonian Democrats. Carlisle's Robert Lee Jacobs became a state senator in 1936 and later a Superior Court judge, and in 1974 Robert Lee Myers III in a special election also won the Senate seat. Jake Myers and Nelson Punt took the entire county away from the Republicans in 1975 and 1979.

These Democratic victories were extraordinary, because in most elections as many as a dozen West Shore Republicans would go unchallenged, as the judgeship and district attorney post did in 1983. West of the Susquehanna was simply the white collar habitat of suburban Republicans. No Taylor-like machine ever developed on the West Shore, because none was needed.

Before the 960s, it wasn't unusual that all the public sinecures in Dauphin and Cumberland counties were held by Republicans, except by law the minority county commissionerships. In the glory year of 1952 when Gettysburg's Dwight Eisenhower went to the White House, the GOP had a registration of 68,358 on the East Shore and 16,753 on the smaller West Shore.

The Republican hegemony was stimulated by the hormonal urges of patronage. Even in early private industry, the railroads, utilities and steel mills were Republican domains, labor as well as management.

The Capitol was the strongest GOP fortress of them all, with 83 years of GOP governors in the 95 years between 1860 and 1955. Before civil service and government unions, there was always room in the bureaucracy for at least 15,000 duly accredited local Republicans. As fashioned by Simon Cameron and made into a fine art by Harve Taylor, and to a lesser degree Sen. George N. Wade, patronage extended from the payrolls of congressmen, legislators, the courthouse, municipalities and school districts right down to getting hired as a playground supervisor.

Folks ate chicken corn soup at the GOP dinners and paid their campaign tithes. Gov. John S. Fine in the early 1950s put a chief fund collector in a Penn Harris Hotel suit, and the state employees paraded by with the checks and cash in the exact amounts of 1 or 2 percent assessment of wages.

96.

AGELESS HARVE TAYLOR

Maris Harvey Taylor, who predated the electric light, automobile, airplane and most of what he called "the indoor conveniences," was last re-elected to the state Senate in 1960. In retrospect, the timing was appropriate. It also was the year of the promises of the Kennedy administration, and they, too, were short-lived.

This was the last election Taylor knew all 290 county district leaders and that his finger was on the pulse of his organization—then one of the most superbly fashioned county machines in American politics.

Margery Scranton, "The Duchess of the Pennsylvania Grand Old Party," was a friend of Harve's. When her son Bill in 1962 ran for governor, Harve gave him 136 of Dauphin County's 145 precincts. Though Scranton was 41 years younger, Taylor soon regarded him as the national GOP's answer to JFK. Harve dedicated the last of his 24 Senate years, a record 16 of them as president pro tempore, to pushing through Scranton's legislation.

By 1964, Taylor was almost 88 and was thoroughly enjoying himself as the Senate generalissimo, cajoling fellow Republicans to give Bill Scranton the presidential nomination and helping Scrantonites ladle out the patronage. Harve was so busy having fun he forgot to attend to his own re-election, and he needed only four more wins to be a senator at 100.

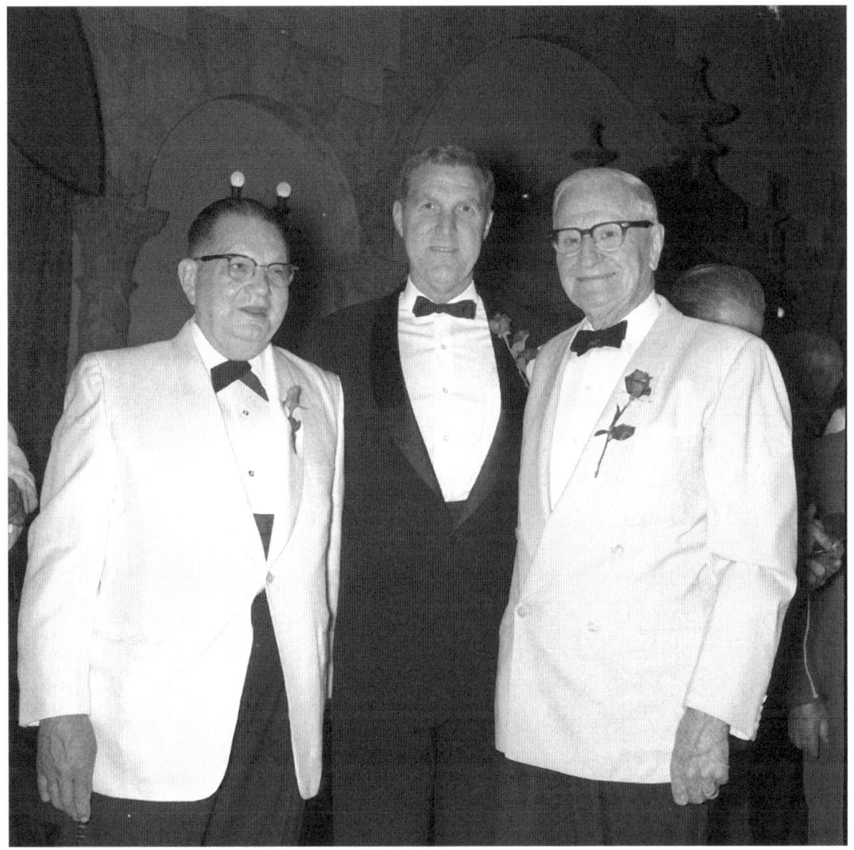

Legendary Sen. M. Harvey Taylor (r) was not as tall as former star basketball player Gov. Raymond P. Shafer (c), but Taylor was conceivably as powerful as the state's chief executive.

Half of Harrisburg assumed Taylor would reach 100; the other half thought him immortal. His agelessness by the 1960s was legendary. When he died in 1982 at 106, he had been a great-grandfather for 20 years, and all his descendants were Republicans. Taylor wasn't even a veteran, because he had been too old for World War I.

What Harrisburgers never expected was that Taylor would foul up his own re-election. Harve had always been the ultimate in political fastidiousness, lullabying every vote he could honestly get and often a few extra hundred that in Heaven or Camp Hill wouldn't be counted.

But in 1964 the old man arrogantly insulted the League of Women Voters by not answering its request for the Voters Guide. He crossed an old pal, Rep. Blaine C. Hocker of Oberlin, a power in the House, by backing an unknown Hershey teacher to oppose Hocker in the primary. This was just when the free Hershey Junior College was closing for the advent of the tuition-paying Harrisburg Area Community College, and Derry Twp. voters were irate.

Taylor's mind was so far from his constituents that he missed smothering a reckless Harrisburg school proposal to tax commuters $5.

The primary returns brought the most startling upset in local history. William B. Lentz, 43, a real estate broker from outside Millersburg, took 82 of the 90 suburban and rural districts and sweetly bumped off the master by 3,249 votes. What the Fighting Five of 1948-50 and the United Arabs of 1962 couldn't do, jolly Bill Lentz did in a campaign that featured him passing out lollipops to kids at shopping centers.

The joke the next day was, "There's sure a traffic jam on the William B. Lentz Bridge."

Taylor was broken-hearted. He personally hadn't lost an election in 30 years. Waiting four years until he was 92, he then sought to be an elected delegate to the GOP National Convention so he could ballot for his friend Richard M. Nixon. Voters knocked him off again, the guy who had a record 16 years as state Republican chairman.

Taylor remained an alert and witty man almost until his last breath.

His smile was as big as Shipoke when his own organization, though half in shambles, maintained control in the jobs Taylor always emphasized: the courthouse, judgeships, commissioners, district attorney and state Senate. But Harve had barbs for all the Democrats he saw emerging: Milt Shapp's eight years as governor, Harold Swenson's and Steve Reed's mayoralties, Reed's and young Pete Wambach's legislative victories, and the insidious wins Democrats made to briefly capture the Harrisburg School Board, Derry Twp. and the mayorship of Paxtang.

Taylor went out in 1964 and big-time Pennsylvania patronage followed in 1970. There also was a new wave of voters—the post-war baby boomers. This crowd, 50 to 60 years younger than Taylor, scoffed at the sacred principle of straight-ticket, straight-party voting. Their nonconformity clearly insured that Taylorism was over for good.

97.

POST-TAYLORISM

Harrisburg's conservatively tailored leadership of a half-century began to fray and its magisterial robe no longer seemed so invincible after Sen. M. Harvey Taylor departed office in 1964.

The Grand Old Party that once had been so masterfully controlled from the devoted ward heelers up, became confused and chaotic. Thanks to the voters' habitual Republicanism and the continued disarray of Democrats, the GOP had five years of grace before the 1969 Riot cost it City Hall.

Although an accident of history, it seemed symbolic that not one of Harrisburg's three Republican mayors of the 1960s finished a full term.

Nolan F. Ziegler died before his second term was completed in 1963. Dr. William K. McBride, in ill health, resigned before the end of his term in 1967. And Albert H. Straub, elected for four years in 1967, bravely pushed the referendum for a new strong-mayor form of government, settled for a foreshortened two-year term, and was defeated for re-election in 1969.

What had once to Republicans looked so promising—Nolan Ziegler as the innovative mayor, William W. Scranton as the popular governor, and Harve Taylor as the octogenarian baron of the Senate and Dauphin County—vanished precipitously.

The crazy Sixties followed the Kennedy assassination. The white middle class evacuated the cities for suburbia. Vietnam erupted. The emergence of blacks and women stirred uneasiness, especially in traditionally Teutonic white male Harrisburg. Municipal and school problems no longer were amenable to temporary overhauls, for though budgets climbed with the mid-Sixties' local wage tax there still wasn't enough money to fulfill all the expectations.

Even Taylorism, had it lasted, would have had difficulty coping with such change, but for the first time the GOP itself lost its majestic presence. A City Hall scandal burst that was comparable with the shenanigans of Philadelphia Democrats. While the miscreants slipped away, the Taylorite remnants indulged themselves in a bitter 1967 fratricidal City Hall primary. And across Walnut Street, the embroiled Shafer administration was splitting the statewide Republicans asunder with deficits 27 of its 48 months in office.

The horrendous decade ended with a nine-month-late Shafer Republicans red-ink budget on Capitol Hill and the Harrisburg Riot. The Democrats couldn't have bought the governorship and mayorship cheaper. And the student president at HACC, Stephen Russell Reed, watched it all and saw opportunity ahead. At 20, he was the same age as Napoleon when Frenchmen stormed the Bastille.

Ironically, the one local positive achievement in the 1960s came billed with the word "disaster" written all over it.

The Defense Department during the Thanksgiving weekend of 1964 announced Olmsted Air Force Base in Middletown would be phased out over a five-year period, the end of the 50-year establishment and 10,333 jobs. Though the terms "snowbelt" and "sunbelt" wouldn't become common until the next decade, Olmsted's misfortune was a result of the emerging South and West showing its Washington political clout over an atrophying Northeast.

Harrisburgers, so often contentious in their civic life, rallied to recover from the Olmsted loss.

The Harrisburg Area Industrial Development Corp. was formed, and within 20 years attracted 68 new firms, including Fruehauf trucking, and encouraged 102 others to expand operations. The Harrisburg International Airport, replacing Capital City Airport, was a direct result of Olmsted's closing and so was Penn State Capitol Campus [now Penn State Harrisburg, Capital College], which opened in 1966 in the very Air Force headquarters where once major generals strode. The year after Capitol Campus, Penn State's Hershey Medical Center admitted its first students.

Though the Olmsted loss was the nation's largest military depot demise of the decade—the base supplied the 1949 Berlin Airlift—Metropolitan Harrisburg didn't buckle. So prosperous was the local economy that the 1964 unemployment rate was 3.4 percent, or 6,200 jobless out of a 180,000 work force. A decade later, that joblessness was down to 2.8 percent, the state's lowest.

98.

NOLAN ZIEGLER, RARE MAYOR

Many successful politicians, like actors and artists, have an embedded sliver of insecurity as their Achilles' heel. That is one reason Boss Harve Taylor loved appointing his followers to jobs, but he seldom promoted them.

Mayor Nolan F. Ziegler rated as a logical choice to be the Dauphin County Republican chief. He was capable and popular, was single without many family obligations, and luckily was a lawyer without a heavy practice to divert his attention.

Yet Taylor never made the proper nod to this winner 27 years his junior, and then Ziegler died of cancer in 1963, a year before Taylor was dumped in the senatorial primary.

In the conservative Taylor organization, Ziegler was a rare figure not constricted by doctrinaire thinking. He also was unusually passionate for stolid Harrisburg, especially as a champion golfer. Once at his home course at the Harrisburg Country Club, he became so angry he threw his putter up into a tree and then shook the tree to get it back. Another time at the Colonial Country Club, he flipped his club into the lake and then picked up the caddy and tossed him in.

Ziegler had the silver hair of a leading man and the self-important presence of a Hugh Scott. "Even his critics admitted Mayor Ziegler had what it takes to win elections—"good looks, poise, personality and a booming voice which captivated audiences," wrote City Hall reporter Bill Zeidler.

He was another of Dauphin County's political bachelors—a strange anomaly for a family-oriented community—but Vance McCormick, Judge James S. Bowman and William W. Lipsitt, Mayor William K. McBride, George W. Gekas and Mayor Steve Reed all let their youth air out before they married, if they did, and none fathered children.

Ziegler relished people, as an old riverboat banjo player, Republican hob-nobber, inveterate party-goer and four-term legislator. "I loved the man," said crony Johnny Durbin.

The voters liked him, too. They first elected him in 1955 by a 3,055-vote majority, and four years later more than doubled it by 6,705. When Ziegler suggested himself for governor in 1958 and Judge Robert E. Woodside Sr. of Millersburg also jumped into the fray, Taylor foolishly ignored friends and let the Grand Old Party select an unqualified Reading pretzel manufacturer who couldn't beat a highly qualified Pittsburgh Mayor David L. Lawrence.

Ziegler was the first new mayor after Harrisburg's population in 1950 had stopped growing. Understanding the city couldn't stand still as it had in 1930s and 1940s, he formed "CORE," or the Committee for Organized Renewal Effort. "The city cannot thrive without a healthy business district," he said.

Out of CORE evolved the 1961 "Lifeline Plan" of wide access roads to the Capitol for funneling the traffic off the recently opened Harrisburg Expressway and South Bridge. Inexplicably, Taylor, never saying a public word, had his wardheelers defeat the bond issue at the polls.

Ziegler did his best to awaken Harrisburg. He began the first renewal project, razing much of the old Bloody Eighth Ward for the Towne House site. His predecessor, Claude R. Robins, had enticed his other East Shore communities to join the Sewage Treatment Plant, and that and the Community College are the only two major endeavors they ever cooperated with Harrisburg.

Ziegler argued Harrisburg shouldn't be isolated from the 16 boroughs and 23 townships in Dauphin County, or for that matter, the 12 boroughs and 22 townships in Cumberland County. In 1957 he told the Legislature it either should make payments on its tax-exempt properties or give Harrisburg permission to annex neighbors.

Swallowing his "Lifeline" defeat, Ziegler launched the $100,000 city traffic plan on Labor Day of 1961, though the Penn Harris Hotel ownership screamed that he made Third and Walnut streets one-way away from its marquees. The 1961 plan was a gem—but 22 years later as many of its light sequences and patterns remain as they originally were, the system is frustratingly antiquated.

Before more could happen, the mayor was dead at 53. Harrisburg was hushed. It hadn't had a mayor die in 46 years or a governor in 115 years.

Colleagues gathered at his funeral, and off to the side they noticed a tall, fashionably dressed young woman wearing a black veil. She wouldn't give her name, but wept that she was Nolan's friend from New Jersey. His closest pals were startled. All the big guy ever told them when he periodically left town was he was "going to New York to attend a little business."

99.

THE NOBLE AND LOFTY IDEAL OF HACC

The local civic achievement of the mid-1960s was strictly non-political. The founding of Harrisburg Area Community College represented an outflanking of the old-guard politicos who seemed indifferent to Harrisburg as the last major city in Pennsylvania without a college.

Harrisburg High's Professor L.S. Shimmel as early as 1902 wrote:

"The capital city of Pennsylvania is not abreast of most other state capitals. While there is abundant opportunity here for the rich and poor alike to acquire an elementary education, there is none for obtaining a higher education...Aid is given to secure factories, because factories increase wealth and population. Where wealth and population are increasing, colleges are needed to raise the standards of life and create noble and lofty ideals."

Front Street for decades maintained its noble and lofty ideals by sending its offspring to Yale, Princeton, Penn and occasionally Dickinson. Only the rare and ambitious from the rest of town made it to college. As late as Sputnik in 1957, the Harrisburg area shamefully endured a high dropout rate and fewer than 20 percent of its seniors entered post-secondary education.

Though imported college night-school courses were offered since the early 1930s, there were no state or Catholic colleges here. York, Lancaster, Wilkes-Barre and Williamsport were college towns, but not Harrisburg.

To make the "Herculean effort of bringing school districts together," in the words of HACC solicitor Frank Haas, it took a combination of the Russian scientists and Harrisburg capitalistic lawyers. The 1957 Sputnik shot insulted America, shaking education out of its torpor. Then the lawyers got busy.

John D. Killish, as deputy attorney general for education, put together the Community College Act, signed by Gov. William W. Scranton on Aug. 24, 1963. Meanwhile, two pugnacious youthful attorneys, Bruce E. Cooper, 40, and James W. Evans, 35, were busy making Harrisburg's the first community college in Pennsylvania. Cooper had been an Eagle Scout and the protégé of Rabbi Philip David Bookstaber. Evans had been a coal-cracker quarterback and a Marine who worked his way through Dickinson undergraduate and law schools. Both were on the Harrisburg School Board, and neither was shy or submissive. They talked fellow lawyer Carl B. Stoner Sr., school board president, into forming a college-planning committee that included themselves, Superintendent Fred E. Bryan and the scrap-iron king and civic leader, Sam Abrams.

The minute Scranton signed the legislation, Cooper and Evans hit the boondocks like two collegiate hucksters. Somehow they cajoled, or bamboozled, 64 of the then 84 school boards in Dauphin, Cumberland and Perry counties into joining as partners. The timing was perfect for the Cooper-Evans roadshow, as the school districts by 1964 would be flush with their new local wage-tax money.

Harrisburg Area Community College was founded in 1964 and grew to over 9,000 students by 1984. By 2010 there were 23,000 at five campuses.

Cooper and Evans were never charged with larceny, but within eight months they had the Hershey Foundation's Jim Bobb closing the 26-year-old free Hershey Junior College for HACC, had Mayor William K. McBride giving away 157 acres of Wildwood Park for $1, and signed the nation's leading community college expert, Dr. Clyde E. Blocker, once from Flint, Mich., to be president. Blocker as an added favor brought with him Maurice Overholt to be financial vice president. Overholt, who prudently kept his pipe tobacco in plastic sandwich bags, set the groundwork for raising HACC's assets from $1 to $37 million in just two decades.

Cautious Central Dauphin heard the Cooper-Evans song, but waited a year before joining HACC.

On Valentine's Day of 1964, HACC was commissioned as a college. The board held its first meeting 13 days later, composed of such outstanding citizens as Mrs. Helen Swope, Mrs. Gertrude Nauman, James Rowland Sr., William Davis, Robert Rubendall, James R. Doran, and Paul Guyer. Cooper was chairman for 18 years, and then in apostolic succession Evans followed.

Classes for 425 students opened in September 1964 at the old Harrisburg Academy. Blocker, president the first 10 years, predicted steady growth, but after the college in 1967 moved into its Wildwood Campus enrollment soared. HACC began its 20th year last September with 9,139 students, or the equivalent of 4,460 full-timers. Over a full year the college has classes for 16,000.

A baby of Sputnik, HACC soon will begin building a $5.6 million high-tech center.

100.

NOT DEAD YET

In early spring of 1966, two years after Harve Taylor left the Senate, the Dauphin County Republicans held a rally in a Cloverly Heights union hall. When the unendorsed, independent GOP legislative candidate tried to get in, Joe Demma, a trusted Myrmidon of the Taylor organization, barred the door.

George William Gekas, 36, shrieked, the public and press responded, and seven-term incumbent Bob Ogilvie got dumped. In 16 years Gekas went on to become the only Harrisburger ever to complete the unassisted triple play going to state House, Senate, and Congress.

Gekas was not only the first of Greek heritage to make it big in local politics, but also this former assistant district attorney was the first to conquer the post-Taylorites. As ebullient a politician as staid Harrisburg ever had, Gekas simply out-campaigned the old boys. His success wasn't a matter of ideology. In the 1960s, Gekas was more conservative than Taylor himself.

Gekas' 1966 upset inspired pundits to write about the demise of Taylorism, but this establishment with a national reputation wasn't dead yet. Youthful Robert F. Smith was the first independent GOP county chairman after Taylor, but the machine slapped him down in 1970 when he sought to retire Williamsport's Herman T. Schneebell from 10 years in Congress.

Taylorism fostered the self-made image of being inexpugnable, but like most of Harve's wonderful yarns the truth was stretched a bit. In fact, the machine had fights on its hands five times in the final 20 years of Taylor's reign.

Taylor's worst embarrassment was in 1961 when he endorsed septuagenarian Col. John Smith, but Lee F. Swope floored him to be the first elected Democratic judge since the Civil War.

The "Fighting Five" of three dozen conservative Republican businessmen sent Steelton's Walter M. Mumma after Harve's Senate seat in 1948. In the "Pappy v. Pop-Pop" contest, Mumma lost by only 1,150 votes, but two years later won Congress as ally Ed Swartz, "the caveman from Indian Echo," defeated R. Dixon Herman for the Legislature.

The "United Republicans," or "United Arabs" as they were nicknamed, tried to seize county control from Taylor in 1962. Young John J. Shumaker made his public debut in that losing effort, only to resurface 21 years later as Gekas' Senate successor.

Within his own Harrisburg precinct, Taylor got the needle from Dr. Howard Milliken, still remembered as a fine physician and free-spirited character. Taylor didn't want to re-endorse Mayor Milliken, so Doc took a coffin to the GOP rally at the Penn Harris Hotel and jumped out shouting, "I'm not dead yet."

Milliken was the World War II mayor when the city kept its movie theatres dark on the Sabbath but had such a thriving red-light district—at least 38 bawdy houses and speakeasies—that John Gunther in his Inside U.S.A. reported Harrisburg was the nation's one city both the Army and Navy threatened to close down. Doc's view of sin was it was bad when it was followed by a rash. If the dispensaries reported too much venereal disease, Doc dispatched the vice squad.

Taylor finally got rid of Milliken in 1947 by running wholesale jeweler Claude R. Robins. Wallpaper salesman John E. Peters lost to Robins in the GOP primary by 3,713 votes, but then signed on with the Democrats, headed by Ramsey Black and Pat Kerwin, for the general election.

Peters blitzed the town in a campaign tagged "Just Himself" by manager Pete Wambach. A startled Taylor wished he had slated his own pal, Dr. William K. McBride, or even McBride's Polyclinic partner, Doc Milliken, again. Peters pulled a record 80 percent of the electorate to the polls, lost by only 2,614 votes and garnered 18,108 himself—still a record Harrisburg losing vote.

Happily for Taylor, Johnny Peters was a one-shot migraine. It would be a long 20 years before the disorderly Democrats would rise again, when young John M. Lynch almost seized the town from GOP control.

More to Harve's liking was the 1951 mayoral race of Democrat John G. Durbin, who in a mere four years turned Peters' all-time high Democratic vote into the town's all-time low Democratic vote of 4,084. Durbin, then 35, had come to town in 1935 from Somerset County as a state bureaucrat. He left public service to be a haberdasher and finally was the wet-water Irish proprietor of the Senate Hotel, where his Republican friends like Taylor, Demma, Marty Lock, Nolan Ziegler, Bill Lipsitt and Ed Henry supped on chicken corn soup and told Durbin he was wiped out because he was feared as the most awesome opponent local Republicans ever saw.

101.

GALLANT FORCES

M. Harvey Taylor was boss emeritus only three years when Harrisburg Republicans for the 1967 mayoral election got to sucker-punching one another.

Worse yet, the Republicans permitted a Democrat to seize the high moral ground, to be the Lochinvar and "no carpet knight so trim, but in close fight a champion grim."

John Michael Lynch was the first viable Harrisburg Democratic leader in a half-century. He certainly was the first who hadn't previously either been bruised or misused by Taylorism. The nation was still in its apotheosis stage with memories of President John F. Kennedy, and Lynch at 36 was a Philadelphia Irish-bred version of JFK sans greenbacks.

This was the last election Taylor went to campaign headquarters, and the returns he saw were surprising—Lynch lost by only 1,095 votes, carried 23 of 60 districts and his 10,371 votes almost doubled Harrisburg's Democratic registration. If the GOP hadn't spent a record $145,000, according to Harold A. Swenson in the Lynch camp, it might not have won.

Tall, lean and athletic, Lynch only recently had quit the Associated Press after 18 years. He came here for the 1949 legislative session and then in 1959 settled in Harrisburg with his family. Using his sharp reportorial skills, he cited data and talked issues in his campaign—a marked contrast to the usual local palavering politician.

Lynch attacked tax rates on the new Towne House Apartments, the mistakes of redevelopment, the abhorrent housing inspection record, a city budget almost doubled in 10 years, and the true residencies and voting habits of such renowned ward leaders of the Taylor machine as Joe Demma and Irv Harrison. Lynch showed pictures of empty lots that had produced voters in the April primary.

For the first time since Vance McCormick, the Democrats had a figure who could draw a crowd.

Unheard of before for any election in the area, this campaign produced intelligent platforms by Lynch and his opponent Albert H. Straub.

Straub ran the most detailed GOP campaign ever.

Bill Keisling, a Scranton administration whiz kid at 26 and later of Harristown fame, as Straub's manager was making his Harrisburg political debut. Lynch and Straub favored a new form of city government. "Council could be composed of the Three Wise Men, King Solomon and Abraham Lincoln, and the system still would not work," said Straub using Jesuit-educated Keisling's lines.

Popular "Big Al" Straub almost was in the unique position of being a Harrisburg Republican underdog.

He came off two terms on the school board to defeat Councilman Tim Doutrich in a bitter primary by a mere 64 votes—and Doutrich loudly charged Straub's winning margin was provided by the cemetery, prison and phantom-house electorate and by most of the absentee ballots filed for 150 people not in the armed forces and for those patients comatose at the county home. On primary day, four people were arrested and later indicted, including a ward leader placed in jail for allegedly assaulting a woman voter.

Lynch claimed Straub was the "Taylor candidate," though one of Doutrich's business partners was Harve's grandson. "Anyone who knows me knows I am not owned by any group," Straub exploded. Fearing his characteristic bluster could hurt him, Straub toned down and became almost genteel. He re-emphasized his "Plan of Action" that included "Demolition and Rat Control," because Keisling estimated the city had 40,000 nonpartisan rats.

Though the 1967 election was one of the good things to happen in Harrisburg's Sorry Sixties, both candidates ended up star-crossed.

Straub became a fine mayor, but served only two years because of the reform he instigated. Straub also launched the independent audit that uncovered a previous City Hall scandal—one that had it been known earlier could have elected Jack Lynch, but then unfairly rubbed off on Straub in 1969.

The defeated Lynch led the ticket for the City Charter Commission in 1968 that Straub espoused. In 1969 he became deputy state auditor general, helping "The Original" Bob Casey win that office twice but lose to Milton Shapp in the critical 1970 gubernatorial primary.

Lynch eventually moved to Susquehanna Twp. and was elected supervisor before he died of cancer at 43 in 1974. His passing was a huge loss to the gallant forces seeking intelligent and decent politics in the Harrisburg area.

102.

BIG AL STRAUB

As if Howard Cosell metamorphosed into Cary Grant, Albert H. Straub evolved from a loud, one-of-the-boys Harrisburg politicians into a statesman.

With magisterial panache, he became one of the town's fewer, dapper boulevardiers, a senior-citizen sex symbol with a square jaw and a thick silver mane. Whether strolling down the street or presiding over his beloved Tuesday Club, the clangorous "Big Al" was now the stately "Mr. Mayor."

The clock stood still for this once evening-school student at old Harrisburg Tech. When he retired from public service as a councilman in December of 1973, the Patriot-News editorialized he was "a young 68." After that, he accelerated his race with Ponce de Leon and often was mistaken as the slightly older brother of his son Robert, the cuisineur of the French restaurant in Shipoke.

Until Straub was 62, and ran for mayor, he usually sounded like an overdue freight pulling 60 coal cars. Noise and macho had been his style during his 14 years as the city circulation director of the Patriot-News, 22 subsequent years as an insurance man, and 10 years as a school director. In those days, Straub never stepped quietly into any room.

The nickname "Big Al" reflected his early career. Like "Big Red," or "Gov. Jim Duff," he was about 6-foot-1, though chesty, but not truly huge. It was his presence that was formidable, and he had a way of expressing his opinion that could shake the chandelier.

Caught in the 1967 GOP primary that he won over Tim Doutrich by only 64 votes and then in the general election with a 1,095 margin over Jack Lynch. Al Straub lowered his voice and became a gentleman. A sweetness enveloped the guy, but he didn't lose his judgement.

In his first day as mayor, he carried through on his pledge by introducing the resolution for a strong-mayor form of government. It would cost him a full term, but he didn't flinch. Then he helped launch the Greater Harrisburg Movement, which in turn gave birth to Harristown.

With intrepidity, Straub ordered an independent audit and out of it came the greatest City Hall scandal in Harrisburg history.

District Attorney LeRoy Zimmerman's investigation unearthed 19,599 missing traffic tickets, phantom names like "Findley" and "B. Findley" on invoices, illegally split and varied priced biddings, various purchasing irregularities and duplicate payments, and underpriced leased lumbering in the Clarks Valley water preserve. Not included in the alleged offenses was the $563,022 missing over 18 years in redevelopment or the fact that Harrisburg, soft on patronage, was among national leaders per capita with 865 City Hall jobs.

Even a defense attorney alluded to other miscreants' slipping justice's net, but the police chief pleaded guilty to five counts of larceny and two lieutenants were convicted in another case for U.S. income tax evasion. The local jury cleared two City Hall officials and two businessmen of the charge of conspiracy to defraud after Judge William W. Lipsitt's precise but sardonic obiter dictum: "A mere error of judgment or departure from sound discretion is not a crime."

As the scandals unfolded, Harrisburg by a 9-to-1 margin approved a charter commission for strong-mayor government. The Doutrich forces from the 1967 primary were in opposition. Lynch led the ticket for the commission and served as vice-chairman under James A. Evans. In May 1969, a month before the riot, the commission's referendum was approved, 6,614 to 4,665.

Straub took the heat for the scandals and the riot—though completely innocent of both—and in November 1969 he lost the mayorship to Harold A. Swenson by a mere 50 votes.

In his salad days, Big Al's reaction would have been heard as far away as Enola, but now he took his bad luck gracefully. Two years later he even accepted a seat on council. William Maclay 170 years before had gone from the U.S. Senate to the Pennsylvania legislature; but no other Harrisburg politician until Straub was so interested in public service and so humble about status.

Councilman Straub vigorously refused to indulge in petty politics. At last when he retired in 1973 saying, "I feel that I have in some small way made a contribution," Mayor Swenson added, "The city is going to miss Al Straub."

103.

THE SWENSONS

"You all think I'm licked. Well, I'm not licked and I'm going to stay right here and fight for this lost cause even if all the Taylors and all their armies come marching into the place. Somebody'll listen to me."

The unforgettable words of Harold A. Swenson in 1969? No, they're the unforgettable words of Jimmy Stewart in his 1939 classic movie, "Mr. Smith Goes To Washington."

Harold Swenson was Harrisburg's Jimmy Stewart playing Harold Swenson. The two resemble each other—the trim 170 pounds on the lanky 6-foot-2 frames, the sauntering walks, the conservative wardrobes and the low-key manner. Swenson and Stewart of Indiana, Pa., could do the role of the likeable hotel desk clerk and Swenson once was that. Stewart is better at saying, "Ah, shucks," but Swenson behind his gleaming glasses could flash the merciless fish-eye stare at the guest making a single reservation for a tryst.

Stewart and Swenson are the unpretentious guys who should be taken for what they appear to be, and neither needed a nickname—certainly not "Haps" nor "Happy" for Harold.

Strange for an actor or politician, neither insists upon talking very much. Swenson as mayor stubbornly put a 12-minute limit on his speeches and seldom orated that long.

Out of such basics, Swenson fashioned his "Impossible Dream," his theme song and as a career strategy, his rectitude was as studied and almost as perfected as Stewart's.

The key to Swenson's personality and political planning was to stay one step ahead of events and rivals, yet appear to be a casual onlooker. He had no ideology nor old-boy ties, nor even spiteful enemies to chisel a reputation for him. His most effective attack was light ridicule.

The image Swenson was comfortable with was that of being a studious, methodical manager. It fit. Now president of Harrisburg Rotary, Swenson still impresses colleagues as the solid type with one foot in the public sector and the other in the private sector.

Within a month of being mayor, Swenson established his magisterial presence, and within his first year he was regarded as mayor of the entire Harrisburg area, invited to cut many of the ribbons in suburbia. No mayor since Vance McCormick earned this sort of esteem. The irony was not lost upon Swenson, however, that while he was accorded high respect by suburbanites, few had much regard for the city he so zealously promoted.

Though Swenson supported Hubert Humphrey for the 1972 presidential nomination, he was the opposite of the exuberantly expressive Minnesotan. Swenson had no instincts for machine politics and wasn't a capital "D" democrat. Everybody knew who Humphrey was, but Swenson for burgomaster never mentioned he was the son of an immigrant Norwegian banker from Brooklyn—it wouldn't have mattered, as ethnic Harrisburg has a minimal Norwegian vote, doesn't distrust bankers and couldn't care less about Flatbush.

Neither did Swenson publicize he was a Syracuse University graduate, had once worked for the Chamber of Commerce, was a top bureaucrat in the Leader-Lawrence administrations for eight years, and was only 41. His one boast was that he was a private businessman in the city. He and his wife ran a Third Street travel agency for 16 years until late 1970.

Spouse Elsie, many said to Harold's delight, was "the politician in the family." Because of Harrisburg's tradition for bachelor and lone-wolf mayors, Elsie, once a farm girl from the Monongahela Valley, became the city's first "First Lady" and excelled at it. She had come to Harrisburg in the late 1950s as a legislative assistant, married Harold when he was the first director of the state Tourist Business Development Bureau, and became the youngest president of the Federation of Democratic Women.

No female commoner perhaps in local history matched Elsie's public service over two decades, a HERCO director, president of the Symphony, Arts Festival, Girls' Club and Pilot Club, and a Capitol lobbyist.

Chatty, quick-witted, and an exquisite hostess, Mrs. Swenson in the Harrisburg male preserve was careful not to make her husband's mayorship a partnership. Yet in a ranking of Harrisburg's articulate seven sisters, the public protagonists might be Cordelia Pinchot, A. Jane Perkins, and Rosemarie Peiffer, while the distaff diplomats could be Judge Genevieve Blatt, Ginny Thornburgh, Mim Menaker and Elsie Swenson.

104.

THE CLOSEST ELECTION IN CITY HISTORY

When Harold A. Swenson lost his bid for a third term as mayor, he said, "I wasn't a good street politician." That might have been so in 1977, but not in 1969 and 1973. As to his 1969 upset victory, he explained, "I didn't win. The people voted against them." Well, that was partly correct.

Swenson had a penchant for self-deprecating his political acumen. Seeking re-election in 1973, he said, "I may not be too good a politician, nor do I claim to be a statesman, but my record as an administrator has made it clear that I will not permit spending more dollars than are actually available." He was a first-rate manager, but he also wasn't simply a junior-grade politician.

Here was a man who brilliantly devised the strategy to be the first Democrat elected mayor in 58 years. He led the city through the potentially disruptive "Harrisburg 8" Berrigan Trial of 1972 and two months later the Hurricane Agnes Flood. He triumphed over the first City Hall employees strike, avoided any scandal whatsoever, and calmed racial anxieties to avoid confrontations such as the 1969 Riot.

He husbanded the city into its most daring investment of all time—Harristown and the rebuilding of center city—and he so mastered the intricacies of municipal finance that only two minor property tax increases were required during his two terms. Somehow, too, he got along with a Republican council six of his eight years. Unlike his more famous contemporaries, Richard Nixon and Milton Shapp, he didn't infuriate half his electorate either.

The 1969 election took place less than five months after the week-long riot. The town was virtually without ambulance service, because the Harrisburg and Polyclinic hospitals discontinued theirs. The stench of the City Hall scandal was still in the air, and there was additional GOP discord because of the Straub-Doutrich primary brawl.

Swenson seized the opportunity and used three effective tactics: He rung 2,600 doorbells, he developed Republican maverick financial support but insisted not a penny more than $100 from each contributor, and in a series of small but adequate newspaper ads he set forth the plight of the city.

While Mayor Al Straub regrouped Republicans—accepting more than $50,000 from City Hall employees, Harve Taylor, Col. John B. Warden, Joe Bihl and other old warriors—Swenson was saying: "The Harve Taylor machine got so strong that it literally controlled every facet of your government. But the Taylor machine has crumbled. Now it's time for the one-party system to crumble."

As Straub sought to redress the riot by promising a moderate crackdown on crime, Swenson in this year after the Nixon presidential victory, vowed "law and order." When Republicans espoused their business ways, Swenson pointed to Harrisburg's five tax increases in six years, a fouled-up $12.5 million incinerator, and a $5.6 million city debt almost as high as the $7.4 million budget.

Even The Patriot-News helped. When it endorsed the Republican with "After 23 months in office, Mayor Straub is intimately acquainted with urban revolution," readers remembered tear-gas guns and took a second look at the alternative skinny guy. Swenson later estimated he got 65 percent of his vote from Republicans.

It was the closest election in city history, 8,753 to 8,703. Swenson took 29 of 60 districts, losing the notorious Sixth Precinct of the Seventh Ward by 231 votes.

The day-after margin was only 33 votes, but there were absentee ballots and Dauphin County, in its quaint fashion, messed up the new law that they be counted on Election Day. HACC student senator Steve Reed stayed overnight outside the courthouse vault to guard the ballot boxes, while Swenson recklessly agreed the late votes be tallied. To his surprise he netted 17 more votes, though in all he garnered 1,618 fewer votes than Democrat Jack Lynch lost with in 1967.

105.

CHICKEN CORN SOUP POLITICS

The Harrisburg public and pundits complain endlessly about "politics" and "politicians." But paradoxically if a Pennsylvania politician doesn't perpetually play politics, the public and pundits retire him.

Traditionally, "playing politics" in the Harrisburg area has meant not addressing the big issues such as flood control, racial relations, mental health, delinquency, poverty and municipal cooperation—questions Harrisburgers never have taken a statewide leadership in.

"An officeholder's chances of re-election are in direct proportion to what he has done while in office," wrote Cole Atwood in his York County book, *Lafayette's Pigeons* of 1971. "If he has been progressive, aggressive and accomplished much, made many changes, instituted reforms and abolished costly or inefficient practices, his chances of re-election are extremely small. If he has done little or nothing, his chances of re-election loom extremely large."

Atwood was a confidant of Gov. George M. Leader and Mayor Harold A. Swenson, both political doers who had their careers terminated.

The Harrisburg area thinks its "chicken corn soup" styled politics as refreshingly nonpolitical, when often they are the politics of negligence and lethargy. The public, with its bureaucratic bent for neutrality, encourages lackadaisical leadership, and too many local politicians smilingly respond. Why have hassles?

As the late Jack Lynch once quipped, "The people here are difficult to arouse and even when they're aroused, they're not very aroused."

Swenson won a reputation as one of Harrisburg's most astute mayors, even one of Pennsylvania's finest. He put managing first and politics second, and that helped cost him a third term or a seat in Congress. Virtue ended up being its own reward, to Swenson's chagrin.

The Swenson eight years were exceptional. Had all he done was prevent any serious recurrence of racial tensions—and Swenson had almost perfect pitch in his sensitivities to this matter—his would have been a remarkable mayorship.

This mayor was low key almost to a fault, and during some bouts of serious illness he was removed even farther from the public limelight. Mayors Al Straub and Tim Doutrich said more in a week than Swenson did in a month. Mayor Steve Reed says more in a day.

Swenson's first emphasis was to get the exchequer in shape, a trick he did so well that a dozen years later the new Mayor Reed consulted him as a volunteer business manager for the first six weeks of his administration.

"Heartless Harold," as 425 unionized City Hall employees called him, took a weeklong strike in May of 1971 to underline his fiscal responsibility. After Swenson scaled down workers' demands by $100 a year, he raised water rates by $70,000, a utility levy that the state and other tax-exempt properties also would pay.

One of Swenson's first actions as mayor in 1970 was to close the two public comfort stations on Market Square, community heritages from the turn of the century but now costly policing liabilities. When council passed the pull-out trash bill in 1972, this additional city expense became law without the mayor's signature.

He started the first city capital budget of $3.6 million in 1972, and then matched Federal flood funds and revenue-sharing to "modestly upgrade certain vital public services and continue to maintain a stable tax rate," as well as keep the city's then AAA credit rating. He assisted in putting together the Capital Area Transit Authority, or CAT in 1973, after Harrisburg Railways threatened to close the lines in Dauphin and Cumberland counties. Fluoridated water—an emotional issue for decades—was approved in 1970 and at last began in September 1972 after the flood.

During the 1973 election year, council's 1-mill tax reduction took effect without Swenson's signature, and he suffered a veto override on a pension increase to police and firemen. Swenson during the 1968 campaign had tabbed Big Al Straub as "the budget un-conscious mayor," so now Councilman Straub had reason to retaliate. But Straub didn't. His was the one "no" vote on the pending override.

The first Swenson term was packed with achievement. Council President Tim Doutrich acknowledged he and the mayor agreed 90 percent of the time. Swenson raised the figure to 95 percent.

106.

ONE GOOD TERM DESERVES ANOTHER

There was no mistaking that Harold A. Swenson was the managing mayor of Harrisburg, but about his politics there was an elusive quality. Some called him a "Republicrat" for his almost invisible party allegiance and his disdain for the weak Democratic county organization.

At his first mid-term in 1971, Swenson never turned a hand for fellow Democrats running for council and the school board. "I didn't feel it was necessary for me to say that I endorse the Democratic candidates," he nonchalantly explained.

So LeRoy Robinson, a respected young black and a Bell Telephone executive, lost his council bid by only 86 votes, while city treasurer Joe Bihl, an old Republican warhorse with a popular luncheonette at Kline Village, kept office by a mere 357 votes.

Democratic upsets were possible, because the once mighty Harve Taylor organization was disintegrating. One of Taylor's most reliable reservations, Derry Twp., actually elected its first Democrat ever as township supervisor in William Stover, a Hersheypark employee.

By 1972 the Dauphin County Democrats did something they hadn't done since Vance McCormick used to open his wallet—they outspent Republicans in the primary by $15,667 and in the general election by $9,086.

What helped was having Milton J. Shapp as governor, Swenson as mayor, and the local Democratic payrollers in the state Auditor General and Treasurer offices. The GOP, however, still won a majority of elections in Dauphin County and, of course, in Cumberland County.

Embarrassed, the Republicans in 1973 quickly regained their financial pre-eminence. For his re-election, Swenson wouldn't permit City Hall dunning, while courthouse Republicans contribute .05 percent of pay toward their standard bearers.

Swenson and Shapp hadn't much in common, but they did share one distinction: Each ran for his office three times, and each was outspent by the opposition all three times.

The Patriot-News called the 34th mayoralty election in 1973 "more of a scrimmage than a campaign." Having survived the Berrigan trial and Hurricane Agnes, having neither any racial disturbances nor a property tax increase, and proudly flaunting a $20,000 budget surplus, Mayor Swenson was as near to being cocky as his sober Lutheranism would permit.

Swenson casually announced he would run, not having told Democratic city chairman Steve Reed in advance, and then he and wife went gadding to Jamaica.

The primary fight again was left to Republicans, and Councilman Albert S. Schmidt Jr. defeated the Al Straub entry, David E. Wade. Wade, 29, the publisher of a weekly in Port Royal, had been on the City Charter Commission and made his political debut by winning a delegate button to the 1968 GOP national convention, a bid Harve Taylor lost.

Schmidt, of Bellevue Park, was councilman for three years and vice president of the family's Capital Bakers and "Tender Touch" bread. He was the nephew of Monsignor Joseph Schmidt who for 50 years headed the Catholic Diocese Mission Board. Jack Lynch had been the Democrats' first Catholic mayor candidate in 1967, and Albert Schmidt was the Republicans' first. To Harrisburg's credit, religion wasn't an issue, though it had been in the 1960 Kennedy presidential election.

This was Swenson's only easy election. He surmounted a Schmidt registration lead of almost 4,000 to win 7, 742 to 5,777.

The hardest attack the reticent Swenson made was that Schmidt's business was situated outside the city while he was in it. "One Good Term Deserves Another" was the best slogan Swenson could think of, but it convinced the Patriot-News to endorse him as the first Democratic mayoralty candidate it backed since the Vance McCormick era.

For his $20,000 job, Swenson raised $18,180 spent $18,024, and gave the $156 balance to plant a city tree. After his inaugural ball at Hershey, he returned to lay off 50 employees because of the impending recession.

107.

GOING CRAZY EVERYWHERE

"The two-party system in the Harrisburg area was reborn Tuesday," The Patriot–News prematurely editorialized Nov. 8, 1973.

There was some substantiating evidence that year when Harold A. Swenson became the first two-term Democratic mayor since 1890, and Milton J. Shapp the following year was re-elected easily to be the first consecutive two-term Democratic governor since 1847.

By 1975 the Democrats had Cumberland, Perry, Lebanon and York counties, and for the first time in a century would have had the Dauphin County commissionership with a mere 2,129 switch in votes.

Paxtang got its first Democratic mayor in Robert P. Shavor in 1973, and there were Democratic mayors in Middletown, Millersburg, Elizabethville, Halifax and Gratz. Though a workingman's town, Steelton in 100 years had only four years of a democratic burgess and four years of Mayor Baynard Reider. Spike Reider in 1973 lost getting the job back by just four votes.

That same year the Democrats took over in Swatara, Hampden and East Pennsboro, and for the first time ever controlled Derry Twp. Two Democrats won in Lower Paxton, and one each in Upper Allen and Wormleysburg. Jack Lynch, Harrisburg's 1967 mayoralty loser, captured a commission seat in Susquehanna Twp. and four years later, though by then Lynch was dead, the Democrats took charge in that suburb.

Even Camp Hill budged. By a 1-0 write-in vote, H.C. Erickson, 70, became assessor, the first Democrat elected to anything since Robert L. Myers II in the 1930s. "He's one of the cleanest Democrats I know," laughed Christian Siebert Sr., 84, the civic leader who founded the park in 1940.

Politics were going crazy everywhere in the mid-1970s and the Harrisburg area, as it rarely is, was in step. Dutchmen bolted their old patterns, because this was a wild era when an American vice president and then president abruptly departed office, there was an Arab oil boycott and energy crunch, and the economy tightened but inflation soared.

So in Harrisburg the Democrats won two school board seats and a new face, Leon Feinerman, became a councilman. The following year, Steve Reed, only 25, upset four-term Rep. George W. Gekas by 484 votes, though Gekas had a 1,769 registration lead.

It was Harrisburg that had the most startling reversal in political allegiances. Shapp in 1974, with a margin of 537 votes, became the first Democratic governor in the century to take the city. Two years later Jimmy Carter tallied a 621-vote plurality and was the first Democratic president to win the city since Franklin D. Roosevelt in 1936.

The tide continued in 1976. Feinerman in City Council was joined by Marianne D. Faust, Dick Stabinski and LeRoy Robinson, and for the first time in 50 years Democrats had the majority. Probably for the first time in a century, the Democrats ran the school board with Tom Connolly as president.

But was all this local ticket-switching merely a curious passing fancy? The Republican Harrisburg area, after all, was immune to the Roosevelt New Deal of the 1930s and wasn't fazed by the Kennedy-Johnson era of the 1960s.

Today a decade later, it is clear that the situation of a two-party system remains far from being clear. Even in 1973, despite all the Democratic cheering, there were 16 municipalities, mostly on the West Shore, where the Grand Old Party candidates ran without opposition. Bill Goodling was re-elected to Congress in 1976 carrying every precinct in Cumberland County, and he doesn't even live there.

In hindsight, the Democrats never established a leadership base. Republicrat Swenson and Maverick Shapp epitomized the Independent strain in the party. Steve Reed, too, is a mugwump, or a Reedocrat who couldn't make peace with seven Democratic council members in 1962 and 1983. Whatever the promise of Cumberland County Commissioners Jacob Myers and Nelson Punt in their victories of 1975 and 1979 vanished with their deaths in 1983.

108.

A HOTBED OF SOCIAL REST

Bridges incite Harrisburgers' vanity, as John O'Hara recognized in his 1949 novel, *A Rage To Live.* The town's Republican mayor in 1919 is completing 14 years and decides a bridge needed at Washington Street should be named for him, "Laughing Gas George" W. Walthour, a dentist. The district attorney as party boss becomes so irate he has Walthour canned, and the doc is one of the few Harrisburgers in the novel with otherwise high morals.

The M. Harvey Taylor Bridge opened in 1952 after the full Senate, including Camp Hill's George N. Wade, voted for the name, while Taylor abstained. "They named it for me because I always took people across," Taylor joked about the 30 remaining years of his life. He was especially proud because it was his bridge, not Wade's, that led to the West Shore.

Wade didn't get his bridge until six months before his death in 1974, and then, as if it were a comment on the traditional anonymity of West Shore politics, the span usually is referred to as the "I-81 Bridge." Furthermore, the bridge was to have more prominence by connecting at Maclay Street for the Farm Show, but Mayor Nolan Ziegler was overruled and the flood-drenched Governor's Mansion was built there instead.

Dapper George Wade was the "Old Smoothy," in reporter John Scotzin's words, but he had the misfortune to be Taylor's contemporary and to represent Cumberland County, which during his day was about as eventful as the kingdom of Nepal.

Wade was 17 years Taylor's junior, but like him was self-educated, keen-witted, sold insurance, hobnobbed with bankers, and was a conservative, diehard Republican. In his youth, Wade was on the Camp Hill School Board, president of borough council, and put two terms in the state House.

Wade and Taylor joined the Senate together in 1941, and Wade went on to serve 33 years—the longest reign in the 200 years of the Senate. As Highways Committee chairman for 12 years, Wade presided over the largest road-building program ever in Pennsylvania. In 1950, he sought the lieutenant governorship and in 1962 he suggested himself for governor.

Taylor became Senate boss in 1947 and blocked Wade's advancement by being president pro tempore 16 years. He knew that to keep his statewide GOP clout, he couldn't share power with a neighboring suburbanite such as Wade. Even after Taylor departed in 1964, Senate Republicans rejected Wade as president pro term by one vote.

For all his seniority—he died as a senator at 81—Wade didn't have Taylor's passion for power. Somnolent Cumberland County wasn't like that anyway. It had neither a boss nor a "War Board" of politicos such as Delaware County, but rather was led by a synod of elders.

The county is divided between Carlisle and the West Shore. As once America's gateway to the frontier, Carlisle until recently thought of the West Shore as nouveau riche. After all, George Washington slept in Harrisburg and Carlisle, not Drexel Hill or Good Hope Farms. If the West Shore were a city, it would be Pennsylvania's fourth biggest, but also the biggest without a county courthouse.

The elders kept Cumberland County pleasantly balkanized, decently governed, and "a hotbed of social rest," as humorist Russell Baker once described Richmond, Va. Wade played a large role in this continuity and stability. So did Sam Williams, Wade's office aide who was mayor of Camp Hill for 20 years until he was beaten at 79 in 1973; the New Cumberland mayor for 21 years, Gerald E. Kaufman, and such stalwart courthouse figures as Sheriff Clyde E. Fisher and commissioners Oliver J. Dickey, Herb Stewart and Ray Sawyer.

Dale F. Shughart was a leading elder. He was district attorney, 1964-65, and then judge for a record 34 years, as well as president of Dickinson Law School since 1962. The wise and courtly judge perfectly complemented the nattily attired, gadding Wade.

Cumberland County provincialism began fading in the 1960s with school consolidation, shopping centers and interstates. Wade died the year before Jake Myers and Nelson Punt captured the county for the Democrats in 1975 and just before women such as Rosemarie Peiffer, Ruth Wrye, Marie Phillips and Pat Vance disrupted the old-boys network.

Maybe it was a sign of the new commotion or a last gasp of old-time mulishness, but when Spiro Agnew left the vice presidency in disgrace in 1973 he received a write-in vote for mayor of Camp Hill.

109.

NO HIGHER OFFICE

If Harrisburg is "dead as a doornail" how come the town makes the headlines so often? Mayor Harold A. Swenson used to ask.

It was during his second term that the state police, using a 1972 law, infiltrated the "Boulevard of Broken Dreams," or North Third Street, and arrested Johns as well as Janes in retail prostitution.

With a chic police woman decoy, nicknamed "Honey Bear," the troopers apprehended their first 44 men on Sept. 17, 1976. After their names appeared in the newspaper, the gents paid $226 in fines and costs, though all they had done was respond to a saucy wink.

Gendarmes prowled for 21 months, in all booking 129 hookers and 214 hookees, including a Philadelphia lawyer, a borough politician, a minister, a visiting rabbi, a TV commentator, a state Justice Department investigator, a doctor, a restaurateur, a 70-year-old Camp Hill sport and a 77-year-old nightowl from Penbrook—civic pillars mostly married and mostly embarrassed.

As sinful Third Street became known as the "Special Intensity District," the West Shore with moral vigor cleaned out X-rated movie houses. After District Attorney Ed Bayley and Rep. Hal Mowery got busy, Harrisburg City Hall reporter Don Sarvey quipped, "You'll need a variance in the zoning to have sex in Camp Hill."

Sex if legalized might have kept Harrisburg solvent, but otherwise Swenson spent a second term, 1974 to 1977, unspectacularly but diligently keeping the old burg afloat. He had to be the compleat manager, a task that suited Childe Harold's nondramatic tastes.

By the end of 1974 the city budget and incinerator deficit was a startling $850,000. Swenson avoided any tax increases in his first term. Now he raised water, sewer and trash bills, which the commonwealth and the nonprofit, tax-exempt organizations also would pay. One battle he lost was his court case against B'nai B'rith and Presbyterian apartments for in lieu of taxes, worth $141,000 annually.

Swenson fought valiantly against heavy pay and pension raises. On the advice of consultant actuary Conrad M. Siegel, he was able to reduce the pension red ink by an amazing $4.5 million, yet the unfunded liability was still $23.4 million when he left office—and seven years later it is more than $30 million.

In retrospect, Swenson suffered politically because of his fiscal prudence. He was a better mayor than ever when he lost his 1976 bid for Congress and his 1977 third term.

An issue like the city employee residency requirement hurt, while there were steps forward that produced few votes, such as the Historic Districts Ordinance of 1974, the Hamilton Health Center development, the hiring in 1976 of the first policewoman in Elida M. Beard, and the $4 million project for the PP&L two-mile steam line to the incinerator.

Interestingly, the mayor had his defeated rival, Al Straub, in his first council and in his second term he had his next defeated rival, Al Schmidt, there, while all the time Councilman Tim Doutrich was awaiting his turn to be mayor. Harrisburg went through the 1960s with no mayor completing his term, but from 1971 to 1978 it had an ex-mayor and would-be mayors in council providing experience in city affairs.

When Williamsport oil dealer Herman T. Schneebell announced his retirement from Congress in 1976, Swenson filed for the Democratic primary. He expected to defeat Lycoming County District Attorney Allen E. Ertel, but then HACC Professor Anthony Petrucci and Hershey businessman Don Rippon jumped into the fray and diverted 10,452 votes. Republican State Rep. Joe Hepford gave up 14 years' seniority expecting to take on Swenson, only to lose by 3,066 votes to Ertel, a candidate who hadn't carried a precinct in Dauphin County's Democratic primary.

No Harrisburg mayor has ever gone on to higher office, but none, not even Vance McCormick who lost the governorship, was as disappointed as Swenson. He had every reason to feel disgruntled with his "dumb Democrats." The next year, less than half-heartedly, he filed for a third term as mayor. His reluctance showed, and when he lost it hardly hurt at all.

110.

SWENSON'S SINCERE RELIEF

A barometer of successful American politics is for incumbents to serve at least two terms. There were six consecutive one-term American presidents, and then came the Civil War. From John Kennedy through Jimmy Carter, there have been five straight presidents who didn't make it through full anticipated tenures.

Harrisburg, too, has had five mayors, or back to 1955, who left office either through death or defeat. Harold A. Swenson was the only one of them to seek a third term.

The city raised the pay for the winner of 1977 from $20,000 to $30,000, though that remuneration was hardly adequate for the heartburn that goes with responsibility.

For the first time in modern history, city Democrats in 1977 had a registration lead, and 2,209 amounted to almost 20 percent of the voter turnout. All Swenson had to do was pull three out of every four votes he got in his original 1969 victory, and he would have a third term.

Swenson organized well enough for his campaign. Republicans like Al Straub—who at 71 wouldn't run against him—and realtor Frank Foose were on his reelection committee, as well as the noted elderly black neighborhood activist, Mrs. Sara Jones. Swenson spent $14,812, or less than before and less than half what his opponent invested, but after eight years as a scandal-free mayor he didn't need much introduction to the community.

But a mayor gains enemies as he adds gray hair, and Swenson had a packful. He supported police tests, so a portion of the black electorate went against him. He signed the short-lived residency requirement, so many city hall employees, police and firemen weren't in his camp.

Though only 51 and off a bout of bad health, a tired Swenson seemed more imperturbable than his usual imperturbability. His fighting spirit might have been drained 18 months before when he had been sandbagged out of becoming a congressional candidate.

Tim Doutrich, wanting the mayorship for a decade, became the Republican standard bearer. He was the well-known hometown boy, 16 years on City Council, and the last of the Harve Taylor organization lads. "Elect a Friend" was Doutrich's slogan, and his messages always began, "I have lived in Harrisburg all my life."

It was to be a Republican year. Watergate was three years past, and in Harrisburg lameduck Gov. Milton J. Shapp made it worse for local Democrats when he gave away his clout in his absurd bid to be president in 1976.

So Doutrich triumphed, 6,578 to 5,128, and City Council went Republican and all three winners for the school board were Republican.

Around the community, only Swatara Twp. stayed Democratic in Dauphin County, and only George W. Davidson Jr. in Carlisle could win a Democratic mayorship—a paradox, because Carlisle long had been one of the most GOP-dominated towns in the nation. Of all the Republican victories, however, Robert G. Reid's upset of Middletown Mayor Harry H. Judy by 89 votes was the sweetest. Reid, a civics teacher and former athlete, is black in a borough with about 100 black voters. So he got the job just in time for the Three Mile Island incident.

A regretful Swenson left his last budget of $11.65 million unsigned—a puzzling precedent that his successor also would follow in 1981—and he departed the Mayor's Office of Room 100 a day early. "My hitch is over," he told reporters. "I have given a good eight years of my life to this city as its elected leader and I am pleased at where we are, compared to where we were."

Swenson's "sincere relief" was shared by fellow retiring Democrat John Lawler up in Lewistown. Both had been mayors during the 1972 Flood, but Lawler at 83 had campaign ribbons for two floods. He held the state record for being mayor 34 years, and before then had been a councilman during the 1936 Flood.

Harold Swenson's parting remarks were: "I severely misjudged the physical and mental drain that the round-the-clock bit does to anybody. There's nothing that reaches the mayor's desk that's easy."

111.

SPOILS INHERIT THE VICTOR

"I don't intend to fail," Paul E. Doutrich Jr. exclaimed in his inaugural address on Jan. 3, 1978.

The four following Doutrich years were not so much crashes as ones of high winds and rough terrain, with the old wartime paratrooper in a desperate struggle to land safely.

A decade before, Lyndon Johnson quipped: "When the burdens of the presidency seem unusually heavy, I always remind myself that it could be worse—I could be a mayor."

Doutrich had the mettle, the optimism and more elected city experience than any of his 30 predecessors as mayor, but he underestimated the demands of the job. As a former athlete, he would agree he wasn't in top shape for the fast play required.

"The last few years have not been particularly good ones for me," he conceded as he became mayor. Troubles with marriage and alcohol plagued him, and his personal debts piled high after the demise of his retail clothing chain.

There was a haggard and occasionally befuddled look to this mayor, accentuated sartorially by the ex-haberdasher's image. In an age when politicians, as well as puddlers, potato peelers and even political reporters, all preened themselves to be Beau Brummells, the personable Doutrich remained pristine dishabilled.

Time magazine in a 1979 article about Three Mile Island even took a shot at the mayor without knowing who he was, describing Doutrich as looking "a bit like bug-eyed comedian Rodney 'I don't get no respect' Dangerfield."

Doutrich's strong point was his disdain of pretense in a town where vanity often is rampant. He was the seasoned sandlotter, the hometown boy from the neighborhoods and clubs. Nobody ever disliked Tim Doutrich, not even at the end of his mayorship when he was like a bedraggled Willie Loman due some smiles and fulfilled promises.

His love of conviviality earned him a career of two years on the school board and a record 16 on City Council. As an enthusiastic baseball fan, he argued during the 1960s that Harrisburg needed a modern public sports stadium.

His dream was to be a congressman like his grandfather, Isaac Hoffer Doutrich. Ike, a farmboy from Middletown, was a proud Downtown retailer from 1908 until his death in 1941. He was on City Council for three years and then in Washington for 10, or until Guy Swope defeated him in the 1936 Roosevelt landslide.

Ike was a comfortable Front Streeter with a chauffeur and style. Young Tim as the oldest grandchild idolized the guy. In fact, he made his first political speech for his grandfather. He was a sixth-grader at the Steele School and the teacher caught him talking in the back of the class. "Paul, if you like to talk so much, suppose you come up front and talk to the class," said Miss LaVene Grove. So Tim instructed his friends to have their parents vote for his grandpa.

John C. Kunkel, Walter W. Mumma and Herman T. Schneebell preempted Ike's congressional seat and Jesse D. Wells bought out his business in 1956, so Tim—almost never called Paul Jr.—had to make his way up in local politics and start his own business. One of his partners was M. Harvey Taylor II, the grandson of the senator.

The mayorship is the mountaintop for one path in Harrisburg politics. None who held the job since 1860 went farther. Doutrich readjusted his sights for it.

In 1967 he lost a bitter primary to Al Straub by only 64 votes, an election that resulted in fraudulent-vote court cases and had Republicans—the loudest of whom was I. Emanuel Meyers, the Darrow of Harrisburg—flinging obscenities at one another. Never a quitter, old sandlotter Doutrich in 1977 finally topped two-term Mayor Harold A. Swenson. The spoils inherited the victor.

112.

SKIDDING ON THE ICE

As a teenager, cultural savant Jacques Barzun was a student at Harrisburg Tech just five years before it became City Hall. In a recent book, Dr. Barzun defined government as "hasty management under stress"—a perfect description for the Doutrich administration, the last to use the Old Tech building.

Tim Doutrich was mayor in 1978 only three weeks when a 15-inch snowstorm hit, atop a prior 5 inches covering the city's 450 miles of streets. Disorganized crews were late in responding, and the $300,000 price tag for snow removal created the first of many budget crises.

"Harold Swenson got us a flood. Tim Doutrich had to do something to top that," quipped Bern Sharfman in his Patriot-News Cynic's Corner.

Snow falls on the just and the unjust alike. Exactly four years later, in 1982, the new Mayor Steve Reed was greeted with a 9.5-inch blizzard that was misplayed into a motorists' rhubarb.

The Doutrich administration started skidding on the ice of its first storm, and it never stopped.

That following July of 1978, Doutrich tried for a "Harrisburg—A Clean Scene" campaign. When it backfired, it only made more obvious how squalid some of the aging neighborhoods had become. Within a month the city, rather than being scrubbed, was forced to live with a lower bond rating by Moody's Investors Service.

Doutrich was at his best warning about Harrisburg's potentially troubled water system. He said the main line from Clark's Valley must be replaced and a reserve filtration reservoir be developed on the 31.5 acres behind the State Hospital that Governor Shapp transferred to the city's domain two months before he left office. Right though he was, neither the mayor nor anybody else had the slightest idea of how to finance such a $30 million project.

With not a penny to spare, Doutrich was forced to conduct a holding operation. His big plus is that he avoided serious racial disturbances, but, on the other hand, there was little, if any, middle-class migration, white or black back to the city.

He did obtain a $2 million bond for two new fire stations. Harrisburg for library service followed Lower Paxton of the mid-1960s in adopting a special property tax, one-third of a mill.

For half his tenure, Doutrich presided over a depressed, bombed-out Downtown. Mary Sachs after 60 years joined others in closing. Finally for the Christmas season of 1980, Strawberry Square was ready to compete for customer's attention that only a few years before the pundits said was lost forever to the suburbs.

Doutrich, like his predecessor Harold Swenson, coexisted with Harristown. He was agreeable to some of its suggestions, but was obstinate when the nonprofit, non-elected corporation wrangled a commitment for a $12.5 million city hall after the Dauphin County commissioners wouldn't be partners.

As an alumnus of the old Esquire Bar, the mayor was a great champion for getting a new version of the Penn Harris Hotel, especially after the Harrisburg Marriott opened in 1980. Yet valuable time was lost to realize this top priority—though the record annual inflation of 12.5 percent for those four years, prime interest rates that peaked at 21 percent, and the hotel industry's preference for interstate road linkage contributed more to Harrisburg's being shut out than the local bumbling.

Had fate been gentler, Doutrich might have had a successful "Tim Doutrich's" men's fashion store in Strawberry Square and a reserved table at the new Esquire Bar in the Harrisburg Grand Hotel.

But fate was punishing. Like Herbert Hoover, Jerry Ford and Jimmy Carter, but without the presidential aura and profits, Doutrich was defeated for re-election in 1981 and unceremoniously ushered out. He left virtually insolvent, without a job, and only a $13,500 municipal pension to sustain him.

For more than a year, Tim Doutrich's health was so precarious he almost disappeared from public view. By mid-1983 he resurfaced with a cane and was trimmer than he had been since high school. Then he married for a third time. His new bride, once a fellow nursing-home patient, affirmed that the old pol first approached her "wanting to talk." Tim Doutrich never lost that gift.

113.

UNSAVORY DAYS

Mayor Tim Doutrich had his shortcomings, but hypocrisy and hyperbole weren't among them. He left office in January of 1982 never proclaiming his four years were the golden age.

For a year afterward the ex-mayor, though bedridden and fighting for his health, was in the news, because his successor, Stephen R. Reed, kept him there. As Gov. Dick Thornburgh excoriated former Gov. Milton Shapp, Reed socked it to Citizen Doutrich. In the past, ex-governors and ex-mayors were peacefully forgotten—the Republican and Democratic state committees sometimes even lost their addresses.

Ten months into his own administration, Reed drew up a 25-page "Fiscal Recovery Report," itemizing the mess he inherited: "years of unchecked spending, poor budget planning, inadequate record-keeping, inflated revenue projections, growing carry-over and unretired debt and serious managerial, operational and maintenance deficiencies."

These charges had some basis, because in 1984 City Controller James J. McCarthy reported deficits of $535,000 and $474,000 for the last two years of the Doutrich administration. Yet Mayor Doutrich shouldn't be the scapegoat, as other City Hall officials and council members shared in the ineptitude of a beleaguered city to cope with multiple urban crises.

Doutrich did leave an essentially un-workable incinerator that was a $1 million annual liability and a Chicago consultant said needed $3 million in improvements. He also left behind $2 million worth of uncollected delinquent taxes and utility bills—two City Hall public servants owed $11,400 themselves and one also had the nerve to have his brother on the payroll.

The last budget, which Doutrich proudly refused to sign, was brazenly under-financed and required 3.5 mills more after it was revised. Bond payments weren't covered. The payroll was fat, there was no new hotel, and no solid prospects for municipal growth. Management was so sloppy the city was paying the schools $3,100 for a census it couldn't use because it had repealed its head tax five years earlier. The blundering was such that $337,301, the equivalent of a biweekly payroll, was found hidden after two years in a forgotten bank account.

Yet Mayor Doutrich met more than his share of tough decisions. Property taxes went up during his four years by 41 percent, as compared to 31 percent for eight years of the Swenson administration.

Those days from 1978 through 1981 indeed were unsavory. The warden at the county prison went to federal prison for taking at least $1,350 in bribes from inmates. The assistant police chief pleaded guilty of accepting as much as $6,000 in bribes for not closing down illegal poker games. One city GOP leader was acquitted of tampering with the public records and the election code. But Doutrich was clean—and poor to prove it.

For such a lifelong politician, Doutrich wasn't sharp as a political manager. To win office, he made too many promises that resulted in lifting payroll restraints Harold Swenson insisted upon.

Thirsting to be in command again, hometown Republicans got smashed on patronage—not just in City Hall but in the school district. The spoils system flourished. Two Republican school directors even ended up in paying jobs in city government. Once during 1979 there were 15 lawyers sharing City Hall's legal largesse. That same year, the payrollers made so much use of the 100-car municipal fleet that the city pumps registered 940 gallons of unbilled gasoline, priced then at about $1.30 a gallon.

The scene around good-natured Tim was out of control.

Dauphin County's two major Republican figures kept clear and didn't use Harrisburg as their base.

Rudolph Dininni, a prominent contractor from Rutherford and a legislator since 1966, was so persuasive he could effect the defeat of the 1980 county Home Rule Study Commission referendum, even though the GOP Executive Committee approved it, 27-3.

LeRoy S. Zimmerman, after a record 15 years as district attorney, became Pennsylvania's first elected attorney general in 1980. No local politician had achieved such high office since Boss Ed Beidleman won lieutenant governor in 1918.

114.

A NEW GENERATION

The Steve Reed election of 1981 was a blitzkrieg—a Democrat sweeping the 15 wards and would have had all 42 precincts if eight votes switched in the famous "Goldwater precinct" of Sibletown.

Incumbent Mayor Tim Doutrich not only lost 8,782 to 3,731, but also he ran 3,521 city votes behind Republican Judge Clarence C. Morrison, and he had the worst showing for a GOP mayoral candidate in the century.

Yet this Reed triumph was anything but an easy coronation. It took grit, keen strategic planning and ambition for him to pull it off.

Only 32—and just 32 months older than Mayor Vance McCormick of 1902—Reed was minority county commissioner after a six-year stint in the Legislature. Never defeated, he risked his career for the mayor's job and took on a rough primary to get there.

Councilman Earl F. Gohl, only 31, might have been the favorite, as he enjoyed the more traditional Democratic backing from the Shipoke-Midtown districts. He had a master's degree from Penn State, five years experience as a Senate staffer, and had been an assistant to Mayor Harold Swenson in 1975.

Stephen R. Reed took to the microphone and high office easily. Beers wrote that opinions he'd heard placed Reed "between Herod and St. John the Divine," but there was "never a satisfactory explanation of who the man is."

The Reed-Gohl contest threatened to split Harrisburg Democrats, especially after Reed hesitated to say he would support Gohl in the general election if the councilman won the bid. "I have never had an opponent so personal and insulting," claimed Reed, while the quiet, almost shy Gohl charged Reed with "inaccuracies and just plain lies."

Reed won by 292 votes—his closest election. A third candidate, Raymond Talley, pulled 428 crucial votes. Reed did carry 25 precincts to Gohl's 14, and three were a tie.

As mayor, Reed in his first two years contended with Council President Gohl, who presided over a council bloc that remained impervious to Reed's smiles or his steamrolling tactics. Buttons saying "Earl" even appeared. "When Steve really wants to talk to me," Gohl said, "he calls me on the phone and we have a constructive conversation, but when he wants to take a political shot he usually writes a news release, calls it a letter, and distributes it to the media."

The Reed-Gohl impasse contributed mightily to City Hall's notorious fissures of 1982-83.

Republicans in 1981 had all the makings of a blood battle, too, but luckily lacked the energy for one. Incumbent Doutrich was challenged in the primary by Julius McCoy and former policeman, Ernest J. Napoli. McCoy, once All-American basketball star from Farrell and Michigan State, was the first black ever to seek the mayorship.

For the often-heard charge that the blacks were "taking over" Harrisburg, the 1981 campaign proved blacks were above noxious racial politics. McCoy, Judge Morrison, council candidates William A. Robinson, Reizdan B. Moore and Calvin E. Gilchrist and school board incumbent Clarice Chambers didn't form a "black ticket," but ran as individuals and all but McCoy won.

Religion also wasn't a factor. Reed became the first elected Catholic mayor of Harrisburg—40 years after Pittsburgh had its first and almost 20 years after Philadelphia.

Doutrich called Reed a "job hopper" and added, "He talks a good game, but has failed miserably in his previously elected office." The intense Reed, then a taut 165 pounds on his 5-foot-9 frame, said the election was "Harrisburg's future at stake." He outspent Doutrich, $33,500 to $30,800.

Strawberry Square had a debate, sponsored by the Junior League, National Council of Jewish Women, the University Women and the League of Women Voters. Reed, once Bishop McDevitt's champion debater, was crisp and in command. It was a spectacular performance, not an exaggeration to claim Reed rivaled John Kennedy or Ronald Reagan on the podium. As Thaddeus Stevens had done in the Legislature 150 years before, but without Old Thad's caustic wit, Reed left his opponent stammering.

In his inaugural, Reed proclaimed "a new generation" for Harrisburg. That was true. He was young enough to be the town's first post-war-baby mayor.

115.

REVEALING GLIMPSES

At a groundbreaking ceremony, Steve Reed flashed a gleaming smile and mused about his "days of innocence" 22 months before when he became mayor.

Stephen Russell Thomas Reed wasn't innocent—not naïve nor angelic—when he was 3.

He shares with such local illuminati as Simon Cameron and Harve Taylor a precocious worldliness, savvy and go-getting alertness that must have originated at conception and was operative by puberty.

Reed will be 35 in August—a Leo by the Zodiac sign, wouldn't you have guessed. He has been in public life 21 of those years, or since he became a volunteer in the Lyndon Johnson presidential election.

He has been the "Enfant Terrible," "Stevie Wonder" or just plain "Steve Reed," said with a teeth-clenched sneer by opponents.

Yet who he really is can only be deciphered by swirling events and a few revealing glimpses. Like Cameron and Taylor, he doesn't get frankly personal. You can bet he'll never emote publically in the Richard Nixon style. Partly by his design, partly by his apparent self-moral necessity to be boss, and partly by his vehement inner drives, he is both blessed and cursed with a mystique.

Only such a psyche as Reed's, at its best and worst, could challenge Harrisburg's usual lackadaisical politics of accommodation with the activistic heretical attitude he doesn't mask.

This columnist has heard hundreds of curbstone and barroom opinions that place Reed anywhere between Herod and St. John the Divine, but never a satisfactory explanation of who the man is.

The first of two previous columns about Reed was back in 1972 when he turned 23 and already was Dauphin County registrar of vital statistics and chairman of the Board of Assistance. The joking was that by 1982 he would be eligible to run for governor and by 1984 for president. The big stuff, however preposterous for anyone, appeared reasonable for Reed's aspirations. The mayorship seemed so implausible the column never mentioned the job.

Like Cameron and Taylor, Reed essentially is self-educated. They never got out of grammar school. He was president and champion debater of his 1967 class of 394 students at Bishop McDevitt and he attended, but never graduated from Dickinson and HACC. He was the 1979 student president at HACC.

As Cameron always thought of himself as a humble printer and Taylor as a hometown small businessman, Reed's alter ego might be that of a lawyer. He affects the style of an attorney, not just the pragmatic mind but sometimes the irritating all-knowingness. Had he ever taken the time to earn a law degree—an omission he must regret—his unremitting dealing could have made half the local legal fraternity seeth with enmity and the other half with envy. In public rouses, Reed relishes legal repartee and isn't servile to any solicitor's learned opinion or vexation.

Reed was born Aug. 9, 1949, in Shippensburg. He became a Harrisburger when he was 11, the year John F. Kennedy, possibly his only idol, was elected president. Reed was the middle child of three in a broken family, and he remained not just a bachelor but close to his mother until her death.

At age 15 in 1965, Reed managed a losing candidate's City Council bid, but discovered politics his vocation. "It will kill you if you don't like it, but when you love politics, it's wonderful," he later said.

Reed worked the 1967 Jack Lynch mayoral campaign and the 1969 and 1973 Harold Swenson victories. By age 27 he got the idea he would like to be mayor, threatening at the last minute to face Swenson in the primary fight.

His youth, Reed knew instinctively, was his asset, so at age 25 he gathered followers from Bishop McDevitt, HACC and River Rescue of which he was chairman, and he made his big move. That was 1974 and he upset four-term Rep. George Gekas by 517 votes. A consumer-type, anti-crime and neighborhood legislator, Reed served six years, doubling his final year on the Hill as a Dauphin County commissioner.

He had seven years of elective office when he became mayor Jan. 4, 1982, and he was only 32.

116.

SUCH A WHIRLWIND

"One is not finished when he is defeated; he is finished when he quits. Always keep fighting. When one door closes, another will open."

This could be Stephen Reed's philosophy, but the words are Richard M. Nixon's from his 1979 introduction to his reissued *Six Crises*.

Nixon had six crises in 13 years. Reed, by this column's count, had eight crises in his first year as mayor and at least 12 in 1983.

Reed personalizes his politics and explains himself a great deal, sometimes humorously but invariably knowing in his heart he's right. He has assuredness and resiliency that rivals New York's Mayor Ed Koch. Occasionally politicians lend themselves for apt comparisons. With Reed, you need a library of history, literature and psychology books.

Take Sophocles' Philloctetes Principle, as Jacques Barzun applied to Abraham Lincoln: "Superior strength is inseparable from disability." Commonplace politicians usually conceal themselves in mediocrity. Gifted leaders like Reed often unabashedly expose their wounds as well as their brawn.

Take Lord Byron: "To create, and in creating live a being more intense, that we endow with form our fancy, gaining as we give the life we image." It fits.

Take Disraeli: "I am one of those to whom moderate reputation can give no pleasure." Perhaps a bull's-eye.

Take Robert A. Dahl's 1961 study about American mayors and how they must have "centrifugal thrust" to pull power to themselves. Beleaguered Harristown confirms Reed's fierce preoccupation with centrifugal thrust.

Take Harrisburg scholar Arnold A. Rogow's 1963 study of "game politicians"—the ones who seek respect and rectitude, not riches, from their gaining power. Periodically Reed disdains approval, but he always has been hyperbole's child and lightning-fast with media releases and camera readiness.

After nine years of elective office in three jobs, Reed—with a cool sense of his own purpose—has positioned himself where he can change things. The "economic notables," in Professor Dahl's words, don't run for mayor. Young Steve grasped the post to become the most significant, if not the most beloved, Central Pennsylvanian since Harve Taylor.

This workaholic bachelor is a dogged activist. Yet, strangely, he has few confreres, no mentors or running mates, few old legislative friends and is that rare type not munificent to fellow politicians' need of flattery.

"There are risks and costs to a program of action. But they are far less than the long-range risks and costs of comfortable inaction," wrote Reed's idol, John F. Kennedy. Both Reed and JFK learned from Machiavelli's Prince, "It is better to be impetuous than cautious."

Reed is a vigorous, ultra-intense optimist and an informed, persevering advocate of his city. Differing from many contemporary public figures, Reed is not shallow. He has a keen mind, and much of his urban thinking is sound.

Best of all, Reed isn't fazed by opposition. Ironically for a man whose inner motivation might be self-esteem, he won't wallow or backslide for slack-jawed approval—not from the power structure, the press or the electorate.

If Reed were simply a composite of these admirable traits, he'd be Abe Lincoln. But he isn't—"not yet," he would joke.

The mayor can be divisive, accusatory, and possessive, an infighter who often prefers confrontation to conciliation. Even for a Democrat he has an exaggerated compulsion for what compatriots have called "hard-edged tactics."

Reed the politician is paradoxical: his incessant visibility yet his mystique, his creative vitality but tendentious one-upmanship, and that entire hue of "shadow versus substance" that Kennedy borrowed from playwright Sean O'Casey.

This Harrisburger should be honored for having some of the enemies he has. To critics who said area politics for a century needed a new voice and ideas, Steve Reed is willing to lead with his jaw for that distinction.

Yet as the Reed career unfolds, the question is can the best of constituencies—which Harrisburg isn't—keep up with such a whirlwind?

117.

REED'S VISION

As an innovator, Steve Reed leads the Central Pennsylvania league. Ideas flick through the fertile imagination of this political virtuoso.

In Reed's first 25 months as mayor, this columnist counted 24 serious Reedian action proposals. During his six years as a legislator, Reed sponsored or co-sponsored almost 200 pieces of legislation or one every three legislative days.

Even his detractors agree Reed is a "quick think," but argue many Reedian proposals can be hasty and poorly prepared. At times Reed's impulsive buoyancy is all too evident, yet the mayor's winning percentage is impressive.

What Reed has is a comprehension—so vivid it is almost a revelation—of Harrisburg's basic needs for the rest of the 20th century. The imperatives are a low-tax reputation and attractive investment incentive so the town becomes again, as it was from 1900-1920, an income-creating and jobs-growth community. "It is crystal clear that Harrisburg must develop new revenue sources and that such revenue cannot be dependent upon the outdated state tax laws," Reed said in August [1983].

Better economics, the mayor believes, would directly benefit not just blacks and the poor, but the powerbrokers in suburbia who still retain affection for the city.

In his insights about social economics, Reed is a decade in front of most local politicians, a century ahead of some. But with the Reed vision goes mulish. It took a humiliating peace treaty with Harristown in July 1983 to avert economically Beiruting Harrisburg.

Reed battled city council unremittingly his first 25 months, but the two did advance in the right direction. Their annual budget increases averaged 5 percent and property tax 3 percent, as compared to previous administration's annual 9 and 10 percent, respectfully.

Many of Reed's best proposals are what he called "revenue-enhancers"—steam from the incinerator to Bethlehem Steel, electricity from the Dock Street dam and the sewerage treatment plant, Allison Hill enterprise zone, Fox Ridge moderate-priced housing, low-mortgage home repair loans, and a City Hall Office of Economic Development.

Some of Reed's ideas fit into the sound-management category—city and school cooperation, Hershey-to-Carlisle economic development unity, City Hall merit pay, and perhaps even volunteer police and fire auxiliary corps.

However, like Fiorello LaGuardia, when Reed falls on his face, he makes it a beaut.

Harristown in 1977 thought it could be a friend to artists, heedless of the age-old wisdom that artists are smarter and shiftier than politicians. When a proposed Arts Center began to assume the proportion of $40 million, Harristown settled for People Place and then exited from that.

Reed devised the Island Concerts, and after the Grateful Dead and Def Leppard each drew more than 14,000, Reed looked like impresario Sol Hurok. But Reed's 45-piece city band has yet to replace the old Commonwealth Band, and his plotting for the Colonial Theater to be an arts mecca ended in comedy.

Divine Providence crumbled the Colonial's 1834 wall into the Tuesday club, saving Harrisburg from a huge arts debt and raising the snoozing consciousness of the Tuesday Club to admit the sisterhood. A month later, developer Bill Alexander unveiled commercial plans for the Third and Market site, and the mayor with chutzpah chortled: "From the rubble of the Colonial Theater comes new life and a new vision."

The Reed baseball Harrisburg Pirates was another dream. Sportswriter Nick Horvath suggested Billie Martin be manager—as if the mayor needed Martin to fight with when he already had Bill Keisling and Earl Gohl.

Reed's recurrent problem is that he so cherishes any of his ideas that he doesn't share them. The Tax and Revenue Study Commission wasn't his project, so he virtually ignored it. He went through two horrendous brawls over a water authority, and Councilman Bill Robinson rightly complained, "Why hasn't the mayor presented us with alternatives so we can make a choice?"

The most explosive Reed idea, however, was to redo Harristown. More on that Friday.

118.

THE BEST LOCAL FEUD

A wise Quaker commended Ben Franklin for "never making an enemy in any majority." During much of 1982-1983, Mayor Reed assailed the two majorities he needed for success: City Council and Harristown.

One civic leader called these clashes "petty bickering," as they involved unarmed combatants and most of Harrisburg slept through them. Otherwise, there was nothing petty about them. "Certain council members consider that their goal is "Stop the Mayor," said Reed with some justification. One of the seven fellow Democrats answered it was Reed's "desire for unabridged control and to take charge without benefit of input from those who may have experience or disagree."

Councils revolve biennially, but Harristown had been a nonprofit entity since 1974 with an operational budget the size of City Hall's, and it nurtured the promise of a center-city Renaissance II if there were to be one.

Harristown featured a glowing present, a past with some forgotten muddles, an economic aggressiveness, a social shyness, and a swashbuckling commander who matched Reed in competitiveness, William Keisling.

Had City hall and Harristown been 200,000 miles apart, not two blocks, and had Reed and Keisling not decided to expend their mid-life crises in mutual anxiety fixations, a punch-out might have been avoided. It was when Reed careened close to staking his reputation on a convention hotel project—a political gamble even Pittsburgh's Dave Lawrence or Philadelphia's Richardson Dilworth would have hedged—that the mayor and Harristown smashed into each other.

Harristown was far from faultless, but it wasn't quite what Reed said it was: a "supergovernment" that has "a monopoly grip on all major down-town real estate," with "preferential relationships with private interests." To the mayor, it had been an "excellent concept" to build taxable properties but now it was the worst Harrisburg-chartered corporate villain since the Credit Mobilier of the 1870s.

To combat "the monster," Reed recaptured the Redevelopment Authority and its power of eminent domain. Council, led by Ear Gohl, voted with Harristown. And after a viable hotel project was lost and the state General Service Secretary Walter Baran warned "We're not going to play games forever" about the Environmental Resources Building, the city's management seemed to be self-destructing.

It took thunder for the drowsy local business and labor chieftains to awaken and arrange a "truce," cutting a deal essentially to get the DER building.

Harristown was a product of the 1969 Riot, the 1972 Flood, the demise of the Penn Harris Hotel, the building of the East and Capital City malls, and the Greater Harrisburg Movement. It was incorporated May 14, 1974, on Keisling's 38th birthday.

Its public commitment and independent financing and managerial scheme are unique in the nation—a brainchild of its solicitor Francis B. Haas and its second president James W. Evans, two masterminds of Harrisburg's strong-mayor government that benefited Reed and of HACC where Reed did his learning.

With the city's contribution of $5 million and another $108.5 million of initial bonding, Harristown began what could be $500 million of demolishing and rebuilding. Strawberry Square and the 333 Market Street Building by 1984 housed 5,200 employees, and the latter vies with the TMI cooling towers as the tallest structures between Philadelphia and Pittsburgh. When the bonds are paid in 1989, city taxes should reap $21.8 million and, because Harristown is the county's top taxpayer, the county, city and schools should total $67.3 million.

Though Reed and Keisling subsequently toned down their personal drama, it was the best local feud since the McCormick-Stackpole tiff of 70 years ago. Both men are sharp, sometimes petty, not always cheerful workaholics. Reed as the incessant political operator and Kelsling as the brooding master builder could be arousing fictional antagonists in the hands of a latter-day John O'Hara.

Often in the past 25 months, the two have distracted themselves pondering what each thinks is the other's psychopathy. Someday, perhaps, they can interrupt their preoccupations and glare at each other in the Keisling Lounge of the Harrisburg Hilton Reed hotel—two demons still belligerent as hell, still striving.

119.

THE HOTEL SITUATION

When Oscar Wilde arrived at the Lochiel Hotel in 1882 dressed in blue velvet knee breeches, he was asked why he brought a fur coat in May. "To hide the hideous sofas in all the hotel rooms," he answered.

After Charles Dickens in March of 1842 stayed at what is today's Warner Hotel, he praised the Innkeeper as an "obliging, considerate and gentlemanly person" and the Inn as "a snug hotel," but he was annoyed that legislators spit tobacco juice on the carpeting.

Harrisburg's hotel industry has had a rousing history, but there is no indication Jenny Lind, Daniel Webster, W. C. Fields, Babe Ruth and other famous guests ever thought this town was special.

"Fort Penn was behind the times in hotel-building, and it was generally agreed that the hotel situation in Fort Penn was a disgrace," wrote John O'Hara in his novel about Harrisburg of 70 years ago.

The Penn Harris, 1919—1972, and the Harrisburger, 1930—1969, glistened with local camaraderie that might never be duplicated again, but they weren't luxury inns.

What Harrisburg had since George Buehler about 1812 opened the Golden Eagle—today's Warner—to accommodate the first legislators was enough rooms, food and booze. As recently as 1965-1972, the Penn Harris, Harrisburger and new Holiday Inn Town provided 960 rooms within three blocks of the Capitol. Mayoral candidate Harold Swenson, once in hotelling himself, suggested in 1969 that Harrisburg should push for a 1,000-person exhibition hall attached to the Forum. The Swenson idea died, so did the Penn Harris and Harrisburger, and by 1973 the capitol city was down to 260 available rooms.

Meanwhile, semi-fancy standard motels opened throughout the area, giving the community 4,143 rooms—more than ever before, but not enough for the big-time convention trade.

As the 12-story Penn Harris was the flagship of Renaissance I in 1919—and celebrated in O'Hara's *A Rage to Live* as the 15-story Nesquehela Hotel—Renaissance II was to be illuminated by a Market Square hotel-convention center of at least 16 stories. In the project would be an office building at Third and Walnut streets.

Harristown was chartered in May of 1974 and in a quick 62 months opened Strawberry Square. Then it collided with record-high interest rates in a fruitless 54 months seeking a hotel developer.

Steve Reed in 1982 took office and assumed personal command: "I think it is my obligation to stick my neck out. What else is the mayor for?

With that began 15 months of what Harristown president Barton Fields called "internecine warfare," but it more resembled a diabolical game of "Monopoly" where nobody could land on the blue-chip hotel properties.

The respected Cleveland developer, Forest City Dillon, was booked by Harristown but in September 1982 bowed out, saying it didn't need Harrisburg politics. Inner City Development from Washington received Harristown's and City Council's approval, but Reed controlled the critical

Urban Development Action Grant. An outfit from Nashville gave Harrisburg the best vaudeville since Eddie Cantor played this town.

At last in January 1984, the mayor and Harristown agreed on Pattison Partners of New York. Their project retained a reasonable price tag of $64.7 million but the UDAG subsidy quadrupled from an earlier Reed estimate to $16 million. Though Harrisburg is one of the nation's last cities without a UDAG, 16 big ones is four times what the Penn Harris cost.

A convention hotel is an absolute imperative for Harrisburg's future. Even if all goes well, it wouldn't open until 1987, or 15 year after the Penn Harris closed.

The 1834 Lochiel became the Colonial Theater in 1912 and the theater dramatically collapsed last September [1983]. But the 172–year-old Warner Hotel remains as one of the nation's oldest on the National Register. With go-go girls, pastrami on rye, and an erotic boutique where once Charles Dickens signed the guest list, the Warner admittedly is "far less splendid than many," in Dickens' words, but it is obligated to hold fast until the tragic comedy of a Market Square luxury inn is resolved.

120.

THEY CONQUER WHO BELIEVE THEY CAN

Toward the end of his long life, Sen. M. Harvey Taylor was discovered by The New York Times as an American political tyrannosaurus. "What's different?" Pulitzer Prize winner Homer Bigart, a fellow Pennsylvanian, asked. "People are changing," snapped Harve. "They don't take baths anymore."

Taylor so mirrored his constituency that even his jokes were its jokes.

From 1900, when Taylor was 24, until 1982, when he died at 106, the Harrisburg area changed immeasurably—so many changes that even 100,000 words in this 120-column series haven't been able to anatomize a tenth of them.

One of the most serious changes is the citizenry as a political force became more "principled." Ironically, that's not necessarily an improvement, as many of the new attitudes rebut old Harrisburg values that made it such a dynamic community at the turn of the century.

How good, how valid, is such new thinking as:

Harrisburg has contagious rot and should be isolated? The East and West Shores can get along without each other, and certainly without Harrisburg? Neighborhood and small-town stubbornness is worth more than area unity? Job growth and business encouragement aren't essential when this place seems to be recession-proof? The white collar should tend to its private and professional aggrandizements, as civic endeavors are no-win?

Or, this community is doing state government a huge favor letting the Capitol be here? Why be concerned with the threat of government's moving jobs out of Harrisburg? What harm is there in archaic boundaries, ridiculous local taxation and almost nonexistent cooperative ties in flood control, waste disposal, crime prevention, recreation and the arts?

Or, blacks, though no longer regarded as inferior, still should be kept separate? And blacks for their part, as they emerge from the old servitude "plantation politics," should prefer separatism with the excuse to grab part of "the action" as new urban spoilsmen?

With the exception of racial equity, the City Beautiful reformers of 1900 attacked all these "principles" as irresponsible. For a golden age, or until 1920, the civic leaders triumphed over such narrow-mindedness. And then for a dross age, or since the 1950s, these "principles" surfaced and hardened into a widely accepted ideology that often reflects nastily upon the entire community.

"There comes a time when every man must learn to rise above principle," the legendary Dan Flood, the old congressman from Wilkes-Barre, used to say before he started dealing for his people. Dan Flood had it right, and Simon Cameron, Vance McCormick and Harve Taylor would agree.

Historian Henry Adams though t himself high-minded a century ago, but he couldn't help admiring "The Pennsylvanians," as he called the Harrisburg Camerons.

"Practically, the Pennsylvanian forgot his prejudices when he allied his interests," wrote Adams. "He then became supple in action and large in motive, whatever he thought of his colleagues. When he happened to be right—which was, of course, whenever one agreed with him—he was the strongest American in America."

When is the last time someone said the Harrisburg area has strong political, business, labor, professional, black or white, or male or female leadership?

It wasn't in the last 10 years, when a desperate city considered selling not only its city hall, middle school and water system but also its sculpture "Crystal." It wasn't when the capital city lost all those hotel proposals to replace the Penn Harris and almost lost the Environmental Resources and PHEAA buildings. It hasn't been in the legislative chambers when hometown voices were muted for meaningful urban tax reform and relief.

It wasn't when a worried business and labor coterie at the last minute settled the 1983 city hall crisis but rabbit-like kept such a "low profile" that something lasting, like the Greater Harrisburg Movement, wasn't revitalized. Can the new "Partners in Progress," to meet Tuesday on their regional economic plan, fill the vacuum of civic vacuity?

Harve Taylor was right in a way he didn't mean. Lots of local "principles" need a bath. There's scum on too many values. The worst grime is the negativism. And few individuals have the commitment, or courage, to offer alternative examples.

The dauntless steelworkers in Steelton have a sign on the wall of Gornik's Tavern: "They Conquer Who Believe They Can."

INDEX

D

E

F

G

H

O

P

R

V

W

Z